A Guide to Eva

A Guide to Evangelism

Clive Calver   Derek Copley   Bob Moffett   Jim Smith

Marshalls

99
269 · 2

Marshalls Paperbacks
Marshall Morgan & Scott
3 Beggarwood Lane, Basingstoke, Hants, UK

First published by Marshall Morgan and Scott 1984

ISBN: 0 551 01111 4
Phototypeset by Input Typesetting Ltd, London
Printed in Great Britain by Camelot Press, Southampton

Contents

Foreword

The great need of the hour in Britain today is for men and women who will ask God to move their hearts with the same compassion that moves his heart.

When he saw the crowds, he had compassion on them, because they were harassed and helpless, like sheep without a shepherd.

The greatest dangers we face as Christians are cynicism and a cool detachment. We must not forget the actual people – including those we know and love – behind the statistics who live 'without hope and without God in the world.'

The harvest is plentiful, but the workers are few. Ask the Lord of the harvest, therefore, to send out workers into his harvest.

The urgency of the hour stares us in the face. The task before us is massive. The time is short, therefore let us 'make the most of every opportunity' to evangelize. I trust God will use this book to move you with compassion to join in this great harvest.

Luis Palau

About the Editors

Clive Calver

After graduating from London Bible College, Clive spent eleven years as a full-time evangelist and bible teacher. He worked from 1975–82 as National Director of British Youth for Christ and then spent a year as Programme Director of Mission England. In the spring of 1983 he was appointed General Secretary of the Evangelical Alliance.

Clive has continued his involvement with British Youth for Christ as Vice President. He is a Governor of Moorlands Bible College, and serves on the Federal Board of Mission England and the Executive Committee of Mission to London. He is an ordained free church clergyman and serves as one of the leaders of Milton Keynes Free Church.

Clive is 35 years old, married to Ruth and has four children.

His previous books are
   Getting it Together co-written with John Oliver
   Sold Out (Marshalls)
   With a Church like this Who Needs Satan? (Marshalls)
   God Can Use You co-written with Eric Delve (Marshalls)
   Now That I'm a Christian (Scripture Union)

Derek Copley

After graduating from Manchester University (Bsc and Ph.D. in Chemistry) Derek did Post-doctoral research at the University of North Carolina, during which time he was involved in planting four churches and worked among American Indians.

Since 1970 Derek has been the Principal of Moorlands Bible College. He is on the Personnel Committee of BMMF, the Executive Committee, and Council of Management of the Evangelical Alliance. He is an elder in his local church where he is involved in teaching and pastoral work.

Derek is married to Nancy and they have two children.

His previous books are
   Home Bible Studies (Paternoster)
   Shock Wave (Moorley's)
   Building with Bananas (Paternoster)
   My Chains Fell Off (Paternoster)
   Ears to Hear (Kingsway)

Bob Moffett

Bob is the Training Director of Youth For Christ-Europe. On leaving the insurance world of London after five years, Bob trained at London Bible College. He spent the next seven years working with young people and local churches in Newcastle-upon-Tyne and Essex.

Living in North-East London, Bob is married to Jill, and they have two girls.

He travels widely in Europe, lecturing to ministers and youth leaders, as well as, in Bob's words, 'keeping his feet on the ground'.

His previous books are
Crowdbreakers (Pickering)
Power-Pac (Scripture Union)

Jim Smith

Jim has served 13 years in the Anglican ministry, the last five of them as Vicar of two former mining villages in County Durham. He is now full time evangelist with CPAS.

As well as doing evangelism, he is very keen that others should do it as well!

He is married, and has three children.

His previous books are
Breakthrough Training Kit (CPAS)
Time to Share (Kingsway)

Acknowledgments

The editors gratefully acknowledge the contribution and work done by Gavin Reid, Gordon Bailey and Eddie Gibbs, particularly in the early stages of this book's development.

Section 1

Foundations

1.1

The theology of evangelism and gospel of the Kingdom

The Spirit is on me because he has anointed me to preach good news to the poor. He has sent me to proclaim freedom for the prisoners and the recovery of sight for the blind, to release the oppressed, to proclaim the year of the Lord's favour (Luke 4:18–19).

Every eye in the meeting was fixed on the carpenter as he read Isaiah 58:6 and 61:1–2. It was not the young man's learning or sophisticated erudition which riveted their attention for he was an artisan with no more formal education than the average Jewish boy; yet there was something different. Those Scriptures, well known to every Jew, somehow seemed alive today. Of course, they knew that Jesus was a local home-grown lad who had caused quite a stir elsewhere in Israel, Capernaum for instance (Luke 4:23). There was power in his teaching, he was healing and casting out demons. Already reports had filtered back to Nazareth and Jesus' fellow-villagers were basking in the glory of them. What was it then, that was different today? Somehow the Scriptures just fitted him. This young Nazarene was coming out into the public eye with scriptural clothes which everyone could see were made for him. They were kingly robes, moreover, as he indicated when he spoke of the anointing upon him. And he certainly was acting like a king, declaring the manifesto of his reign – good news to the poor, freedom to prisoners incarcerated in dark dungeons, and liberty to the oppressed. God's age of favour was here. It was not only that he preached these things as God's good news of the Kingdom (Luke 4:43), but he seemed able to effect them by the power of his proclaimed word. In the five-point manifesto in Luke 4:18–19, proclamation of the word is emphasised three times.

At the start of the Christian age, Jesus came into Galilee proclaiming, 'The kingdom of God is near; repent and believe the good news' (Mark 1:14–15). There is no such thing as Christian evangelism that is not rooted in the ideas and context of God's kingdom. In fact, this evangel is called the gospel of the kingdom (Luke 4:43; Matt. 4:23; Mark 1:14–15). If we do not understand the biblical use of the phrase 'the kingdom of God' (or heaven), we are unable to appreciate the evangelism that Christ brought and taught. Moreover, to say, as is often repeated, 'Jesus preached the kingdom of God and Paul preached Jesus', as though there were two gospels, one by Jesus and another by Paul, is manifestly a shallow assessment. Jesus clearly preached himself (Matt. 5:27–8, 9:6; 10:37–9 etc), identifying himself with the kingdom (Matt. 12:28; 16:27–28). Paul preached the kingdom of God (Acts 14:22; 20:25; Rom. 14:17 etc), even though Jesus Christ was the content of his message (1 Cor. 1:23). Jesus and Paul preached the same gospel – the good news of the kingdom of God which Jesus ushered in.

It will help in defining the kingdom if we first clear the ground of popular misunderstandings and state what it is not.

1. The kingdom of God is not:

(a) *The Church, the Body of Christ*

It is rather the power and activity of God expressed through that body. If I punch someone on the nose it might well be said, 'The kingdom of Roger Forster is at hand,' especially if I leave an impression on the nose punched. In a similar way, the Church, the Body of Christ, is the present vehicle of God's kingdom just as Jesus' physical body was while he was on earth.

(b) *The rule of God in men's hearts*

This would make God's kingdom depend on our obedience. When we pray 'Your kingdom come, your will be done on earth as it is in heaven,' we may be wanting God's will to have its way in us by our willing obedience, but this prayer extends far beyond that and asks for God's intrusion into the affairs of this age amongst the obedient and disobedient alike. The force in the form of the verb 'come' does not suggest a gradual pervasion or process, but it is an event which is prayed for.

(c) *God's gradual over-ruling in history leading us to a beautiful society*

It is a sudden interruption, an invasion of the future age and powers into the present scene.

The first century Jew, hearing Jesus' proclamation of the kingdom, would have responded as we should, with excitement. He would have known that Isaiah spoke of the good news in terms of God coming to reign (Isa. 52:7–8). The kingdom of God implied the drawing near of the reigning God, or even 'the kinging it of God', as it would sound in the language of the Jews. The gospel of divine activity meant, and still means, that a new age has dawned.

2. The kingdom of God is where:

(a) *The SPIRIT is poured out*

God has come by his outpoured Spirit. This was foretold by his prophets, 'I will pour out my Spirit on all people. Your sons and daughters will prophesy . . .' (Joel 2:28ff). 'I will pour out my Spirit on your offspring and bring blessing on your descendants' (Isa. 44:3). The Holy Spirit, anointing Jesus as King at his baptism, is now flowing from this fountain head, available without measure to all mankind. 'I baptise you with water' said

John, 'He (Jesus) will baptise you with the Holy Spirit and fire.' God is now totally accessible by his Spirit, available without limitation. Jesus spoke of a baptism he was constrained to accomplish before he could fulfil his mission of bringing fire on to the earth. This pentecostal fire was accompanied by wind, foreseen as God's breath, 'For he will come like a pent-up flood that the Breath of the Lord drives along' (Isa. 59:19), while Paul describes the kingdom of God as 'righteousness, peace and joy in the Holy Spirit' (Rom. 14:17).

Evangelism is serving this same Holy Spirit to mankind (2 Cor. 3:6).

(b) SATAN is defeated

Satan has been defeated and his kingdom-power broken. This is clearly depicted in the wilderness temptation conflict (Matt. 4:1–11), where Jesus emerges as victor. However, it is at the cross that the evil forces of the universe are finally confronted and put into total disarray (Col. 2:15). Now Satan, the strong man of Matthew 12:24–9, may be bound, and God's liberating forgiveness released through his servants (John 20:21–3). This victory was prophesied in the beautiful Isaiah passage in which the enemy's weapons, sickness, sin and death are wrested from his grasp and a stronger champion divides the spoil of his resurrection triumph with his followers (Isa. 52:13–53:12; cf. Luke 11:22).

Jesus' words in Mark 10:45 contain at least four allusions to this 'servant' passage of Isaiah 52 and 53. 'For the Son of man came not (52:13) to be served but to serve (53:10) and to give his life as a ransom (53:4–6) for (53:11–12) many.'

As Moses, God's servant, was used to ransom Israel from Egypt, so Jesus would ransom his people from man's greater enemy. 'Now is the time for judgement on this world, now the prince of this world will be driven out. But I, when I am lifted up from the earth, will draw all men to myself' declared the new king.

Evangelism is demonstrating that Satan is defeated (Luke 10:17–20)

(c) SALVATION has dawned

The salvation powers of the coming age have arrived. Jesus makes it clear that the salvation prophesied by Isaiah (Isa. 26:19; 29:18 etc) is evident enough in his ministry for John the Baptist to be satisfied that Jesus had brought in the kingdom. 'The blind receive sight, the lame walk, those who have leprosy are cured, the deaf hear, the dead are raised and good news is preached to the poor' (Matt. 11:5). In this way Jesus announces the fulfilment of God's purposes for men and the consummation of the age. Further, 'Blessed is the man who does not fall away on account of me' (Matt. 11:6), is then presented as a challenge to the disciples to continue to trust him. The bridegroom is with us (Mark 2:19), the wedding garments are put on

(Matt: 22:4), the new wine (the best kept till last (John 2:10) is being poured out (Mark 2:22). The harvest is waiting to be reaped (John 4:34–8). God's gifts of bread, water, life and peace are all freely offered in Christ. For the hour is coming and now is, when the spiritually dead shall be raised and when men will worship in Spirit and truth (John 4:23; 5:25). The new covenant where sins are no more remembered (Jer. 31:33–4) by God has arrived at last.

Two symbolic actions, based on Zechariah's prophecy, performed at the beginning and end of Jesus' ministry declare how completely the New Age had intervened. First, Jesus cleansed the temple (John 2:13–17; Mark 11:15–17) 'that there should be no longer a merchant in the house of the Lord Almighty' as Zechariah declared (Zech. 14:21). The age of pure worship had come. Secondly, he rode into Jerusalem as Zechariah had predicted, 'See your king comes to you, gentle and riding on a donkey' (Zech. 9:9; Matt. 21:5; John 12:15), and the prophet goes on to describe the universal peace his kingdom would bring by removing the war machine and proclaiming peace to the nations (Zech. 9:10).

Evangelism is evoking faith in men and women to enter Christ's kingdom and be saved (Rom. 5:9, 10, 21).

(d) *A new SOCIETY is born*

The poor have good news preached to them. In Luke 4:18, 19, Jesus is using verses which Isaiah has coined on the basis of Leviticus 25, the jubilee programme of Israel, known as the year of restoration. Beginning with the day of national atonement with God, Israel has this fiftieth year to express with each other that atonement. If they were right with God and reconciled to him, they were reconciled with their brothers also! Leviticus 25 shows that:

(i) Since they had ceased from their own works and entered into God's rest they were to give rest, sabbaths, to their fellows also.

(ii) Since God had remitted all their debts, all debts were anulled throughout Israel.

(iii) Since God had given them a new inheritance, each man was to have his family inheritance restored to him.

(iv) Since God had set them free, all slaves were to be freed and work contracts released.

All this was very good news to the poor and disadvantaged. The love of God restored him to a proper position in society. Jesus interpreted the spirit of the jubilee teaching of Leviticus 25 in his sermon on the mount. Moreover this kind of society came spontaneously into being after Pentecost (Acts 2:42–7; 4:32–7) as the disciples practiced jubilee living.

However, Jesus' preaching of good news to the poor went beyond just the materially disadvantaged. He included the spiritual bankruptcy of tax collectors and prostitutes (Mark 2:16; Luke 7:37–49). The title of derision given by his enemies to Jesus sums up beautifully his own interpretation of good news to the poor, 'the friend of tax collectors and sinners' (Matt: 11:19). These poor could come near to God for God had drawn near to them. They could receive his rest, forgiveness and life by faith, for no price. This same condition made it hard for the financially and morally rich ruler to inherit eternal life (Matt. 19:16–26).

We need empty hands to receive Christ's resources, as dependents with no independent means to fall back on! We come as new-born children into the Father's kingdom. The 'poor' include the sick, the oppressed, the brokenhearted (Isa. 61:1–3), the prodigal son and the dying thief. All these are welcomed into the kingdom of God to find release, healing and forgiveness in the new community of God's people.

Evangelism is introducing people into the richness of Christ's new society (Acts 2:41–7; Heb. 12:22–4).

The advent of Jesus means the Father's kingdom has intervened into the affairs of men.

This does not mean God has never reigned before. He has an *eternal* kingdom and rules in the kingdoms of men from the beginning of history (Daniel 4:32–4) leading men to REPENTANCE.

But now God's kingdom is also *present* and able to be received as it rescues and delivers with signs and wonders. (Daniel 6:26–27). This kingdom is received by FAITH.

But God's kingdom is also *future* (Daniel 2:44), when all opposition is removed, and sorrow and tears disappear in his heavenly kingdom, while his servants reign with him in the New Jerusalem golden society for ever; our lives are orientated there in HOPE.

Therefore, in the light of God's reign, mankind is called to repentance, faith and hope in order to fully participate in God's good news of the kingdom.

3. The Kingdom is:

(a) Received by grace

'Fear not, little flock, it is my Father's good pleasure to give you the kingdom' (Luke 12:32).

(b) Seen in the life of his people

The love and justice and forgiveness of God, seen in the society of his people, reveal the heart and character of the Father to a broken-down world. This new society acts as salt in the old society, hindering corruption and fertilizing spiritual growth (Matt. 5:13–14). It lights up the world to relieve its darkness and check its evil ways, so that the structures of society find God's kingdom in his people getting his will done on earth (Matt. 6:10).

(c) Expressed in power through his people

By works of healing (Luke 10:9) and forgiveness (John 20:21–3; Matt. 18:18) the mission of Jesus continues through his people, bringing his kingdom into the lives of men and women.

(d) Extends to all nations

'This gospel of the kingdom will be preached to the whole world . . .' (Matt. 24:14).

(e) Has a consummation

'. . . and then the end will come' (Matt. 24:14). At the final consummation of all things, Jesus will return to root out all that offends in his kingdom and will divide into wise and foolish, good and lazy, faithful and wicked, sheep and goats, for his eternal reign of righteousness and love. The King will reply, 'I tell you the truth, whatever you did for the least of these brothers of mine you did for me . . . take your inheritance, the kingdom prepared for you since the creation of the world . . .' (Matt. 25:2, 21, 26, 40, 34).

But first, *this gospel of the kingdom must be preached in all the world.*

1.2a

The sociology of evangelism

Sociology can never replace the sovereignty of God nor the spiritual dynamics involved in evangelism. Nonetheless, it can offer many insights which are relevant to the work of evangelism. In itself sociology is a neutral tool which can be used in the service of God or the devil. So why not use it for God? Sociology is the discipline which studies people in their relationships in an objective way. In doing so it often debunks common sense ideas about those relationships and provides us with a more reliable understanding of our society.

How can sociology help in evangelism?

(a) *It sees man in relation to man*

It is futile to try and evangelise a person as an isolated individual. Christians have long recognised that the social circumstances of the hearer affect his ability to hear the gospel. Most would accept that 'empty stomachs don't have ears' so we need to feed a hungry man before we preach to him. Sociology broadens this point. Healthy, normal people do not exist in a vacuum any more than the homeless and hungry do. People all belong to a network of social relationships which help to shape their attitudes and responses to life generally as well as to spiritual truth. The primary network to which they belong is the family and secondarily to school, an office or factory network, a peer group and numerous other networks of relationships which vary in their significance for the individual.

An understanding of these networks of relationships should teach us two important lessons for evangelism.

(i) Our method of evangelism needs to be appropriate to the dominant social network in the area we are trying to reach. Paul's change of strategy when he moved from preaching to Jewish synagogue congregations to Gentile pagan congregations is a biblical illustration of the point. Today it is no good inviting neighbours to an evangelistic dinner party in an area where neighbours never eat in each other's houses. Sociology helps us to identify what is appropriate.

(ii) It stresses the need to aim evangelism at the significant people within the networks of relationships. Praise God for the individuals who are converted when none of the rest of their social network are. They are the exceptions and their survival often depends on their rejecting their former social network and moving into a new and foreign one. Too often their spiritual interest is only temporary because the dominant social network to which they belong crowds it out. These networks need to be recognised and our evangelism aimed at the significant people within them just as Paul aimed at key people in the community or household. So, for example, to evangelise children in isolation from their parents it to pretend that reality is other than it is.

(b) *It identifies relationships*

Sociology helps to identify the assumptions which lie behind these networks of relationships. People see the world and their own lives through spectacles which most are not conscious of wearing. So in evangelism the gospel is not introduced into a blank mind but one already filled with assumptions and interpretations which often need to be overcome before an individual can turn to the living God. This is an aspect of repentance.

In our society two basic interpretations are encountered. For most, particularly urban dwellers, there is an underlying belief in the power of technology to solve our problems and improve our tomorrows. For these people, belief in natural abilities has rendered resort to supernatural answers irrelevant. These people also live in a world where they are spoiled for choice. In supermarkets they can choose from fourteen varieties of breakfast cereals and in religion they can choose from x varieties on offer. Faced with such variety many are dazed and make no choice at all or perhaps first choose one brand only to be converted to something else shortly afterwards. As man's life has become mobile so has his thinking. Our evangelism often fails to reach such people because we assume an acceptance of the supernatural or a knowledge of the facts of Christianity they do not possess. Our evangelism needs to start further back than it often does.

Other areas, however, particularly rural and isolated ones, still have a layer of folk religion. Christian tradition lingers, mixed with superstition and pre-Christian practices. They still observe the importance of rites of passage being 'done' in church and may attend church or chapel for special occasions. They have faith in 'faith' and prayer and believe that if you live by the golden rule God cannot complain. If they attend church or chapel it is because it is a community institution rather than a spiritual institution. Belief in the living God is as difficult for these as it is for their secularised contemporaries.

(c) It can give confidence

Recent studies have shown people are not attracted to watered-down religion which has so compromised with the world that it has nothing different to offer. Churches that grow are those which preach a clear alternative message. As in Acts 15:12–14 it seems that churches which are feared are still those which win converts.

(d) It analyses group functions

Sociology analyses the functions and dysfunctions of groups, getting behind their stated purposes and formal structures and looking at what actually happens, what their real achievements are, and how they actually work. It can do this too for our evangelism. In doing so it might point out that certain music or literature is dysfunctional and certain rearrangements could lead to greater effectiveness. More generally, it might point out that many evangelistic campaigns have functioned as celebrations for the faithful rather than communications to the unbeliever. The penetrating analysis which it can provide should not be destructive. It should serve as an incentive to change in order to achieve our goal.

The school of Church Growth has used sociology best of all in relation to evangelism and the reader is referred to other chapters and books which outline its thinking. In addition to the areas mentioned above this school looks at leadership and decision-making, group dynamics and goal-setting.

It is an excellent illustration of the way in which sociology can be used to glorify the God who made not just man but man-in-relationship.

Further reading

The Homeless Mind, B. Berger, P. L. Berger and H. Kellner (Penguin, 1974)

Between Pulpit and Pew, D. Clark (Cambridge, 1982)

Churches and Church-goers, R. Currie, A. D. Gilbert and L. Horsley (Oxford, 1977)

I Believe in Church Growth, E. Gibbs (Hodder, 1981)

The Making of Post-Christian Britain, A. D. Gilbert (Longman, 1980)

Why Conservative Churches are Growing, D. Kelly, (Harper and Row, 1977)

Religion in Sociological Perspective, B. R. Wilson (Oxford, 1982)

1.2b

Strategy and goal-setting in evangelism

Most churches and Christian Fellowships have spent the last ten years either lurching from one crisis to another or leaping from one special event to the next. Few churches do any strategic medium-term or long-range planning. Most ministers haven't the time; they are too busy keeping the machinery of the church system running. Most leadership groups haven't the courage to ask the serious question, 'Is what we are doing having any effect?' It is seen as tantamount to challenging old Mr Blogg's position as leader of the Youth Fellowship. And so the work goes on and on, faithfully but not very fruitfully.

Now is the time to take a basic look at the areas of strategy-thinking and goal-setting. It is not unscriptural to do so. After all, in the early church the Holy Spirit set the strategy in terms of time, areas and patterns (Acts 1:8; 16:6). The Father himself had set the target – the redemption of the world and the bringing of all things in the universe back to himself (Col. 1:20).

Principles of strategy-thinking and goal-setting

(a) Listen to the Lord

Any attempt at strategy-thinking and goal-setting must start by seriously listening to the Lord now – not to what the Lord has said and done in the past. Tradition in the area of theological insight is invaluable. Tradition in the area of activity is usually harmful. Edward de Bono says, 'Organisational patterns tend to outlive their usefulness and become powerful negative weapons. All organisations seek to maintain their own existence, they finish up existing on sentiment not on rationality.'

Encourage yourself with the words of Isaiah: 'Do not dwell on the past. See, I am doing a new thing! Now it springs up' (Isa. 43:18). Listen seriously to the Lord. The priority of prayer cannot be over-stressed.

One thing is guaranteed: as you pray, the Lord will teach you to take a serious look at the lost. The work of the Holy Spirit is to prove to the people that they are wrong concerning God and sin and Jesus Christ (John 16: 8).

(b) Look at society

Take a careful look at what is happening in our society and especially in your own town and area. There are certain new trends; the first signs of an increasing birth-rate, but falling rolls in the middle and upper schools; more boys than girls; increased leisure activity; long-term unemployment and larger numbers of senior citizens and those in 'early retirement'.

Think about some of the questions which are worrying people at a deep level. Again you must research not only the national mood but also the special feelings of people in your own community. The threat of nuclear warfare troubles many young couples with young children because they naturally wonder if there is any future for the little ones they have brought into the world. Questions of law and authority trouble those living in high-rise flats and elderly people who wonder if they can collect their pension without being attacked on the way home from the post office. Inflation and unemployment impose a high burden of insecurity in certain parts of the country. Face up to these issues; this is where people outside the churches are troubled.

(c) Take action

Now you are ready for some careful goal-setting. 'If you aim at nothing you will be sure to hit it.' So says the old slogan.

(i) *Set some faith targets.* Only a few, two or three are sufficient at the start. If your faith is small then only push it one step beyond its strength. Don't allow the devil to make you so ambitious that he discourages you with your total failures and prevents you from ever setting any targets again. There are so many needs. Accept the fact that you cannot meet them all at once.

You haven't the manpower, you haven't the finances, you haven't the premises. Ask yourself, 'Where are people hurting?' This is where the Christian gospel will have power.

(ii) *Learn to major on your strengths.* If you have a large number of active, alert, mature senior citizen Christians then ask yourself if you should be doing a major work amongst the senior citizens outside the church instead of complaining that you cannot get the youth work off the ground. Face up to the fact that people are different. Are you reaching the obvious 'your kind of people' or are you a Daily Telegraph church trying, unsuccessfully, to communicate to Daily Mirror readers. The answer lies in strategic church planting rather than continued frustrating non-communication.

(iii) *As a whole fellowship agree your priority goals* for the coming year. Gather the fellowship together for prayer. Divide up into small groups – no larger than six people in a group. Ask them to write down all their daydreams and hopes for the growth of the church. No discussion, just write down as many goals as possible. Crazy ideas are allowed, but just put them down, don't try and evaluate them individually. After ten or fifteen minutes ask each group to choose from their list (the list should be about twenty ideas long) the two top priorities which the church should seek to achieve in the next twelve months. Then gather everyone together. Write up all the top priorities on your overhead projector. Some groups will have overlapped; you are unlikely to get more than ten different ideas. Everyone then has two votes (one with their left hand, one with their right!) in order to vote for the top two priorities.

'How many believe that out of the ideas listed on the screen, number one should be one of our two goals for the next twelve months?'

'How many vote for idea number two? . . . and so on. This simple choice procedure will result in a decisive vote for two or three of the ideas.

(iv) *Check each month on progress*. Rejoice at every success, it will lead you on to more successes for the Lord.

When you have made your choice, make a major commitment in the agreed areas. Don't nibble at the ideas take a real bite.

(d) Reflection

There is an obvious value in standing back from your situation to get it more clearly into perspective. Never be afraid of setting a whole day aside for prayer. Use every bit of outside help you can get. Utilise secular expertise in your fact-finding as you discover the real 'felt needs' of the people in your area. Harness the creative tension of differing ideas within the fellowship in order to set your goals strategically. Then go and grow for God's glory.

1.3

The evangelist – an appreciation

Samuel Moffett's father was a pioneer missionary in North Korea when great areas of that country had never seen a white man. He took one of the first bicycles up into that section and, dressed in black with a white face, he was a strange sight indeed in a country of white clothes and darker faces. One day, he came to the top of a pass and began to coast down toward a small village. Some children were playing a game similar to hopscotch at the edge of the village, but when they looked up and saw the strange being in black clothes with a white face, coat-tails flapping in the breeze, swooping silently down on them on an infernal machine at a rapid rate, they scattered to the far corners of the village shouting, 'Look out, look out! Here comes the devil riding on a pair of spectacles.'

The idea of the evangelist can produce a similar reaction among some Christians. He is considered to be a variety of uncomplimentary things – a money-grabbing charlatan; too emotional; a high-pressure salesman; a glib-tongued con-man; the preacher of a superficial easy-believism; an opponent and disrupter of the local church. If only one of these charges were true it would be serious enough. Undeniably, some evangelists have acted unworthily and irresponsibly in the past, but that should not make us denigrate the gift of evangelism. These are major criticisms which are a mixture of truth, legend, error and lies. But the troublesome factor is that this kind of reaction against the evangelist has tended to paralyse the church in respect of evangelism!

The commission given to the Church is to 'go and make disciples of all nations' (Matt. 28:19); to 'preach the good news to all creation' (Mark 16:15) is to be Christ's witnesses to the ends of the earth (Acts 1:8). In other words, we make Jesus known as Saviour and Lord so that he can be loved and obeyed. To refuse to do that for whatever reason is to disobey Christ. If a football team refuses to play football it has no right to call itself a football team. The same could be said for any group of Christians who fail to evangelise. Thus we need to examine the role of the evangelist and his relationship to the Church. Our appreciation of the gift and its function will bear a direct relationship to our involvement in evangelism.

1. His function

According to Ephesians 4:11–13, the evangelist is a gift of grace bestowed by the ascended Christ on the Church. He comes before pastors and teachers not because he is in any way superior to them, but simply because people need to be converted before they can be shepherded and instructed as Christians.

(a) Called by God

No one can determine to become an evangelist just because he can speak well, has a great personality and relates well to all kinds of people. God certainly uses natural ability and it has a place in the ministry of the evangelist. But God of his own free choice calls and equips men to be evangelists.

The gift of the evangelist is marked out by a clear understanding of the content and nature of the gospel and, consequently, an intense desire to communicate it clearly and simply to all people everywhere (Acts 17:16–17).

(b) A proclaimer/herald

The evangelist is a proclaimer. Paul describes himself as 'a herald' (2 Tim. 1:11). The word he uses means 'a person who makes public announcements on another's behalf'. Heralds had to have a good voice to summon warriors to battle and the people to the assembly. They had to refrain from exaggeration and garrulousness because both lead to the danger of delivering false news. The message was to be delivered as it was given to them. They could not amend or alter it, even if they did not like it. The message did not originate with them. It had royal authority and power behind it. The herald was a spokesman for another. He was the mouthpiece of his master.

The evangelist is under the same constraint as the herald of God's good news. He proclaims God's activity on behalf of men in Jesus Christ. He does not deal in generalities but in glorious specifics. There is only one way to God Christ is the only mediator between man and God (John 14:6; 1 Tim 2:5); 'the Father sent the Son to be the Saviour of the world (1 John 4:14). He calls them to repent and believe the gospel. As J. I. Packer says, 'Evangelism is the issuing of a call to turn, as well as to trust.' He proclaims Jesus as Lord and Saviour. Jesus is not a model to be admired or a martyr to be remembered. He is the Lord to be worshipped, trusted and obeyed.

(c) He is an instructor

The passage in Ephesians 4:11–13, shows that the task of the chosen specialists is to exercise their ministries so as to 'prepare God's people for works of service, so that the body of Christ may be built up'. Thus the evangelist has a duty to lead, train, equip, identify and encourage the gift of evangelism. Evangelism is not the task of a few professionals but the responsibility of all Christians.

When the gospel is preached and no one responds to the call to repent and turn to Christ, some Christians tend to feel that the evangelist is losing his power. They forget that shepherds don't have sheep – sheep produce sheep!

The largest sit-down strike in the world has taken place in the church, where those who claim a relationship with Christ seem totally disinclined to share that experience with anyone else. The church has taken on the appearance of a comfortable dormitory for lethargic saints rather than a training camp for spiritual soldiers.

With the right kind of encouragement and training, Christians can be led into effective evangelism. They need to be shown the potential of their lives; the possibilities of service in their factories, shops, schools, colleges, offices and homes; the importance of building relationships with neighbours and friends and friendship evangelism. God has given each Christian a place in the gospel lifeboat and he expects them to row, not just put their oar in! But most people don't row automatically, they need to be taught how to row.

Good training is essential but that needs to be enhanced by the enthusiasm of the evangelist for the gospel. Believers need to appreciate the glory of Christ in the gospel and the fact that with God there are no negative experiences because to him all things are redeemable. He's in the redemption business. No person is too hard for God to save. The evangelist will encourage Christians to share their testimony. It is a most powerful apologetic. All testimonies are valid, not just the spectacular ones. There are no boring testimonies, only boring Christians. Help Christians to be interesting human beings and interested in others. Show them the value of spontaneous testimony that is not locked into a witnessing system. Let them know it doesn't matter if we blush, stammer, falter as we witness. It doesn't matter whether the cat is black, grey or ginger so long as it catches mice.

The Church is the key to evangelism and so the evangelist must be involved not only in doing evangelism but in producing an evangelising church.

(d) He is a learner

According to James S. Stewart, the first axiom of effective evangelism is that the evangelist is certain of his message. That means refusing to ignore theology. The wise evangelist will learn from the theologian and Bible teacher. He will wrestle with the mysteries of Scripture. He will discipline his mind to read about and understand the gospel at a deep level. As J. H. Jowett warns, 'You cannot drop the big themes and make great saints.' Sound biblical theology will provide the evangelist with the divine guided missile he needs to demolish all their 'fabricated intellectual objections to the gospel'.

A spirit filled heart is not in conflict with a theologically disciplined mind. The evangelist needs both. Severed from its spiritual and doctrinal foundations, evangelism loses its conviction, credibility and power.

2. The evangelist in the local church

(a) He is recognised by the local church

In Acts 13:1–3 the Holy Spirit made known his will to the leadership of the church. In response to that divine direction Saul and Barnabas were set apart for this special service of evangelism. The leadership identified with them by the laying on of hands and as a recognition of their being sent out by the church. After fulfilling the commission they had received, the team returned to report to the church all that God had done through them (Acts 14:27–28).

He is accountable to a local fellowship for his actions and is prevented from becoming a law unto himself, recognising no authority but his own.

He should be the object of prayerful support and fellowship. He cannot urge men to join the body of Christ if he is simply a floating rib in it.

(b) *Relationship and other ministries*

There should be no conflict or competition between the ministries of pastor, teacher and evangelist. The evangelist recognises his God-given place in the church and his inter-relationship to the other gifts and ministries. He does not underestimate their value or overestimate his own importance. He respects and recognises that all have been given to equip the saints for service.

As G. Campbell Morgan puts it, 'the fullest fact of ministry includes the whole church, and the men within it who have received special gifts, have received them in order that they may perfect the church to its work of ministry.' The gifts of ministry are given to enable the church to do the work of the ministry. Thus the various special gifts work towards one united end.

(c) *Sphere of activity*

Philip was an effective evangelist and exercised his ministry in a number of ways. He was a mass evangelist. In the city of Samaria he preached to the crowds (Acts 8:5–6). Later we find him moved by the Spirit from the city to the desert and here he exercises a ministry of personal evangelism (Acts 8:27–35). Later on we discover that he is taken away from the Ethiopian by the Spirit and becomes an itinerant evangelist as he 'travelled about preaching the gospel in all the towns until he reached Caesarea'.

It is important to notice that there is no New Testament distinction between the mass evangelist and personal evangelism. Peter preached to crowds in Jerusalem at Pentecost (Acts 2) and to Cornelius the soldier (Acts 10).

Apart from Ephesians 4:11, there are only two other New Testament references to 'evangelist'. In Acts 21:8 we read that Paul 'stayed at the house of Philip the evangelist' and in 2 Timothy 4:5 we find Paul urging Timothy to 'keep your head in all situations, endure hardship, do the work of an evangelist'.

Spurgeon summarised it well when he said, 'among men, God's richest gifts are men of high vocation separated for the ministry of the gospel. From our ascended Lord come all true evangelists: these are they who preach the gospel in divers places and find it the power of God unto Salvation; they are founders of churches, breakers of new soil, men of missionary spirit, who build not on another man's foundations, but dig out for themselves. We need many such deliverers of the good news where as yet the message has not been heard. I scarcely know of any greater blessing to the church than the sending forth of earnest, indefatigable, anointed men of God, taught of the Lord to be winners of souls.'

1.4

A contemporary history of evangelism

At the beginning of the twentieth century Britain stood at the peak of her imperial power. Few of her citizens would have believed that within fifty years India's independence would start the unravelling of the greatest empire the world has ever seen, and that Britain herself would be facing the future as a second class power in the world. At the same time, few evangelical Christians would have believed that the mighty movements of God in the previous 200 years would be wiped out by a tidal wave of unbelief and cynicism.

The eighteenth century

In October 1733 a meeting between two young men was the spark of a fire which was to set the whole nation ablaze: George Whitfield and John Wesley. At twenty-two George Whitfield had London and Bristol at his feet. But he turned his back on all this and went to America to preach to the Red Indians. He had received the vision to do so by hearing from John Wesley, who had gone to America for exactly the same purpose, but by now John Wesley was returning in despair, saying, 'I went to America to convert Indians, but oh, who shall convert me?' While Whitfield was in America, John Wesley finally understood what it was to trust in Christ alone for salvation and an assurance was given to him that all his sins were forgiven. Released from the crippling shackles of doubt, fear and guilt, Wesley began to work and preach with all the power of his enormous abilities. By the middle of 1739 Charles Wesley commented, 'The whole nation is in uproar.' A sleepy church and a nation almost dead to the voice of God had begun to awaken and that Great Awakening itself was to become the most important social phenomenon of the whole century.

Having returned to England in 1738, Whitfield began to preach in the open air. It was not long before he had persuaded Wesley to do the same. The most important thing to realise about the movement which these men set in train is that they inspired a great army of imitators; the vast majority of those who went out to preach the Gospel following them were ordinary working people, and most of them were vigorous witnesses. Most of Whitfield's converts were recruited into already existing churches, but Wesley could not bear to leave his converts without some after-care, so he formed the class system. The classes were, in effect, tiny house churches. By 1798 101,000 people belonged to Methodist classes – one in every thirty Englishmen. This movement of ordinary working people in the years after his death saw a remarkable growth, and it was in the nineteenth century that the most outstanding results of Wesley's work were to be seen.

The nineteenth century

In 1823 a young Cornish miner called Billy Bray was converted and immediately began to preach all over Cornwall. Over the next forty years this ex-drunkard was to set up several chapels and to be instrumental in leading thousands to Jesus Christ. His story was typical of many men who were raised up by God at that time to preach the good news of Jesus to the ordinary people of this country. However, the most famous of the 'working men's preachers' was Richard Weaver. At the age of seven he began work as a miner, working from five in the morning till nine or ten o'clock at night. Working under dreadful conditions like these, the men with whom he mixed were bitter, wild, violent and knew only one consolation, that of getting drunk. By 1852, when he was converted at the age of twenty-five, he was a famous drunkard and a prize-fighter, known as Dick the Undaunted because he never gave in until he had beaten someone. His ministry was one of the most powerful this country has ever seen. He regularly drew crowds of five to ten thousand men and preached all over the British Isles. One man who heard Weaver was a Lancashire man called Harry Moorhouse. He was a pickpocket who had served time in gaol before he was twenty-one. Soon after his conversion he began to preach and was in Dublin when the famous American evangelist D. L. Moody was preaching there. With typical Northern cheek Moorhouse informed Moody that he would be going to America and that he would preach for Moody at his church in Chicago. At this time, although a well-known preacher, Moody was still based in Chicago and had not yet begun his worldwide evangelistic ministry. It was Moorhouse who was to show him the way to that greater ministry. Moorhouse duly arrived at Moody's church and in his absence began to preach on the love of God for sinners; something which Moody himself had never preached about. Moody had preached that God hated sinners. Over the next few days Moorhouse turned Moody's church upside down and revolutionised Moody's ministry forever. After meeting Moorhouse Moody could never forget that God loved sinful men and women, and he went out to proclaim that glad message to a world that needed it. It is significant that Moody himself was an uneducated man of working-class origins.

Meanwhile, back in England in 1865, William Booth resolved that though the church of his day had failed the ordinary working man, he would not fail to take the message of Jesus to the people of the East End. Methodism was his background, but by his day it had forgotten its working-class origins and become far too respectable for such a scheme. Thus the Salvation Army was born, and through its ministry hundreds of thousands of ordinary, working-class people, formerly disregarded by the vast majority of the established church, found their way into the kingdom of heaven. Booth's concern for social justice shook the nation on several occasions and caused several chapters to be rewritten in Britain's law books. He died in 1912, one of the mightiest warriors for God the world has ever seen.

The same period saw the birth and astonishing initial growth of the

Brethren movement, particularly in the West Country and in Ireland. This movement brought thousands of ordinary people into the kingdom of God, and liberated hundreds of working men to become leaders and preachers in the church.

The twentieth century

In 1905 a man called Evan Roberts emerged as the major preacher of the Welsh Revival. Over 80,000 were converted, of which at least 60,000 persisted in the Free Church of Wales and many of the others went into Pentecostal churches. At the same time the Welsh Revival spread into England and touched every major town and every county. By 1914 it was possible to look back at nearly 180 years of expansion of the gospel – an expansion at its most powerful amongst the working classes. Hundreds of thousands of them had heard the good news and had come to Christ.

However, while this great movement was going on, much of the mainline Church was losing its confidence in the great theme of the 'evangel' – the good news. In nineteenth century Britain most clergy paid lip-service to an unthinking orthodoxy; among many, this was not based on clear biblical thinking. The Church was to pay a devastating price for its state of unreadiness. After twenty years of sitting on the manuscript, Charles Darwin published *The Origin of the Species* in 1859, and followed it up in 1871 with *The Descent of Man*. Both in England and America the initial reaction of the clergy was of unthinking conservatism. Meanwhile, discoveries in astronomy indicated that the universe was much larger than anyone had ever believed; the notion of an always-existing universe swiftly became scientific orthodoxy. To thinking men and women it appeared that the Church was simply the last bastion of reactionary thought, refusing to face up to scientific truth. Gradually the idea began to penetrate through society from the philosophers that science and religion were in direct contention. Many theologians, in order to accommodate new ideas, felt they must abandon orthodoxy: modern liberalism had arrived.

In the golden days of the growth of empire many had found it easy to believe in the goodness and love of God and in the inevitability of human progress towards the victory of the love of God. The 1914 to 1918 war put an end to that. As men watched their mates drown in mud and blood, and fought off rats that chewed them while they still lived, they simply ceased to believe. They had been asked to join Kitchener's army to serve God first, then King and country. It's no wonder that it became clear to the vast majority of the soldiers that the Church was part of that great machinery of state which had sent them to France to die. The alienation and bitterness which that produced helped to produce the feeling that if a working man becomes a Christian he has thereby betrayed his origins. After the Great War the whole of Europe breathed a sigh of relief. Everyone wanted to forget the war. The middle and upper classes had the money to enable them to do just that, but it was still a time of grinding poverty for the great mass of people.

From an obscure village in Wales God called two brothers – Stephen and George Jeffreys. They had begun preaching before the First World War but they came into their own during the 1920s and 1930s. The most significant mass movement in evangelism during that whole period was the new movement of the Pentecostal churches. In one legendary crusade in 1930 in Birmingham, George Jeffreys preached for ten weeks. During that time 10,000 people came to Christ and over 1,000 were baptised immediately, and there were hundreds of astonishing cases of healing.

Meanwhile, others were thinking strategically about the upper classes. One man had a profound influence in this area – 'Bash' Nash was responsible through a system of camps and other work with public schoolboys for the conversion of a stream of young men from public school background who have gone on to Anglican training colleges and become leaders of evangelicalism, especially within the Church of England. He, more than anybody else is responsible for the fact that today evangelicalism is a powerful wing in the Anglican Church. But this has not as yet resulted in a powerful mass movement at any level, and there are many in the established churches who still react as Archbishop Fisher did in 1954 when Billy Graham came to Harringay. His thirteen-week crusade at Harringay Arena shook the whole nation, and it seemed clear we were on the brink of revival, but the Archbishop, along with other church leaders, begged Billy to go back to America. By the time he returned the following year, the moment had passed.

After the departure of Billy Graham in 1954, it seemed as though evangelism in Britain went into the doldrums, but in the last ten years there has been a transformation. During the 1950s evangelists often laboured faithfully without seeing any fruit. Today we rarely give an invitation without a response. There are more people coming to Christ now than ever before in the memory of the current generation of evangelists.

We are faced with a new opportunity. Two factors demonstrate that God is moving in a special way in our country. Firstly, there is a greater awareness in the mainline denominations of the need to evangelise. More and more leaders are saying, 'Yes, we must get involved in mission', and for more and more of those leaders it is becoming apparent that mission must involve the direct proclamation of the great message of the gospel. Secondly, the legacy of the first world war is dying. Church and Christianity are no longer seen popularly as the mechanisms of oppression. The generation that grew up in the fifties and sixties threw itself into selfish consumerism. That generation became a new establishment in the media, standing for materialistic and secularistic values, and having a perceptible anti-Christian bias. So we have a new generation of young people, among whom an increasingly influential minority is seeing Christianity as a revolutionary option. As young people always do, they are rebelling against the parental norm. This means that we in our generation must show them a radical alternative, a Christianity that mirrors Christ.

Few Christians would deny that in spite of some excesses the Charismatic movement has had a great influence for good on the mainline denominations. It has encouraged people to examine what they do and to ask the question, 'Is this God-ordained or simply a tradition of men?' and it has spawned the house-church movement, which in years to come may well prove to have been the most significant thing that has happened during this decade. The charismatic renewal has had enormous influence in the Roman Catholic church, resulting in a new evangelistic zeal which in some areas has put hundreds of young people on the streets witnessing for Christ.

Exciting as all this is, it pales beside what God is doing in the Church worldwide. Put simply, the Church is exploding. In South America it is growing at one and a half times the birth rate. In Africa, south of the Sahara, it is growing at twice the birthrate, and in Muslim North Africa there are cracks in the apparent monolithic structure of Islam. All over the world, except in Western Europe, the Church of Jesus Christ is on the march. It is the most exciting organisation in the world today, growing faster than it ever has done before. And we who are the people of God must act as his prophets. First, we must call his wandering people back to him. There is a desperate need for Christians in Europe to repent of their allegiance to the trappings of religion and to love the Lord himself. Our God is good and merciful and he longs to do a miracle in our countries.

We stand on the brink of what I firmly believe could be the greatest outpouring of the Holy Spirit that our country has ever seen. We must evangelise, because it is only as we evangelise those outside the Church that we will begin to see rising up a generation that does not know what cannot be done. When we have a generation like that, then God will be able to do whatever he wants to do because he will be no longer restricted by our unbelief. Let us make the victory of Jesus ring through our nation as never before.

1.5

Signs and wonders

1. How Jesus saw signs and wonders

(a) His own ministry

Miracles accompanied Jesus' preaching of the gospel. When John the Baptist sent messengers to inquire if he was the Messiah, Jesus sent the reply, 'Go back and repeat to John what you hear and see: the blind receive sight, the lame walk, those who have leprosy are cured, the deaf hear, the dead are raised, and the good news is preached to the poor' (Matt. 11:4–5).

When confronting the Jews in Jerusalem, Jesus said, 'The miracles I do in my Father's name speak for me' (John 10:25) and he urged them, 'Believe the miracles, that you may learn and understand that the Father is in me, and I in the Father' (10:38).

The word translated 'miracles' means 'works'. Jesus cannot be separated from his words or works. The Father is revealed in both.

(b) *In his disciples' ministry*

When he sent the twelve to evangelise they were commanded not only to preach that God's kingdom is near, but also to heal the sick, deliver people from demonic forces and even to raise the dead. Their ministries were to be an extension of Jesus' own ministry, revealing his Father and the nature of his kingdom.

Jesus gave a similar commission to the seventy-two. They rejoiced that even the demons submitted to them in the name of Jesus. He immediately taught them why: their names were written in heaven. They belonged to the kingdom of God and in the name of Jesus could exercise authority over whatever opposed him.

Faith was essential if they were to see the power of God at work.

'I tell you the truth, anyone who has faith in me will do what I have been doing. He will do even greater things than these, because I am going to the Father. And I will do whatever you ask in my name, so that the Son may bring glory to the Father. You may ask for anything in my name and I will do it' (John 14:12–14).

Such amazing promises are made to 'anyone who has faith'. Greater things still would be possible once he returned to the Father because the Holy Spirit would then live in them.

2. How the early church used signs and wonders

The closing verses of Mark are thought by some to be a later addition to the gospel account. Even if this is so, they reflect the faith and expectancy of early Christians. They were commissioned by Jesus to go into all the world to preach the good news. They expected also to see God at work in miraculous ways, including deliverance and healing: 'They will place their hands on sick people, and they will get well' (Mark 16:18). These are signs that will accompany those who believe. 'Then the disciples went out and preached everywhere, and the Lord worked with them and confirmed his word by the signs that accompanied it' (John 16:20).

There is ample evidence of this in the Acts of the Apostles. Many wonders and miraculous signs were done by the apostles. The healing of the cripple at the temple gate is given as a vivid example. Peter made it clear that such a healing was possible by faith in the name of Jesus.

When the opposition in Jerusalem began to harden, the disciples met together in prayer. They saw their need clearly, 'Enable your servants to speak your word with great boldness. Stretch out your hand to heal and perform miraculous signs and wonders through the name of your holy servant Jesus' (Acts 4:29–30). The Lord answered their prayer by filling them with the Holy Spirit again.

It was clear that, like Jesus, the apostles expected to communicate the gospel of the kingdom in word and power. This was an expectation shared by Paul, used so significantly by God in evangelism. He brought the gospel to the Thessalonians not only with words, 'but also with power, with the Holy Spirit and with deep conviction'. He tells the Romans that he fully proclaimed the gospel of Christ by what he said and did, 'by the power of signs and miracles, through the power of the Spirit'.

The inference is that the gospel is only fully proclaimed when there is the expectation that God will confirm his word with signs following. Certainly Paul impresses on the Galatians their need to exercise faith in the word so that they can continue to move in the miraculous power of God (Gal. 3:1–5). He reminded the Corinthians, 'The kingdom of God is not a matter of talk but of power' (1 Cor. 4:20).

3. Signs and wonders today

We are to proclaim that same gospel and same kingdom today. Does God expect us to communicate the gospel in the same way? There is no biblical evidence to suggest otherwise.

He is the same yesterday, today and forever. The power and authority of his name has not diminished with the passing of centuries. His word and promises are as true today as ever they were. Anyone who has faith in Jesus can do what he has been doing.

(a) Why do we not witness more of God's sovereign power at work in the miraculous?

Failure to respond in faith to the operation of God's own Spirit in his world would be nothing less than foolishness. However, we do need to beware of other opportunities for spiritual immaturity. Any attempt to make the Living God fit into our neatly packaged human formula for his activity is doomed to failure.

God is God and can be no other. It is as we listen to his voice that we gain the revelation as to what and how we should pray. To assert boldly that God must do 'this, or that' is spiritually foolish, but to assert that he no longer performs signs and wonders can be spiritually fatal to life and growth.

Often there is not the faith or expectation that God will confirm his word with signs and wonders. To maintain that such events are not for today contradicts the scriptural evidence and, many would contend, serves only to provide an excuse for not exercising faith for the Holy Spirit to work with such power. If Jesus and the apostles knew they could not proclaim the gospel fully without demonstrating the authority and power of the kingdom, will we be able to convince this generation with words alone? Is not our witness only partial if we speak the words of the kingdom without demonstrating the works of the kingdom?

God is no magician with miracles on tap to suit human ambitions. It is never enough for people to seek signs as ends in themselves, a lesson which Simon Magnus learned to his cost! (Acts 8.20). Jesus stood firmly against the spiritual hucksters of his day, he continually emphasised that signs are not performed by God merely to make people believe, but because they do believe. They demonstrate the love, grace and power of the Lord in whom we believe and are a witness to those who are offered the words of life.

In times of spiritual revival there is renewed faith that God will act in powerful ways. What he is prepared to do in this generation is only consistent with what he has been able to do in every generation of the Church's history. Where there is faith (and sometimes that is only on the part of the preacher) God will confirm his word with signs following. These are the works of power that confirm the word and in no way stand in opposition or competition with the word.

In many evangelistic meetings in Britain today, not only do great numbers come to faith in Jesus, they also see his sovereign hand at work in miraculous ways, often bringing healing to hundreds of people. In all such acts God himself is glorified and faith is encouraged.

Church Strategy and Structures

2.1

Church growth principles

When we speak about church growth principles we are not thinking in terms of success-guaranteed techniques. There are many things that a church leader could do to fill his church, like numbering the seats with a prize for the one occupying the lucky number, or by hiring the best in musical entertainment week after week! But such methods would be inconsistent with the gospel we proclaim and the character of the Lord we profess to serve. A church growth principle is of a different order. It represents a general principle derived from Scripture and demonstrated in the experience of the church. It is a pragmatism which is biblically based. It is a way of working which is consistent with the righteous and compassionate nature of God, and in line with his purposes.

Having distilled a general church growth principle from the statements of Scripture and the experience of the rapidly growing church of the New Testament period, the church growth student then traces its application by the church through the centuries, and learns from the experience of the contemporary church around the world. Closer to home, he will also want to look at growing churches in his own country, in situations which most closely resemble his own. Negatively, he will also be interested to observe whether the neglect of the principle results in non-growth and spiritual stagnation.

Undergirding every church growth principle is a cluster of theological convictions. All these are expounded elsewhere but can be briefly stated here!

● humankind is corrupted and enslaved by sin; lost and under condemnation (Rom. 3:23; 6:23).

● Christ, who is God's only Son, came to this earth to become humankind's unique Saviour (John 14:6; Acts 4:12).

● God wants lost people found (Ezek. 18:32; 1 Tim. 2:3, 4; 2 Peter 3:9).

● once 'found' (i.e. reconciled to God, born again in his family and made sons and daughters of God by adoption) they should be incorporated into the church of Christ, which is his body here on earth (Acts 2:41–42; 1 Cor. 12:13–14).

It is these theological non-negotiables which church growth principles seek to express and apply. As this volume is concerned with practical evangelism, I have selected those which most directly apply, and, to sharpen their thrust, have expressed them in question form.

1. How do we rate our evangelistic effectiveness?

The narrative of the Acts of the Apostles provides an inspiring record of the explosive growth of the Church during the first thirty years of its existence. Peter in the Jewish world, Philip in Samaria and Paul among Gentiles of the Roman Empire all gave top priority to preaching the good news of Jesus Christ, establishing churches and to building up the new converts. Such apostolic concerns were not confined to the leadership but permeated through the Christians they left in each place as the fruit of their ministry. This passion for evangelism cannot be restricted to the pioneering phase of mission. It should be maintained in every church which finds itself surrounded by large numbers of people who have either never heard the gospel, not yet seen a convincing demonstration of its power to transform people's lives, or have, for whatever reasons, rejected the Lord's claim upon their lives. As was the case in New Testament times, most churches in Britain today occupy little more than a bridge-head position in society. It's time to move out, for there is much ground to be possessed and lost territory to be reclaimed.

Church growth insights help us in two important regards – honesty and accuracy. Let us begin by examining the performance of our church during the past ten years:

What priority have we given to the proclamation of the gospel?

What practical steps have we taken to enable as many people as possible to hear the message God has entrusted us to proclaim?

If unbelievers have had a variety of opportunities, how many of them responded to the invitation to commit their lives to Christ as Saviour and Lord?

Of that number, how many have continued to grow in their spiritual lives, to become effective witnesses in the world and responsible members of the church?

These are basic questions, but few churches in Britain are performing sufficiently well to take them as read. In fact, it is those which have the most evangelistic concern, and are seeing increasing fruit for their labours, which are continually evaluating, improving and experimenting in these areas.

Notice that the heart of our concern is not *whether* or not the church is growing, but *how* it is growing. Some congregations are increasing but at the expense of other churches. They are growing by Christians transferring from one camp to another. Their gains merely represent someone else's losses. When new people arrive we must be honest enough to ask where they have come from, why they have come, and has their coming benefited them to the point that they have become a channel through which God's love is reaching other people's lives.

Honesty demands accuracy, which means counting heads and asking questions. We count people because people count. It is a demonstration that the church cares and is undertaken because the leadership recognises it is accountable, for one day there will be a spiritual audit. I have yet to visit a church which did not bother to count the collection after each service! If we value people more than pounds and have what a previous generation described as 'a passion for souls', we will be evaluating our endeavours to win them for Christ. God's ways are most frequently uncovered in the prayer-soaked agony of trial and error. It is those who sow in tears who reap with shouts of joy! It is he that goes forth weeping bearing the seed for sowing who shall come home with shouts of joy, bringing his sheaves with him (Ps. 126:5–6).

2. Have we defined our evangelistic task with sufficient clarity?

This question is posed to stimulate us to ask what we might expect to happen as a direct result of our witness and gospel proclamation. If we do not anticipate any response we are unlikely to see any or to have made any provision to deal with it. For too long we British Christians have masqueraded our predisposition to failure under the pious label of 'faithfulness'. While true faithfulness may not in every circumstance result in instant and dramatic results, it should always lead to effectiveness in the implementation of the will of God. Faithfulness describes a faith-inspired attitude. A faithful person is someone who is both full of faith and is having his faith stretched in the face of fresh challenges. Faith is the assurance of things hoped for (Heb. 11:1). Some Christians seem to regard faith as a fluorescent fog fanned from heaven. In the Bible faith dispels fog – enabling us to see farther and with greater clarity. With the eye of faith our field of vision stretches to the horizon and beyond it, for it embodies 'the conviction of things not seen'. Such faith stimulates us to action, just as Noah invested in a Cammell-Laird sized boat-building project long before the first drop of rain fell as evidence of a flood to follow.

In terms of practical evangelism 'faithfulness' entails prayerfully setting goals and drawing up plans to achieve them. It means looking at our existing congregation in relation to the communities from which they are drawn:

Who can be reached through their network of contacts?

How can we set about motivating and mobilizing God's people so that they are equipped and have ideas and opportunities to embark on the task?

Try looking beyond the existing situation by describing your 'potential congregation':

Are there significant sections of the community which neither you nor any of the other local churches are reaching for Christ: teenage gangs, young marrieds, senior citizens, single parent families, families with the bread-winner who commutes to work or travels long distances, shift works, etc?

What new things could you be doing to reach such neglected groups (or 'hidden peoples' as they are described in Church Growth parlance)?

Then we need to come to terms with the fact that when such groups look inside the church and find nobody like themselves there they will feel 'odd-man-out' and be tempted to slip away unnoticed. As new Christians they will want to meet new people who understand their particular perspective and have had to work through their range of problems in relating their new-found faith to their everyday lives. They will require tailor-made groups and, in some circumstances, the church may need to think in terms of planting new churches to ensure the development of a worshipping and witnessing congregation which is indigenous to the community.

In defining our evangelistic task our objective is not simply to register decisions but to make disciples (Matt. 28:19). Our perspective is not one of a brief encounter but a life-long commitment. Disciple-making requires a long-term investment. Has your church developed on going programmes beyond weekly church attendance to ensure the growth of babies in Christ, or are they destined to a life-time of spiritual adolescence?

Finally, our evangelistic responsibility does not end with the proclamation of the gospel, we also need to understand as much as we can about what is happening on the receiving end. For the response is influenced not only by what we communicate, but also by what happens to the seed of the word of God after it has been planted in the soil of people's hearts. Jesus describes the possible developments in the short, intermediate and long-term in the parable of the sower (Mark 4:1–20). We need to find ways of working suited to different kinds of soil: hard, shallow or weed-choked, as well as maximising the potential yield of good ground.

3. How do we identify our evangelistic resources?

Every good idea carries a price tag in terms of abilities, time and funding. God has given to his body all the functions necessary for it to be fully operational. The problem is to identify and begin to exercise those limbs and muscles so that the church can begin to move in the area of evangelism. In order to help you do this you may want to call upon the services of a visiting evangelist, not to do evangelism on your behalf, but to help you develop an effective outreach programme.

The winning of individuals and groups to Jesus Christ should be the concern of every believer. Therefore evangelism should not be regarded as a department in the church's organisation, but as a dimension of the church's life. All that the church undertakes in its worship, social outreach, community concerns, and children's, youth, and adult educational and fellowship programmes has either a direct or indirect bearing on evangelism. So they need to be viewed on a regular basis from that perspective.

Pursuing the body metaphor, the gift of evangelism has been described as both the reproductive organ and the legs of the church. Without these organs the church is destined to sterility and immobility. Christ's command to his church is to go and bear fruit, for that purpose we were chosen and appointed (John 15:16). All within the church are called to bear witness to the central truths of the good news of Christ and to his working in their lives. Some within the church, which church growth experts estimate to be in the region of 10 per cent, have the gift of evangelism. That is, people who have a God-given ability to present the gospel clearly and persuasively, and to sense when and how to make their approach or seize an opportunity.

How do we find such people who are lurking, undetected and unemployed in our church? The best way to embark upon specific evangelistic projects is to get as many people involved in on-the-job training and then see who has discovered a particular skill in doing it. The remainder will not have wasted their time, because their involvement will have equipped them to become better witnesses. Every world champion swimmer began by helplessly and nervously splashing about in the water.

Having identified your evangelists, the remainder of the congregation can cluster around them to contribute their specific gifts in hospitality, music, encouragement, practical help, organising, teaching and pastoral care, to provide the context in which the evangelist can operate. Any mother knows that a whole medical team is involved in giving birth to a baby. And once the baby has arrived her responsibilities are not over, and other people, including father, have their roles to play at various stages in the infant's development.

Resources begin to emerge as evangelistic principles are taught and prayed through and as the leadership involves the congregation in gathering ideas and formulating plans.

4. Are we developing appropriate evangelistic strategies?

Earlier we drew attention to the need to identify the different kinds of people which make up the community we believe the Lord has called us to serve. In order to show Christ-like love and to begin to communicate effectively we need to begin where they are rather than expect them to jump over to where we are. Consider for a moment our Lord's pattern.

He always had the nature of God, but he did not think that by force he should try to become equal with God. Instead of this, of his own free will he gave up all he had, and took the nature of a servant. He became like man and appeared in human likeness. He was humble and walked the path of obedience all the way to death – his death on the cross (Phil. 2:6–8 GNB).

(a) *Communicating in everyday terms*

In becoming a man, he did not remain aloof and shielded. Rather, he lived in the closest proximity to ordinary people. He taught not in the language of the Jewish religious elite (Hebrew), nor that of the secular scholar (Classical Greek), but in Aramaic, and 'koine' (trade) Greek, the languages of the people. He spoke to people in terms they could understand, drawing his imagery from their everyday world: fishing, well-water, children's games, sowing, harvesting, sweeping the house, breadmaking, storing wine and patching old clothes. Do we use language those around us can understand and address ourselves to their world and concerns?

(b) *Being where people are*

Jesus spoke to people on their territory and in their familiar surroundings where they felt relaxed and undistracted. He addressed the crowds on hillsides, and crowded into a private home. He showed social outcasts such as tax-collectors (the 'Mafia' of his day) and prostitutes that he accepted them for what they were by eating at their table. But his acceptance was always with the aim of changing them.

Evangelistic guest services are commendable when outsiders are invited and some, at least, accept. But they do not begin to exhaust our evangelistic obligation or potential. Like Jesus, the Church today must go where people are – into the shopping precincts, the pubs, onto the golf course, into the hairdressers, the leisure centres and keep fit class. Neither should we forget the need to meet people in their own homes. In making this list I have in mind individual Christians and specific groups who are witnessing in each of these situations and are finding people waiting to be found.

(c) *Special ventures*

The churches in this country need to think not only in terms of varieties of methods but in scales of operation. At the base line is the witness of each individual believer. Then there are the evangelistic efforts of small groups in the neighbourhood, school, workplace and sports club. The local church itself should ensure that it is involved in regular outreach through its Sunday worship and programme of weekly activities.

Then from time to time churches need to get together in a concerted and co-ordinated effort to cover an extensive rural area or to reach a city. In urban society the churches lack community visibility. They need to be seen acting together and pooling their resources to make an impact on the entire community. Such occasional large-scale events become newsworthy and thereby attract media attention. Television, radio and newspaper coverage can cause the gospel to be talked about in the country at large, thus helping to create a God-consciousness which is otherwise inhibited by media disinterest.

5. Have we an effective programme to conserve the fruits of evangelism?

A new baby demands urgent and constant attention. The same is true of a new Christian. He needs more than *telling*, he needs *showing* how to pray to his heavenly Father, how to read and apply the Bible to his life. He requires help in explaining his commitment to Christ to his family and friends. He needs to learn how to witness and introduce those he loves to Jesus. In very few churches is such basic teaching and personal care provided. The new Christian is expected to integrate into the rest of the Christian family like a new pupil with no previous knowledge of French being expected to pick up from a fourth year French class. How many of us had the help of a mature Christian who met regularly with us to pray, study the Bible, providing personal support? It is all too easy for a church to be so busy running its organisations that it has neither time to notice or respond to the real needs of its members.

A growing church requires spiritual foster parents who are trained and set aside from other responsibilities to help new Christians. Larger churches will require a 'welcome group' where groups of new believers can find their feet, learn from one another's experience and about their church's priorities and goals from the leaders. We also need an ongoing programme of Christian education which is not suddenly cut off after the early teens, but applies Christian truth and provides companionship at every stage in life. With increasing social pressures creating such havoc in family life, the church itself must ensure that it is not adding to the problem with its organisation overload. Some churches are already experimenting with inter-operational teaching, where the whole family is together learning from one another and enjoying each other's company. And what about those who are no longer at work? Earlier retirement plus longer life expectation create exciting new possibilities to develop new ministries.

We began this contribution by mentioning some key theological concerns which undergird church growth principles. We conclude by listing vital attitudes with which they need to be applied:

we require honesty in facing issues and evaluating results

expectancy that God will bless in any undertaking his Spirit has inspired within us

consistency and perseverance in recognition that a spiritual harvest requires months of patient toil

humility in acknowledging that as important as our role may be, the major part is in the hands of God to whom we give all the glory.

2.2

Prayer and spiritual conflict

Introduction

'If the labour of prayer does not preceed as well as accompany all of our work in the kingdom, it will become nothing but a work of man, more or less capably done and with more or less effort and agitation as the case may be, but resulting in nothing but weariness both to ourselves and to others.' So wrote O. Hallesby in his book on prayer.

Most of us belong to churches full of meetings and activity but sadly lacking in productivity particularly in the area of evangelism. If the church is like every human institution, organized by man's ingenuity and kept alive by man's activity, then prayer would be of little consequence. But if we see it as the body of Christ able to effect a radical change in our world through ordinary people motivated by supernatural power, then our beginning, ending and middle would be in prayer. Power does not rest in prayer. It is found in God. But God responds to the prayers of his people. If we had one priority in our church today it must be to pray, even if that means stopping a great deal of other activity.

God's promise

The unlimited potential of prayer as seen through the promises in the Bible is staggering as God moves into action in the lives and situations that we bring before him (cf. Matt. 18:19; Matt. 7:7; John 14:13; Js. 4:2, 3; John 15:7; Matt. 21:22; Js. 5:16; Luke 11:5–9; Luke 18:1–8; Luke 18:10–14; Matt. 6:7). The following parables teach us different aspects of prayer, yet despite these promises it's amazing how little we pray.

Why Pray

(a) *To hear God's voice*

The ministry of Jesus was to do what the Father was doing and say what the Father was saying. For many, prayer is an attempt to move God over to our point of view or to get God to do what we want done. In the end it often seems much easier to try and do it ourselves than to get God involved. But the whole concept of prayer is to discover God's point of view, how, when and where he wants to move, to move with him and to obey him. This must be our priority in evangelism. Our strategy must include an understanding of spiritual conflict as we seek wisdom over matters of church direction. If time is set aside to listen to God individually and corporately, not just in silence but in praise, worship and prayer, God will speak to us.

It may be through impressions in our mind, through Scriptures, or direct words of prophecy. Usually God gives a growing sense of direction confirmed in various ways. All in leadership need to be part of a small group of people with whom they're sharing and praying together and listening to what God is saying. In the midst of the clamour of human voices we must hear the voice of the living God.

(b) *To ask of God*

(i) *For others*. Intercession is 'acting as a go between'. We can pray on other people's behalf. The Bible tells us we need to ask

in faith. That is according to the faith God has given us.

specifically. Much of our praying is for vague blessing for vague people in vague situations which means we can never find out if the prayer was answered! We are called to pray and trust him in specific ways for specific situations and specific people so that we can see specific answers. The biblical concept of crying and pleading with the Lord is strange to most of us, yet these are expressions of genuine concern. In times past when the people of God became desperate they cried out to God and He answered them. We must do away with polite praying which expresses truth but which does not come from our heart. We must encourage people in our churches to pray from their inner being and to cry out to God until the answer is seen. This is particularly true in the area of evangelism.

in agreement. When two or three agree in a church situation it is a way of testing the rightness of our prayer. A practical thing to do is to divide the fellowship into triplets and encourage each triplet to pray for nine unbelievers regularly and specifically. This agreement in faith will have tremendous results.

according to his will. As we wait on him, he makes his will plain to us and we can pray accordingly.

(ii) *For the Holy Spirit*. The greatest need today for all of us is an outpouring of the Holy Spirit, first on the church and secondly on the world. History shows us that God sends his Holy Spirit in power upon a praying people. He comes to those who really want him. Pray for revival, for an outpouring of the Holy Spirit on the church which will result in an awakening in the world. Pray persistently so that God realises we are serious.

(c) *To fight*

Evangelism can only really be understood in the context of conflict and warfare. It is in the place of prayer that the battle for the hearts of men and women is won and the direction of nations is decided. We must rediscover the type of prayer that not only asks but also declares. Rulers exercising authority do not beg or beseech, they command. We often feel it is presumptuous to pray in this way, so we ask the Lord to do it. But are told to submit ourselves to God and to resist the Devil (Js. 4:7). Resisting means addressing him head on, issuing a word of command! This is done, not on our own authority, but on the authority of the name of Jesus. We are involved in a real spiritual conflict not against people but against spiritual forces (Eph. 6:10ff.). We must stop attacking one another and start unitedly to attack the real enemy. Jesus said, 'the whole world lies in the evil one.' The Bible tells us that 'the earth is the Lord's and the fullness thereof' (Ps. 24). The enemy has usurped what is the Lord's and that includes men and women. Bringing them into the kingdom of God inevitably involves conflict. Evangelism is rescuing men and women out of darkness and bringing them into light. When we grasp the fact of this conflict our attitude to evangelism will change. It helps us to realise that prayer must be our priority.

How to pray

If we are going to be involved in this conflict there are certain things we need to know.

(a) *Know the enemy*

Paul talks about this enemy being powerful, organized, cunning, intelligent, unseen but finite. Satan himself is the head of a vast array of evil spirits. These are not 'forces of evil' but distinct intelligent beings. We must see the day-to-day conflicts with evil spirits in our own life, the life of our church, and the lives of those with whom we are dealing as well as the real strongholds of evil that dominate our society.

(i) *What is his work?* He leads people away from God: Christians through disobedience and non-Christians by keeping them from seeking him. His prime work is to afflict the church and prevent it from being effective. How does he do this?

He divides. He will always attempt to set Christians against one another. Sometimes in families, or in the family of the church. He notes gossip and negative talk. The first step in dealing with the enemy is to encourage the fellowship to 'walk in the light' with one another. Divided we are ineffective, united we are strong.

He deceives. We need to be careful of doing things that appear spiritual but which in fact are side-issues. He keeps many Christians busy with lots of good Christian activity so preventing them from doing what God is really calling them to do.

He destroys. He comes to break up churches. He attacks physically.

He blinds. In praying for non-Christians we must pray aggressively, claiming the promises of 2 Corinthians 10:4–5, pulling down the stronghold of deception. Teach people to pray for their friends in this way.

(b) *Know your authority*

(i) *What Christ has done* (Col. 2:15; Eph. 1:21–3; John 12:31; 1 John 3:8; Heb. 2:14). Christ on the cross won the victory over the powers of darkness and enabled men and women to share in that victory.

(ii) *The Christian position*. We are in Christ (Eph. 1:1, 3; Eph. 2:6; Eph. 3:10; 2 Cor. 10:3–4). Paul encourages us to stand in our position of victory.

(c) *Know how to fight*

(i) *Defensively*. We need to be alert for the ways in which the enemy attacks, whether through individuals in the fellowship, family units, the whole church, or the work in which we're engaged. For the enemy to leave a situation there often needs to be repentance, as his in road is often through some area of sin in our lives.

Note Nehemiah 4, and see how he set a guard to protect the work. We must set up prayer cells, prayer gatherings, prayer partnerships, to protect the work that God is doing.

(ii) *Aggressively*. This is primarily in the area of evangelism as we seek to take ground for the kingdom of God. We must encourage prayer at several levels:

Personal prayer. Each individual needs to listen to God and to respond to God and to pray for his family.

Prayer triplets. Regular groups of threes meeting together to pray for unbelievers. Everybody in the church could be involved.

Fellowship prayer meetings. Many church prayer meetings are poorly attended. The reasons may be varied: uninspiring leadership, lack of purpose and specific prayer, too few people dominating the prayer meetings, too predictable. Prayer needs plenty of variety.

Suggestions for prayer meetings

(i) *Variety*. Try not to make it just another meeting. Have prayer meetings for a period of time and then stop for a time or change the time and place. Early in the morning is a good time for local prayer meetings as it saves booking another evening in people's busy diaries.

(ii) *Length*. Let people know how long it is going to be. It stops folk getting agitated if it goes on too long. If God leads, it can always be extended.

(iii) *Participation*. Encourage everybody to take part. Stop long prayers which prevent this. Encourage short, loud specific prayers.

(iv) *Content*. Give specific subjects for prayer. Be sure to stay with a subject until it is prayed through. Dotting about all over the place is very destructive in prayer. Remind yourselves the next time what you prayed for and see what answers there have been. It is an exciting adventure together, not a dull routine. Intersperse with praise and thanksgiving.

(v) *Purpose.* Be sure of the purpose of the prayer meeting. It may be for personal needs, or for specific needs in the area. Don't allow it to be too general. Fix targets – and go for them!

Prayer and fasting

There is tremendous value in personal and corporate fasting in relationship to prayer. This is particularly true in areas of conflict. At times when real breakthrough is needed, get the church together to fast for a period of time and come together to pray. Have short fasts to begin with! We must regain this lost weapon. Remember both prayer and fasting develop with practice – don't try to be a giant overnight.

The secret of evangelism

Evangelism is regaining territory that has been taken by the enemy. It is not a process of intellectually convincing people of truth but of releasing them from prison. Evangelism must be approached in the perspective of spiritual warfare. Therefore the priorities are:

(i) *Prayer.* To know the enemy strongholds and strategy; to break the enemy's hold on people and places; to know God's strategy in battle; to cry to God for release of his power.

(ii) *Praise.* A declaration of the Lordship of Christ.

(iii) *Preaching.* A proclamation of the cross of Christ.

(iv) *Perseverance.* Deliverance is not necessarily immediate (cf. Moses and Pharaoh).

(v) *Positive action* The real battle may be in the spiritual realm, but we have to work hard on the ground to reap the benefits. The Lord gave Joshua the promised land, but he had to go in and possess it.

2.3

Planning

Life would be far too colourless if we were without visionaries. We all rejoice at the results of a successful venture. The vision and the results are like the twin banks of a river, getting from one side to the other involves crossing a bridge, the name of the bridge is planning! Short cuts and similar inadequacies will cause the inevitable introduction to the river below!

Is planning, however, an exercise showing lack of faith and limiting the operation of the Holy Spirit? The answer to that must be a very emphatic no. Can you imagine a company embarking upon a sales promotion dreaming of doing so without a plan? If this is good enough for the endeavours of mere humanity, how dare we offer Almighty God any less? The differences comes, however, in prayer. We must plan to pray; and pray to plan. The meeting of a planning committee must have a time (preferably at the beginning and the end) for prayer. This serves as a reminder that the plans must be his from conception to inception. When plans are properly and prayerfully laid they provide the security which facilitates a response to the touches of the Holy Spirit. Absence of those plans can leave us lurching from crisis to catastrophe in such a way that little time is left to hear the still small voice.

Planning itself is essentially a practical exercise and requires practical guidelines. The majority of events are better planned by a group than by an individual. This group should not be fewer than three to ensure a good breadth of opinion and not more than six. Any more will make decision making interminable. The choice of these individuals is crucial. Avoid visionaries since on a planning group preoccupation with vision blurs practicality. Visions and dreams are given to individuals but good plans are the product of corporate understanding. Remember that these people will need to get things done, not necessarily do things themselves. A good planning committee shares the work as widely as possible to maximise effectiveness.

Lastly, the group must be prepared to trust each other completely. If necessary, a good length of time must be given at the first meeting to getting to know each other. A practical way of doing this is arranging to have a meal together prior to the first meeting. The value of this will only become apparent as you continue to work together and sometimes need to anticipate another reaction to a particular situation. If this ground work is laid properly there will be no necessity for 'mutual checking up' when decisions have been reached (the group should be selected for expertise not because they all agree with each other).

Your group must now apply itself to four tasks:

1. Determining and understanding objectives

The setting of objectives is crucial both to the ultimate achievement and the continuing morale of those involved in the project. Each person must understand these objectives because only then will everyone, however seemingly insignificant, be bound together by a sense of mutual purpose. Progress and ultimate success will be measured with reference to the original objectives. Setting too many is a subtle way of making sure you look as if you have done something but the likelihood is that most will be forgotten by the participants and remain unachieved. Imprecise objectives leave no reference points for monitoring progress, hence the team lose heart because they have no idea if they are moving forward. A few clearly stated objectives will provide the right springboard and the right foundation for work to begin.

2. Setting realistic time targets

Many projects falter because the time factor is not given adequate consideration right at the outset. Each step must be given estimated times to ensure each part fits together. Here is another plea: make the time scale realistic. Nobody is going to thank a planning committee who set deadlines which are more likely to result in coronaries and breakdowns than in successful accomplishment. Don't, however, make them too generous or the hobgoblin of procrastination will rear its ugly head.

3. Division of responsibility within the group

The effectiveness of any planning group will be impaired if individuals feel themselves either to be carrying more than their fair share of the work or that they are peripheral to the task. Both are avoided if at this stage responsibility is divided between the members of the group. Each individual will then involve others in their particular area and hence more people become involved and the work load spreads.

Here is a list of some of the areas of work:

(i) *Prayer*. Group leaders spreading information quickly.

(ii) *Publicity*. The campaign must be planned early and carefully brought to a climax at the time of the event.

(iii) *Music*. Book featured musicians as early as possible. Leave the choir as late as practical, as a high level of enthusiasm needs to be maintained and it is difficult to do this in large groups over long periods.

(iv) *Counselling*. How many counsellors? Who? Are they to be trained?

(v) *Speakers*. Book early and have alternatives or disappointment will be guaranteed.

(vi) *Follow up*. Through churches? How do they get information?

These are some of the areas, others are financial control, catering, stewarding and arrangement of venues. Make it clear who is given these jobs and follow up by sending each group member a written list. Remember two things:

There are always many more willing and able people around than you think; a planning committee must find them and not give up and do it themselves.

Don't always expect people to achieve the objective in the same way as you would have done it.

4. Establishing communication

Lastly, the communication network must be set up. How often will the planning committee meet? General progress reports must be circulated as widely as possible for prayer and morale. People must know who to include and how to contact them.

Planning is the art of asking the right questions *and* making sure they are answered. Always plan for the best as Jesus never deserves anything less. Remember, good prayerful planning enables all to respond to Spirit-inspired adjustments and facilitate concentration on the areas of greatest need.

2.4

Human resources

Jesus had no great organisation, no buildings, no pre-packaged programmes or techniques. He chose twelve men, and one of these was a traitor. But through the others he turned the world upside down.

Today our churches are cluttered with organisations, we spend fortunes on buildings and search for techniques. But we neglect our most precious and potent resource – our members.

One glance at the New Testament or at Church history will tell us that God's methods are people. The gospel spread like wild fire across the face of the ancient world because ordinary Christians everywhere 'gossipped Christ' (cf. Acts 8:1–4).

In New Testament times it was the responsibility of all Christians to take the good news to those who were not Christians. Today we appear to feel that it is the responsibility of non-Christians to come into our church premises to get themselves converted.

Let us follow through our thinking about evangelism and human resources in its right context, the church as the body of Christ:

1. The Body of Christ

Sometimes people say 'I wish I had been alive when Jesus was here. How wonderful to see his expression, hear the words from his lips and see him touch the leper. I wish I had been with Jesus in the body.'

The New Testament makes it clear that there is no way of having real fellowship with Jesus except in the body and that body is the living fellowship of his believing and obedient people. It is in this body that Jesus lives and through this body he manifests himself to the world.

When a person is born again he is born into this body and the nitty-gritty of the Christian life is our sharing of the life of Christ in the body and being a living and active member of the body (Eph. 1:22–3).

The New Testament says many things about the body of Christ. I will comment on four of them:

(a) Gathered by God

If we gave a pencil and paper to everyone in our church and asked them to write down why they were there, we would get an interesting variety of answers. But the fundamental truth about any truly Christian church is that its members are there because God called and put them there. They are not there by whim or chance. They are gathered by God.

Doubtless the first apostles would have given different reasons why they followed Jesus. But Jesus said, 'Deeper than any reason you give is the fact that you have not chosen me but I have chosen you and ordained you to go and bring forth fruit' (John 15:16).

Your congregation may not appear to be a company gathered by God. But let no lack of beauty or spots or wrinkles lead you astray. It is here in this ordinary congregation that Jesus intends to live by his Spirit and through which he is to manifest himself to the world. 'You together are the house of God' (1 Cor. 3:16; Eph. 2:19–22) and in that house Jesus lives by his Spirit.

(b) Given to each other by God

Just think of the person you get on least well with in your church (does their face leap to your mind?). God has given that person to you and he has given you to that person that you might in his Spirit learn to love one another, to forgive one another, to pray for one another and to minister to one another. So the body, being of many members, is yet one body: 'God has so arranged the members of the body . . . so that there is no division in the body' (1 Cor. 12:24–5).

People around us are not impressed with our arguments. Most are not thinkers. They see and they feel. And what they need is to see a living demonstration of the presence and power of Jesus in a community of love, forgiveness and joy. And what they need to feel is the warmth of an extraordinary fellowship that is so filled with Jesus, his love, mercy and generosity, that they cannot keep it to themselves so it flows out into every part of life and every part of the community. There is nothing with greater evangelistic power than a living and overflowing church. And this begins when we start to give ourselves to and share our lives with one another in the church (Col. 3:12–17).

What binds us together is not our natural liking of one another or our agreeing with one another or even the mutual faith. What binds us together are the blood bonds of Jesus Christ and these bind us together in him for all eternity. If we have to live together for all eternity we may as well begin to learn to love one another now – 'So will the world know that you are my disciples' (John 13:34–5; 1 John. 4:7–21).

(c) Gifted by God

(i) *All have gifts.* Paul makes it clear that every member of the body of Christ has a gift or gifts: 'The Spirit gives gifts as he chooses to each one', 'To every one is given a gift' (cf. Rom. 12; 1 Cor. 12; Eph. 4).

Gifts are given to do the work and will of Christ. They are to glorify him, not us. They are for the good and upbuilding of the whole body. The more gifted a member is, the more he is the servant of others.

One day we will give an account of how we have used our gifts as well as all our time, talents and possessions. For we are owners of nothing but stewards of everything in Christ.

Paul is not normally thought of as a humorist but in 1 Corinthians 12 he has a series of hilarious but pointed cartoons about gifts. There is the foot sitting over in the corner sulking because it is not a hand. Paul says, 'Don't waste your time wishing you were someone else or had some other gift. Find out your gift and develop and use that.'

Then he has a large eye coming down the road on its own and claiming to be the whole body. 'You are not the whole body', says Paul, 'you may be able to see marvellously but you cannot touch or taste or smell or hear.' (Don't ask me what Paul is doing talking to him if he can't hear!) So Paul points out that no one member can do the work of the whole body, however great his gifts – not even if you call him a minister or clergyman.

The third cartoon is where the head says to the feet, 'We don't need you. Buzz off!' But if they did, the body would fall down. So, says Paul, for every member whose gifts are not discovered, developed and used the body is disabled and impoverished.

How much is your church disabled and impoverished?

(ii) *Discovering gifts.* There are several methods. The best is where a house group have been meeting weekly for about a year and have shared deeply. They study Romans 12, 1 Corinthians 12 and Ephesians 4. Following this they put down on the left side of a piece of paper the names of everyone in the room, including their own. They then put beside each name the gift or gifts they have perceived in each.

The leader collects the papers and reads out to each person in turn the gifts that all have attributed to them. When a group has shared at depth for a year there is usually a pretty good consensus of discernment about the gifts of each.

A second method is to look for someone (or more) in the fellowship who has the gift of discerning the gifts of others. It is usually a quiet, loving and encouraging kind of person.

A firm with as many workers as you have members would have a personnel officer or personnel department to use all the talents in the right place. It is probable God has provided one for you. Other methods are to be found in other papers or books on the gifts of the Spirit.

God has given us the resources for the work he wants done. Our prime need is to discover them and to build our structures around them. We must stop letting the existing structures dictate our needs and pushing people into vacant slots. Organisations eat people and eating people is wrong!

Jesus is the Lord, not the structures.

(iii) *Developing gifts*. It is not enough to discover gifts. We must also develop and use them.

The best way is in gift groups (people with the same gift meeting in groups of three to twelve) who meet once a fortnight to share, pray, reflect, study and to plan further action. Here is the action/reflection pattern so evident in Jesus' training of the Twelve.

What research there is suggests that about 10 per cent of church members will have a gift for evangelism. They should be discovered, set free from everything else to develop and use their gift in a group. They will do the more formal evangelism of door-to-door work, house group or party evangelism.

This does not mean that the other 90 per cent have no responsibility for evangelism. Only some are evangelists but all are to be witnesses in and through the contacts of everyday life. All need training in personal witness. The evangelists need the other gift groups. They will, for instance, soon get bogged down with family, personal and social problems unless they have pastoral, helping and counselling groups to whom they can hand over such problems so that they remain free to exercise their gifts as evangelists.

(d) *Growing in the knowledge and love of God*

Jesus never told us to make converts. He told us to make disciples (Matt. 28:18–20).

A disciple is a convert who goes on growing to maturity in Christ, who is growing as part of the body, in applying the faith to every part of life and is able to share his faith with others. We have too many converts who remain babes in Christ all their days and never grow up.

God's prime purpose is not to make us happy. It is to make us like his Son, to fill us with the Spirit and the purposes of his Son and to make us an able and active member of the body of his Son,

Home groups, sharing God's word and seeing how it works out in daily living, are fundamental in helping Christians grow to maturity and to loving, genuine witness. Most church members believe they ought to witness but they do not know how to begin and are not likely to try unless they are encouraged to learn, preferably in a house group. Most find it difficult to share with people outside the church because they have never been given the opportunity to share with others inside the church.

My own prescription for growth is for all new members to have one year's classes in home groups on Christian faith and life. Then to discover their gifts and join two groups meeting alternate weeks. The first would be a gift group and the other a neighbourhood 'Watch and Pray' group. This consists of those living in three or four adjoining streets who watch for newcomers, births, marriages or deaths, illness or need and visit to give help and to share their faith when opportune. They meet for Bible study, sharing and prayer.

Another major factor is leadership. Bad leadership is like the beech tree. It may look magnificent but nothing grows under it.

Good leaders train others to become good leaders. Good leaders enable a church to become alive in every member.

2. The church in the world

Everyone knows where the church is at eleven o'clock on a Sunday morning. Its members, like the fingers of hands pressed together in prayer, are gathered together for worship, to praise God and to receive his word.

But where is the church at eleven o'clock on a Monday morning? Its members are still in the church – they can never be other than in the church for they are the church. But on Monday Jesus has spread out the fingers of his hands and put them down on the map of your area.

One finger is a man who works in a factory over here. His mates rib him unmercifully about being a Christian but it is to him they go when in trouble and three others have become Christians through his life and witness. Another finger is a woman whom some call a housewife and I call a home-maker. Here she is on a wet Monday morning singing hymns of praise to Christ and all the neighbours know it and know her loving care.

Another is a big businessman making difficult decisions in a world of greys. But every day he dedicates his life and work to Christ, knows his guidance and lives by his redeeming mercy.

Another is a girl in a shop. It is a pleasure to be served by her for Jesus and his care shines through. Another is a teacher whose caring and competence have left a mark for Christ upon a thousand lives. And so on.

The fingers of Jesus, touching every life situation in his Father's world, are his people. Through them all life becomes a love offering of God to people and of people to God.

Theirs is the front-line ministry and witness. They can reach hearts closed to the preacher and speak in accents that touch people in the situation where they are.

The prime ministry is theirs. The job of leaders is to equip all God's people for their ministry and to build up the body of Christ until it is alive in every member and the gospel floods out on a multitude of tongues and through a multitude of lives (Eph. 4:11–12).

Useful books

Discovering Your Gifts (Baptist Union)
Your Spiritual Gifts Can Help Your Church Grow, Peter Wagner (Regal Books)
Spiritual Gifts and the Church, Bridge and Phypers (IVP)
I believe in Church Growth Eddie Gibbs (Hodder & Stoughton) Cf Appendix H
Urban Harvest Roy Joslin (Evangelical Press)

2.5

Budgeting

'Mission costs money!'
'Yes, but the Lord will provide!'
This conversation has been rehearsed time and time again. Both statements are of course true, but both are incomplete.

Mission costs

Budgeting implies that we seek to determine, as far as possible, what an evangelistic mission, project or opportunity will cost, before it takes place.

First, we need to divide the mission/project/opportunity into its constituent parts. Personnel, materials, advertising, venue, administration, plant and equipment. Each item should be individually and realistically costed.

This will achieve three results:

● it tells us how far our faith must stretch

● it unpacks for us why our faith needs to stretch that far

● it gives a basis for ongoing budgetary controls and amendment. It also means that one can contrast the anticipated expenditure on one item as against another.

Once a basic budget has been agreed and adopted, then control procedures need to be established. These are equally simple. For example, if expenditure in each category over an annual budget is expected to be consistent in all four quarters of the year then an item is presented as follows:

		Quarter 1	Quarter 2	Quarter 3	Quarter 4	Total
Advertising	£3600	900	900	900	900	3600

If, however, the advertising is an increasing expenditure then it might need:

		Quarter 1	Quarter 2	Quarter 3	Quarter 4	Total
Advertising	£3600	300	600	1200	1500	3600

In this way a typical budget of expenditure can be presented (based as much on material information as we can gain and subdivided as far as necessary).

		Quarter 1	Quarter 2	Quarter 3	Quarter 4	Total
Personnel	£12000	3000	3000	3000	3000	12000
Materials	£4000	500	500	1500	1500	4000
Advertising	£6000	500	2500	2500	500	6000
Venue	£6000	–	–	–	6000	6000
Administration	£3000	750	750	750	750	3000
Equipment	£2000	–	–	1250	750	2000
	33000	4750	6750	8250	13250	33000

This kind of budgeting not only says what is required, but also when it is actually needed. A useful guide that many have discovered is to take administrative costs at around 10 per cent of the total budget.

God's provision

This is far more difficult to structure and assess. That is why it is helpful to know each quarter how income relates to expenditure. In other words what our cash flow situation actually is. Then if we discover that our projected expenditure represented foolishness rather than faith we can duly amend it.

Here we need real prayer and real wisdom to know the Lord's promise of provision and to break down those areas in which we might receive it, e.g. gifts, covenants, standing orders, sales, seat reservations (all as appropriate).

Correct financial dealing can greatly encourage individual giving. If people are convinced that the handling of finance will be responsible and budgeted so that massive shortfalls do not occur they are more likely to be committed to the project and give accordingly.

Alongside budget should come accounts, so that projected income and expenditure are analysed next to real income and expenditure. In this way we can steward the Lord's gifts to us and by using them properly and responsibly bring honour to his name – even in our finance.

2.6

Coping with growth

That which is alive grows and multiplies. That which is dead does not. This is the nature of things. Living churches grow and remain. Dead ones decline and often disappear. In the living Body of Christ problems of growth must be met and solved. They are problems of life, not death.

1. What is meant by church growth?

There are three aspects:

(i) *Spiritual*. Christians have new life through their new birth and the gift of the Spirit. This must develop as they 'grow in grace and knowledge of the Lord', in an understanding of God's word, in the grace of the Spirit (love, joy, peace, etc.), in their relation to one another in fellowship, and in spiritual maturity (2 Pet. 3:18; Eph. 4:11–16).

(ii) *Numerical*. Numbers may decrease where dead wood is cut away. However, the norm for living churches, as evident in Acts, is to grow numerically. There is no limit. Jesus said he would draw all men to himself. Full Gospel Central Church Seoul is approaching a quarter of a million members!

(iii) *Activity*. Living bodies don't just expand. They develop distinctive organs with special functions. In Christ's Body the Spirit gives gifts and ministries (1 Cor. 12:4–7). So in healthy Christian communities spiritual activities emerge and grow, with gifted people exercising their gifts. These foster other growth forms, all by the working of the Spirit.

2. Problems of growth

As with physical growth so with spiritual. There are problems.

(a) Extremism

In growth situations certain truths and experiences are vivid or intense. They may become overemphasised so leading to imbalance. Spiritual gifts may be overstressed at the expense of spiritual graces. Healing, prophesying, tongues, visions may become too important. But so may repentance, authority, holiness, separation, organization, dress – as though nothing else mattered. Many problems arise from lack of balance. Important truths carried to excess become twisted into error. And extremism inevitably produces division.

(b) *Superficiality*

Numerical growth can result in shallow profession. Crowds draw crowds. Spiritual standards may fall as when the church of the fourth century mushroomed through the 'conversion' of the emperor Constantine. The church may grow proud and worldly. Glorying in success, it falls under judgement. It becomes dry, dead, divisive. Disintegration sets in.

(c) *Disorder*

Milling crowds often cause confusion. There can be physical disorder. But what of spiritual confusion as Paul encountered at Corinth? What if traditional forms are threatened when the Spirit works in power? What if churches have to change? If orderly passive services are invaded by 'audience participation', spontaneous prayers, praises, testimonies and gifts of the Spirit? Without control it can be chaos.

In the 1904 Welsh revival, ministers could not preach for the praying, weeping, repenting, counselling and singing in the congregations. But the churches grew and grew. Today we have new worship forms, new songs, new experiences and emphases, new freedom in many fellowships. All this needs guidance and oversight.

(d) *Accommodation*

Traditional chapels complete with poky entrances, narrow aisles, straight lines of pews are unsuitable for growth that requires space for greeting, sharing and audience participation. In 1855 Spurgeon, facing rapidly growing congregations, said 'By faith Jericho's walls came down, and by faith these back walls must come down too.' Growth means removal of many kinds of walls! These are all problems of growth. Of health and life! Like the baby Jesus, growing churches need to be 'wrapped in swaddling clothes', free enough for adjustment to their growth! Growth requires adaptation.

3. How to cope with the growth

Things will not just look after themselves. I have learned two things in growth situations. First, to recognise the Holy Spirit to be the divine custodian of God's work. I must not usurp his rights, but trust him in both people and situations. Second, to take my responsibility under his control as God's appointed leader to care for that work. Such responsibility involves five things.

(a) Doctrine

Like the bone structure of the body, this must be strong and well fitted together. There must be good grounding in the truth. In the Acts it says that converts 'continued in the apostles' teaching'. Later Paul committed the Ephesian elders 'to the Word of God's grace', and later still urged Timothy to hold fast sound words and teach wholesome doctrine (Acts 2:42 and 20:32; 2 Tim. 1:13 and 4:2).

Sound biblical teaching is all important. It is like the foundation of a building. If it is defective anywhere, the structure will be unsafe. Therefore, if Christians are to grow properly they must be well-grounded in the Gospel and in all aspects of biblical truth.

(b) Discipling

A good programme of discipling is essential to proper growth. This should be supervised by ministers or elders in weekly groups where teaching is applied and problems dealt with. New believers must be taught how to pattern their lives on Jesus their Master. So the fellowship becomes safe and strong. House groups are important. Yonggi Cho in his book *Successful Home Cell Groups* shows how the Central Church, Seoul grows largely as the result of its programme of weekly house groups led by trained men and women. These groups grow, divide and again multiply. They allow free participation. They evangelise, they create fellowship and most important they produce leaders.

(c) Shepherding

Sometimes this is overdone, depriving Christians of personal liberties. Nevertheless, church growth requires pastoral care and in normal situations the Holy Spirit raises up men and women with pastoral gifts. Whoever these may be they must prove to have shepherding qualities. They must be *friends* not *dictators*; people full of love and grace; but they must be overseers. As such they must be recognised and accredited by the local believers and under the spiritual covering of the fellowship. They must guide, but be checked by the church as well. Prayer is essential. We need those who can pray effectively both for individuals and the fellowship as a whole. Those who can wage spiritual warfare against the powers of darkness. Intercessors! Prayer warriors! Without such prayer, growth is hindered. It is only safe where cradled in prayer.

(d) Fellowship

Healthy growth involves right relationships, whether in bodies, families or churches. Where it is very close, fellowship itself may produce problems, which must be faced and solved. Living things grow best in light and true fellowship requires openness and honesty with one another. 'If we walk in the light . . . we have fellowship with one another' (1 John 1:7). In this light we repent and confess our faults to one another. We are open and broken. We forgive and are forgiven. Then God's love flows in to fill our relationships. When this happens a lot of problems are solved. Without this light we simply stagger on from one problem to another.

(e) *Accommodation*

In the USA, churches that are three-quarters full start planning for extension. If not, growth slows down. Our premises must be planned for growth not stagnation, with space for free movement in growing meetings. Semi-circular seating rather than straight will assist fellowship and worship. Areas for musical instruments other than the lonely organ may be needed. Vestibules should be large enough to meet in, talk, buy books and tapes and even refreshments! Rooms for counselling, prayer, teaching and fellowship are a great help. Good lighting and attractive decor create a good atmosphere. We find our church lounge a great asset.

In all these things growth may involve a numerical 'ceiling'. Develop, divide, grow again, is the right process. Calvary Chapel, California is a splendid growth fellowship. Sound in teaching, open to the Spirit, balanced, evangelistic and committed to developing leaders it has established hundreds of other churches. All right for the USA you say? I believe that real life will always produce growth of *some* sort in *any* place. But what grows must scatter to form new growth. As the word says, 'There is that which scatters and yet increases' (Prov. 11:24).

Harry Leemont of Australia tells how, when asking God why so few were converted in his church, he received the reply, 'When you are ready to care for them as I want them cared for, I will send them to you.' God wants souls born again to be brought to spritual maturity. We must keep this goal always in view.

The most important thing in all this is *love*. Love alone can properly cope with the many problems and needs of a growing situation. Love that counsels and cares. Shepherd-love, parent-love, brother-love. Christ's own love, patiently teaching and balancing. Love that heals inner hurts and smoothes rough edges. Love that challenges. Love that reconciles. Love that builds up. Love that never fails.

2.7

Church planting

1. Basic assumptions

(a) *World evangelism is our responsibility*

While the initiative in salvation for mankind is gloriously God's the responsibility for world evangelisation and bringing in the kingdom is yours and mine. Jesus said, 'as the Father sent me, so send I you' (John 20:21). When the salvation and the power and the kingdom of our God and the authority of his Christ have come, it is because 'the brethren' (i.e. you and me) have conquered Satan 'by the blood of the lamb and the world of their testimony for they loved not their lives even unto death' (Rev. 12:10–11).

(b) *Church planting is the norm for world evangelisation*

Jesus founded the Jerusalem church as the vehicle for bringing his kingdom into all the earth. He intended the church to move outward all the time in planting new churches. This was the motivating principle of the early Christians. Paul, probably the most prolific church planter ever, wrote,

> To me, though I am the very least of all the saints, this grace was given, to preach on the Gentiles the unsearchable riches of Christ, and to make all men see what is the plan of the mystery hidden for ages in God who created all things, that through *the church* the manifold wisdom of God might now be made known ... (Eph. 3:8–9).

(c) *Church planting is particularly needed today in the UK*

This is now a virtually unevangelised country with at least 85 per cent of the population still needing the gospel. In the inner city areas particularly there are few existing churches touching the lives of ordinary people. Even in the so-called Bible belts there are areas of great population density in which people have no contact with a live church, and so have little or no opportunity to hear and encounter the gospel in action. We need not allow undue sensitivity to existing established churches to hinder the planting of new ones, for God has always worked both inside and outside the established churches. Some of these themselves are seeing the need of planting daughter churches in neighbouring areas if their spiritual dynamic is to be maintained. Obviously we should avoid unnecessary geographical overlaps with living or reviving churches.

(d) *The New Testament provides us with the necessary principles of church planting and life*

Christians have at times been unnecessarily divided by different interpretations of Scripture. Some of these in turn have tended to limit a proper understanding and experience of Jesus, the good news, church life, evangelism and so on. But a properly Christ-centred method of interpreting and applying Scripture can avoid this (cf. Section 1:1). The central truths of Christian life and experience are simple enough. Jesus gave only three basic commandments: 'love' (John 13:34), 'stay' (John 15:4), and 'go' (Matt. 28:19). We must aim to make these the defining characteristics of the churches we plant:

> God's *love* in Jesus, expressed in the response of loving worship towards God and loving service towards one another and the world;

> the presence of the Holy Spirit in whom Jesus taught us to *stay* ('abide', 'remain'; cf. Greek of John 14:2; John 17:18; John 15:5, 7 etc.), and who brings both the Father and the Son to us;

> a compassion and determination to *go* and share Christ with everyone in every place to which the kingdom of Jesus has not yet come. A community motivated by these qualities will certainly please God and do his will.

(e) *We are still in the age of Pentecost*

Peter described the coming of the Holy Spirit upon the church at Pentecost as 'this is what was spoken by the prophet Joel: And in the last days it shall be, God declares, that I will pour out my Spirit upon all flesh . . .' Whatever else we may wish to say about our present point in history, we must, by definition, still be in 'the last days' of Joel's prophecy. Or they may be 'laster' last days, in which we can expect to experience the intensity of God's kingdom even more greatly! The whole New Testament church planting programme flowed out of the fullness and gifts of the Holy Spirit, and must continue in the same stream today.

2. Getting on with the job

(a) *Where to begin*

Unless you have a specific call somewhere else, begin where you are, or in the nearest unserved place to your home. Experience shows that in a city, an area of approximately one mile in diameter is most suitable for planting a church in. In a country area, this could be extended up to two or three miles.

(b) Research the area to be able to apply the strategy of Jesus thoroughly and intelligently

In order to plant an effective church in a given area, we need to have a good working knowledge of the people and the whole context in which they live out their lives. Use the local library, local council and personal reconnaissance (footslogging, conversations with locals, etc.). Use a map and notes to build up a picture of the area: its housing, amenities, institutions, industries, communication systems, people groups, churches and religions. Some knowledge of recent history will help too.

(c) Setting the time scale

A goal of two or three years (the length of Jesus' own ministry to the establishing of the Jerusalem church) seems an appropriate biblical maximum period for church planting. Once a thriving church is established with mature leadership, the process can be repeated much more quickly (cf. the First Church (Assemblies of God) in Seoul, which now plants six new churches a day!)

(d) Applying Jesus' strategy

Jesus' missionary strategy must be the basis of all church planting. It resulted in the establishing of the church at Jerusalem and everywhere else. I have found it helpful to sum up this strategy from Mark 1 in words and phrases which all begin with W.

(i) Jesus was *well-pleasing* to God (Mark 1:11). A man on whom the Holy Spirit descended and remained. He was the first of that type. Any would-be church planter must be a man full of the Holy Spirit.

(ii) Jesus was a man at *war* (Mark 1:13) He fought with the devil and won, by the word, meekness, worship and service, in praise, prayer and fasting and ultimately by laying down his life. The evangelisation of the world is a fight against Satan, the flesh and the world; a life of spiritual warfare.

(iii) Jesus planted the church *with others* (Mark 1:16–17). From the beginning, Jesus called around him a team of workers. team work is essential to church planting for at least two reasons. The first is Jesus' famous dictum, 'Where two or three are gathered together in my name, there I am in the midst . . . (Matt. 18:20). If you have a team, you already have started church planting, because in those two or three, the church, the body of Christ which he indwells and reigns though, is already in the place. It's just a question of extending it! Secondly, the Gospel of the kingdom is expressed in renewed relationships, man to man as well as man to God. The lack of the former gives the lie to the latter. A united team who love each other are tangible proof of the gospel (cf. John 17:22–3).

(iv) Jesus preached the *word* (Mark 1:14–15). Verbal communication had a central place in New Testament church planting. There is no way that we should retreat from or apologise for this. Nowadays words are devalued among ordinary people by often irrelevant education systems, political rhetoric and centuries of religious hypocrisy. But Jesus' word was different (cf. 1:27). He spoke with authority. Like Jesus we must *proclaim the Word* (κηρυσσω (v. 14), confronting people with the astounding good news in the open air (v. 14), in their places of work (v. 16), in their homes and meeting places (v. 33, 39). We must *teach* the word (διδασκω) (v. 21) in small groups and large, wherever people can be motivated to stay and learn, and we must simply *say* (χεγω) (v. 17; cf. v. 28) this good news wherever we can gossip the gospel. From the seed of this word the kingdom grows.

(v) Jesus did many good *works*. Good works alone do not make us acceptable to God. But they are the living proof and present reality of the kingdom we preach. Good works are absolutely essential and integral to evangelism. Jesus' works were both natural (valuing and receiving the poor and outcast, washing feet), and supernatural (healing the sick, delivering from demons). If we are weak in faith for the latter, we should get on with the former. Soon the needs we face will drive us to faith for the supernatural! But if we ignore the former, we vitiate the latter (cf. Matt. 7:21–3, 10:42).

(vi) Jesus *warned* the religious, political and commercial establishment of the consequences of their hypocrisy and injustice. This aspect of Jesus' strategy is only hinted at in Mark 1 (cf. the context of John's arrest [v. 14] and Jesus' warning to the leper [v. 43]. But it is central to Jesus' ministry throughout the gospels (cf. John 2:13–19; Matt. 23; Luke 10:13–14). It was particularly this prophetic quality of Jesus' strategy that highlighted the alternative authority structure of Jesus' kingdom and brought the confrontation between it and this world at the cross, where the need for repentance was understood and the church planted. We must be true to this aspect of Jesus' evangelism today if we are to produce the kind of shake-up where men and women have to choose between God's way and the world's and plant companies of Christians through which God can reign.

(vii) Jesus prayed and *worshipped*. It was as Jesus communed with his Father that the kingdom was embodied in his life and expressed in the world (Luke 5:16; 6:12; 10:21–22; 11:1–4). This principle was already there in the Old Testament and continues throughout the Acts of the Apostles (Acts 2:47; 4:24, etc; 13:2; 16:25). Paul states it clearly in Ephesians where worship is the means of overcoming evil, being full of the Holy Spirit and becoming a living Christ-centred church (Eph. 5:14–32). A team of church planters must learn to live and work in the context of worship in the Holy Spirit.

(e) *Listening to the Holy Spirit*

Jesus' strategy for church planting is clearly far reaching. The aim is to be true to Jesus in the specific context of the people in a given local area. We become rapidly bogged down by the task unless we have a hotline to mission control; unless we are discovering which particular aspect of strategy to emphasise at which stage in the process. Whether by circumstances, Scripture or direct prophecy, we must learn to apply Jesus' strategy in church planting by listening to the Holy Spirit (cf. Acts 8:29; 10:19; 13:2, 16:6–10).

2.8

Changing emphasis – the evangelising church

'The Church exists for mission as fire exists for burning', said Emil Brunner. If that is so, then there can be no church worthy of that name that does not engage in evangelism; evangelism being one element within the total mission of the Church. Evangelism enables the Church to grow.

A church may be a lively gathering of Christ's people – well taught, encouraged to pray, educated in principles of church growth, giving well to overseas missions, structured for fellowship and pastoral care – but yet not reaching out. All our time and attention may be geared to the membership. But the Church is the 'only organisation on earth that doesn't exist for the benefit of its members'. Luis Palau has said that the Church is only one generation away from extinction. If it doesn't evangelise, it will die. Evangelism is the means God has chosen to proclaim his message of redemption and salvation to those not of his kingdom. It is the Body's means of communication to the world.

After large-scale missions like Mission to London and Mission England, we tend to say 'We've done our bit – we've helped as a church in the much-hailed mission of the century – now we can get back to "normal".' By comparison, everything else must seem innocuous, incidental, maybe ineffectual. On the other hand, your church may have seen such success that you've more than enough to do in conserving the fruit. Or it may be that your church has been almost untouched by the effects of large-scale evangelism. You're too small, or too preoccupied with other things, or in the midst of a change of minister, or structure, or services, or emphasis. So evangelism isn't your priority.

However, whatever the presuppositions from which we start, there is no getting away from the fact of the Great Commission, the importance of proclaiming the gospel, and our church's responsibility in it. But how? Where do we go from here? What other evangelism is valid, appropriate or effective? It does matter that the evangelising process should go on. We can never say 'we've done enough' – there will always be people who need Christ and who need to hear and see something of his love. Evangelism, if seen merely in crusade terms, falls far short of biblical ideals. Of course, there were the public preaching occasions – like Paul on Mars Hill. The one is perpetually fruitful, while the other is spasmodic. Your church may be given a sense of satisfaction at having 'done something' but there may be little to show in the long term, unless there is a continuing emphasis on evangelism.

So we need, in considering the way forward, to start where we are, where relationships already exist, where our church community lives, and where the church building is located. That was the Lord's commission: 'Jerusalem, Judaea, Samaria . . . uttermost parts of the earth' (Acts 1:8). You can't very well man an outpost until you've established a good base.

1. Making the most of relationships

New initiatives in evangelism have made much of the need for individual Christians to pray for and share their faith with those with whom they were in regular contact – people at work, at school and college, and in the neighbourhood. We also build relationships in recreational/social activities at those points where members of the community meet – like pubs, clubs, across the garden fence, at the leisure centre, or at school gates and fetes. Church-based evangelism must continue to emphasise the importance of developing those natural relationships we all have with people in everyday life. Until we become relaxed and used to sharing our faith with those we know, we are hardly going to be able to witness spontaneously to those we don't know.

Inspiration and help needs to be given regularly to help the average Christian become aware not only of his responsibility to witness, but of the way in which it can occur, and what happens when people do give expression to their faith.

Forming a witness cell of those who have an evangelistic concern is one way of getting going in a church on a limited basis. Probably 10 per cent of any congregation would be motivated in this way. But a better means would be to set everyone in a prayer cell – three per prayer group – praying for specific people with whom they have everyday contact. Prayer like this will begin naturally to open up opportunities for faith-sharing.

2. Making the most of the congregation

Church-based evangelism must at times be corporately expressed. The body life of the church is valid when every member is functioning to mutual effect 'to build itself up in love' (Eph. 4:16). That building is from without as well as from within. The five-fold public ministry of Ephesians 4:11 was 'to prepare God's people for works of service, so that the body of Christ may be built up' (v. 12). Numerical growth of one body (growth in size) must be followed by cell growth by that body (growth by reproduction).

There are basically two types of congregation – the community and commuter. The *community* congregation consists mainly of those who are in walking distance of their place of worship, and who can therefore more readily relate to the people who live in their locality. New 'community churches' within some house-church streams, fellowships formed from Christians living in the same village or on the same estate, and Anglican parish churches come within this category.

I've personally found it helpful, as a first stage, to have a day or weekend conference with such groups, during which a brain-storming session in small groups takes place. The groups look at the spiritual needs of the community, the purpose and effectiveness of existing church activities, neighbourhood evangelism, the pros and cons of house groups, and the use of their buildings. The findings of such a brain-storm produce a most stimulating agenda for the leadership to work at! Their job will be to look at the ways the gifts of the existing membership can most effectively be applied to meeting the most obvious needs of the surrounding community, and the way in which the church buildings can be adapted to cater for those needs.

If the congregation is a *commuter* one – where most travel from a distance to their place of worship – the approach needs to be different. Human relationships more easily occur where the members live. So those relationships need to be developed there mid-week – *not* at the church building. Help should be given to enable house groups to be formed, pastoral and teaching needs to be met, and for the needs of neighbours and friends to be catered for. In this way, home-based groups become outposts of the church. When a house group develops, consideration needs to be given to helping a more regular fellowship to be established in that community. For this to happen, the prayers of the church need to be toward such a shared goal. If it is, some transplanting may occur – a few families will move into the area either as a personal/family decision, or as a result of the encouragement of the leadership. In the fellowship I'm at present attending, this has happened. As a result, one new strong church has been established and another one is a target of prayer and interest.

In the same way, some large churches could adopt a spiritual 'no-go area' – like a down-town ghetto area or an inner city suburb. Sometimes an ailing church in such a location would welcome the input of new life to help re-establish it. The Icthus Fellowship in South London is one which has successfully achieved such partnership. There are also many spiritually deprived areas crying out for the missionary interest, prayers and involvement of numerically strong churches who can provide resources to plant a new congregation.

Whatever is done, the objective must be to create 'community' where none exists – a community of Christians who are expressing a community spirit. That's just another way of saying the church is being the body of Christ to its locality – bringing the whole gospel to the whole man. Those groups that have attempted such a strategy have achieved some remarkable successes. A radical new expression of Christianity, characterised by enterprise and initiative, warmth of fellowship, depth of worship and commitment to each other and the Lord, has produced involvement in the communtiy and outreach that is relevant to local need. And a response that has brought steady and in some cases rapid growth.

3. Making the most of the church buildings

Won't such a strategy denude the church building of all its best people? Not if the value of members of the congregation not involved in such developments is seen. And not if a reappraisal takes place of the way the existing church buildings are used. Most British church groups put a disproportionate amount of time into the maintenance of their buildings – maintenance suggests mere upkeep. It rarely includes renovation.

If church buildings are still in populated areas, they are always assets, whatever their condition. Part of the strategy of a local congregation should be for the better use of those buildings for the spiritual benefit of the community around. So often they remain merely the meeting place for the few Christians who still attend. But they could be so much more. Help is sometimes available for renovation and alterations through Manpower Services and the Youth Opportunities Project. British Youth for Christ hold a register of unemployed Christian young people. They could help not only in the renovation but also in witness in the locality. In other words, short-term help is available from outside for weak churches. There *is* an alternative to a slow death – resuscitation!

Working on the principle that the buildings should serve the needs of the community, facilities could then be provided for mums and toddlers, the elderly, the unemployed, ethnic minority groups – or any other relevant need. I even know of one fellowship whose building doubles as a sports hall mid-week. Some provide restaurant/bookshop facilities – if they are located in a good shopping area. All these are contact points for the body of Christ to engage in 'works of service' (Eph. 4:11) as a means of faith-sharing.

If the church building is no longer in a populated area, or in a dilapidated condition, the site could be sold and the money invested in providing facilities for a new fellowship in a new population area.

Transferring resources to where the needs are means that the church is always seen as a living organism – mobile and flexible, being with the people where they are.

So far, this chapter has dealt with strategy for local church evangelism. But the Church is more than local. In a town or city it is made up of many congregations – and, in a nation, of many denominations. Our church strategy for evangelism needs to look realistically at co-operative action in reaching the unreached areas of our land, and in starting new congregations.

With less than 10 per cent of the population claiming to go to church regularly, there are 90 per cent who should be classified as 'unreached'.

Perhaps half of those believe in God, but have not expressed that belief in any tangible, observable way.

(i) In *new development areas*, the churches should plan to cater for at least 10 per cent of the new population to be church attenders. That means moving with the planners in identifying sites for possible Christian purposes and motivating people for outreach and establishing contact with the newcomers as they arrive. (A 'spot-the-removal-van' competition for Sunday School children will yield a contact list for follow-up.)

(ii) In *existing population areas*, target for a Christian house group in every street and tower block. Two out of every 100 homes will have a family of committed Christians, on average. If they can get together for prayer and witness, others would begin to see Christ where he needs to be seen – in everyone's neighbourhood.

(iii) In the *spiritually deprived areas* of Britain, such as minor cities, new estates and towns, and rural areas, a strategy for sending and supporting evangelists, pastors, teachers, and overseas Christian workers needs to be developed. But in that sending process there needs to be a far closer relationship and fellowship link than has previously been the case between the sending church and receiving area, so that the full-time worker or team is seen as an extension of the sending church. As an outpost is established, support is built up, and valid, culturally related evangelism takes place.

'Evangelism is not a sporadic encounter, but a continuous engagement.' That implies there is *always* fresh territory and new people to be reached in Jesus' name.

Mobilising Membership for Evangelism

3A.1

Everybody does it

'In our church ten per cent of the members have to do all the work and the other ninety per cent never do anything.' How often have you heard that remark? Is it true of your present church fellowship? Are you one of the ten per cent or one of the ninety per cent? In all probability you are one of the ten per cent of leaders and doers. That is why you are reading this book. I want to share with you some of the secrets of motivation so that you finish up with more activists and less spectators. This section is not easy reading and it will be even harder to implement, but if you do take it seriously I guarantee that changes will be accomplished.

Reorientate your leaders

This is the first change which must be faced and it may make you unwilling to read any further.

Rule 1 – it is the task of leaders to motivate.

It is not 'their' fault that 'they' are not doing anything it is *your* fault. If there are not enough leaders it is because the leadership has failed to train more leaders. If there are not enough workers it is because the workers have failed to produce more workers. Sometimes this is simply the result of fear. All groups, and churches are no exception, produce a pecking order, in which people know their place and in which due recognition is given to those in authority. If you increase the number of leaders then some of the present leaders may feel they will lose their place and their prestige. If you double the number of workers then some of the present workers may feel that their work no longer looks as good as it used to do because of the new comparisons. This will clearly result in stress. To avoid it, churches have for centuries kept all the work in the hands of the few. So we do not utilise the musical gifts within a church – violin, flute, guitar – to form an orchestra, because to do so would threaten the position of the organist and the deputy organist, both of whom have complained for years that none of the young people are coming along to take on their job and they have to be there every week.

So the first task in motivation is for the present leaders to humbly and honestly face up to the threats which producing more leaders will cause. It will then need a clear act of the will and an act of faith to embark upon the following programme.

Recognise your limitations

Learn to build upon the strengths which you can already see rather than bemoan the weaknesses which the devil keeps reminding you about. We can't all do everything but everyone can do something. Look for the obvious 'somethings' rather than trying to be clever and developing obscure plans or plans which have no realistic hope of success.

The elderly congregation of thirty people was informed that there was to be a meeting to plan the formation of a youth club. The club would invite the local hooligans off the street and share the gospel with them, thus ensuring the survival of the church. It was a recipe for disaster. They didn't have the man-power to take on such a project and the inevitable result, six months later, was a few disheartened pensioners and a number of broken windows. If only they had seen their chance to develop a ministry amongst the senior citizens who had moved into the new sheltered accommodation just down the road. Ah, but would that have ensured the church's survival? Yes, for quite a number of years, because people are living longer than ever before.

The majority of our church buildings and many of our church organisations have become mere monuments to a past age rather than an illustration to the neighbourhood of the movement of God's Spirit.

All organisational patterns tend to outlive their usefulness and to become powerful negative weapons. All organisations seek to maintain their existence. In order to do so, some will finish by existing on sentiment rather than on rationality. In other words, their continued existence will make no sense at all. Changes therefore must be brought about. You can and will accomplish change if you recognise your limitations. Begin with small, acceptable changes. Remember that the greater the change called for by a plan then the greater will be the potential resistance to the plan. Use the old but successful 'thin end of the wedge' technique. Or as my American friends put it, 'inch by inch, everything is a cinch'. You can wince at the wording but the idea is sound. Not everyone will see the need for change all at the same time. Indeed, some may never see it. Start with the more possible and plausible changes. Small successes are still successes.

Realise your opportunities

Do not make the mistake of thinking that nothing is being done. Some of the older ladies may already have built bridges of outreach to neighbours and to social clubs. Their lives have already been a strong witness. What you need to do is to reap the harvest of their endeavours rather that trying to retrain them all to go door knocking in the council estate. Unemployed members of your fellowship will already have made contacts among other unemployed people. Make the most of these opportunities.[1] Find out what really is being done. It may be done automatically – like the church member who always visits the launderette at the same time every week and always talks to the same half-dozen clients. What can be done to turn that into part of your evangelistic outreach? Or the Christian personnel manager who deals with staff problems in the local store. How can you support him in realistic prayer so that he will know which needy cases can be cared for by the church? Stop complaining that he doesn't attend the church's prayer meeting; maybe he would come if you were praying about real people.

God has already given gifts and abilities to the members of your church. Pray especially for the gift of discernment so that you will be able to see the opportunities and the people available to meet those opportunities. You do not motivate people by producing a scheme for evangelism and asking for volunteers. You motivate by helping people to discover the things they can do. By informing them of the possibilities and by producing the evidence and encouragement which deals with their hesitations and inhibitions.

Reassess your targets

The biggest single failure in effective motivation is the failure to set any targets at all. Or, equally, to set such vague and unquantified targets as to be useless for any evaluation of success. The second area of failure is to set definite targets but never to review them. The result is that those who tried to reach the target become disheartened and confused.

If experience shows that your target was unrealistically high then you do not improve your faith by continuing to aim at such a target. Bring it down to where a realistic endeavour, touched by God's Spirit, will bring success within a reasonable period of time. Three to four months is the 'hope' time for most Christians. Remember also that whatever target is set must be worthwhile even to those who are not the 'early acceptors' of the new idea. 'Early acceptors', as the name suggests, are those who will join the initiators (the 'ideas people') as soon as an idea is explained. You are fortunate if you have fifteen such people out of every one hundred members. Then you must encourage and inform and persuade others to give their support. Ask yourself all the questions you would want to know about someone else's idea. Get a friend to play devil's advocate and challenge all that you say. Then present your plan for evangelism and change, graciously and patiently and persistently. Take every opportunity to explain things but do not wait for a two-thirds majority before you put the plan into action. You are doing well if around 55 per cent are with you by the starting time. Another 30 per cent will join you only as the programme is seen to be working.

What do you do with those who never see the ideas as workable? You love them; but you do not wait until you have changed their views. You will have to learn to live with opposition. The 55 per cent majority will back you once you have shown that the returns from all the efforts needed in the evangelism and changes are worthwhile. It is the second golden rule of motivation.

Rule 2 – the potential returns must equate with the effort expended.

Example. We should all give up three nights a week for six months to visit all the high-rise flats in our city giving a copy of the New International Version of the Bible to every householder. It will cost £18,000 to finance the venture. It will *probably* result in some new people attending our church.

What do you say? No, thank you! That is the answer of any rational, thinking Christian.

Alternatively, I ask all the active people attending the mid-week Bible study to join in a one night literature distribution on one of the new housing estates. We will do it two weeks before Christmas and whilst we are out that one night, the less active will still meet to pray for us. We will all finish back at the church for coffee. We are delivering a church Christmas card. It will cost us about thirty pounds and we can reasonably expect half a dozen young couples from that estate to attend our 'Carols by Candlelight' service as a result of receiving the top-class invitation. Assuming the visitors put a pound each into the collection, almost half of the outlay is immediately recovered. In addition, we will have special 'new-comer spies' ready for the evening to make sure that every visitor stays for coffee and mince pies after the service.

The second scheme will win the 55 per cent support. Guess how thrilled we will be when ten new couples turn up and two of them later get converted.

Planning for any change is essential. It is important to set targets which can be aimed at. Constant reviews of your time scale are necessary. If a scheme is taking too long, so that morale is slipping, shorten the end date and replace it with another, fresh programme. Do not grind on to the bitter end; you will only store up bitterness.

In reassessing targets, always be on the look-out for new leadership potential. Give them scope to emerge and as soon as they do emerge, nurture them with responsibility. Of course, nothing ever works out to plan, except by accident. That is the reason why you should constantly check the actual results against the plan; not just to see what is happening, but so that action can be taken to improve the results if they are falling short and so that future plans can be modified if events have proved that you are working on false assumptions.

Remedy your deficiencies

As your programme of change progresses, it will develop a personality all of its own. It will also reveal character defects. Do all that you can to remedy mistakes made and to correct wrong assumptions. A piece of grit in an oyster produces a pearl; in humans it causes a sore eye or a blister.

Lead by example but make sure that your leadership group does not become an exclusive club/clique. Watch your use of language; correct the tendency to give your programme a jargon of its own or to refer to it by its initial letters. Nothing is more hurtful to those who want to join in at a later stage.

Remember that all the parts of the body must function in their rightful places. Do not try to make everyone into an evangelist. *All* are witnesses; around one in ten have the God-given gift of the evangelist. Do not try to hold an outreach meeting in every home; not everyone has the gift of hospitality. Find the gifts of your people and use them. Where you have some gaps, pray for the Lord's provision.

There is no one training course for all; no universal crash course to produce a new generation of super-witnessing Christians. Aim at a gentle, continuing nudging forward rather than attempting one hundred metres in ten seconds. Outreach evangelism is motivated by love. The more love within the fellowship, the more outreach. The more you open yourselves to the fullness of God's love, the more outgoing you will become.

Motivation thrives on encouragement. Thank people for the responses made and the effort put in. If they got half-way to the target, that is terrific. Do not berate those who missed the opportunity, share the success stories of those who took the opportunities.

Rule 3 – never overlook the important in favour of the urgent.

So many churches are only into the immediate blessing or the present crisis. They lack the dimension of eternity. All of our activities must be examined against that background. The supreme task of the church is not to organise itself for the blessing of its members, but to order itself for the benefit of non-members.

We are not to place our primary emphasis upon fellowship but upon going into the world outside our church walls with the good news of a Saviour. Do some serious strategy thinking about the future and measure all that you are doing – however urgent it seems to be – against the important aspect of eternity; that of extending the kingdom for the glory of God. If you take a serious look at what you are doing, then many of your activities may have glaring deficiencies in the light of the importance of saving men. Have the courage to remedy your deficiences.

Summary

Set your targets for change and build in a time limit with frequent reviews. Do not be so far ahead in your ambitions that you are out of sight to everyone else. Get hold of those who always support you and sell your ideas to them first. Take them into your confidence. Then explain, inform and persuade the others until you have your 55 per cent. Keep a check on how it is all working out. Do not be too proud to modify targets. Be daring but also be realistic and remember the three golden rules of motivation.

- it is the task of leaders to motivate, not the job of the others to get themselves motivated
- the expected returns must make all the effort worthwhile

● never overlook the important in favour of the urgent.

Note
1. For a further development of this theme see Maranatha Ministries Project Sheets, The Christian Teaching Centre, Kirby Stephen, Cumbria.

3A.2

Spheres of influence

Evangelism involves a complex interaction between a trinity of evangelistic agents – the Word, People, and Spirit of God – and the unevangelised. This article will focus primarily upon the role of the people of God and concentrate on the carrier of the Good News rather than its content or communication. In other words, this section is aimed at you.

You will find much in this book about what evangelism is, why it should take place and how it may be done. In this section we will attempt to identify the people you could evangelise and discover your potential for evangelism. In order to do this we need to look at your day-to-day relationships.

Understand your network

When man was made, God said, 'It is not good for the man to live alone' (Gen. 2:18), and apart from the rare recluse or the lone sailor we do not. We are social beings and we live our whole lives in relationships with others. Some are lifelong and deep, others are passing and shallow, but these personal contacts form channels of communication that God uses to carry the Good News from one person to another. These 'circles of influence' or 'networks' may be consciously activated by every Christian for he is indwelt by the Holy Spirit and 'takes' Christ to the people around him. As Christ is received by people in this network, Christianity spreads like a virulent infection. The Faith is contagious!

In Africa, 20,000 people are added to the Church every day and the primary cause of this remarkable growth is the uninhibited 'gossiping' of the Good News by the ordinary Christian with his relatives, friends and neighbours. This interpersonal evangelism has always been the major means of making disciples and if you are going to effectively evangelise your network we need to examine your relationships in detail.

Your family

Western families are usually *nuclear families*, which are made up of parents and their dependent children. Great stress is placed upon the marriage relationship and when children are old enough to marry they leave the parental home to form another nuclear family. This leads to continuous fragmentation into very small groups typically made up of husband, wife and two children. With the breakdown of marriage so prevalent in Western society there are also increasing numbers of one-parent families producing even smaller groups.

In the nuclear family, to which you probably belong, close relationships are fewer, but just as Andrew brought his brother Peter to Jesus (John 1:42) so you can share the Good News with your immediate family. You will probably have to try harder to make contact with your other relatives!

Turn to *Figure 2* and write down your name and names of your relatives who are unbelievers and with whom you could share the Good News.

Your friends and acquaintances

Western society is complex with a great variety of associations, institutions and clubs in which people are organised to fulfil certain functions or complete particular tasks.

In all these groups people relate to each other and in any one day you are probably in touch with several. If your day begins with collecting the letters from the front doormat and the milk from the doorstep you have already been served by the Post Office and Dairy and been visited by the postman and milkman. At work, where the division of labour and differences of status are evident within the company but not so obvious to the outsider, you will make contact with a number of people. You may be a banker to those at home but just one of many cashiers at the Bank. Travelling home from work you could be preoccupied with planning a busy evening that includes a brief meeting to discuss this year's Girl Guide camp for your daughter, and an evangelistic home Bible Study group you attend with your wife.

During this one day you will have touched the lives of dozens of people. Some you will see again and some you could get to know quite well. A few of them will be friends, with whom you share various degrees of intimacy, others are only acquaintances, whose faces you know and with whom you merely pass the time of day. Together with your family these people make up your total network and *your potential for evangelism*.

Your ability to activate this network for evangelism will depend on the frequency and ease of contact, the depth of the relationship and the level of common interest. Obstacles to evangelism may be due to differences in class or status, age or sex or even personality. But if you are able to cultivate these contacts and overcome these obstacles by becoming a Christian friend to these people, then the opportunities for effective evangelism are considerable.

Identify your network

We have already identified a most important and key element of your network in your family. As we build up your network we will identify the other people among your friends and acquaintances with whom you could share the Good News. They will fall into four categories, associated with the *work, leisure, social* and *church* areas of your life. (See *Figure 1. Elements of a Network*)

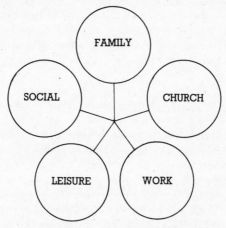

Figure 1. Elements of a New Network

Work

Simon Peter was exhausted after a hard and fruitless night's fishing, and was washing his nets when Jesus confronted him with the Good News of the kingdom and called him to become a disciple (Luke 5:1–11). Matthew was busy with his tax-collecting when he heard the same invitation of Jesus (Luke 5:27). So there is nothing new in Jesus being found in the work and market place.

If you prayerfully reflect upon the people you meet at work (or school, or college if that is appropriate) you can probably identify some who are open to conversations about Jesus Christ.

Turn to *Figure 2* and write down the names of those you can identify at work.

Leisure

The importance of rest from the hectic daily round is stressed in the act of creation and the command to keep the Sabbath (Gen. 2:1–4; Exod. 20:8–11). In addition to the Sabbath, on at least one occasion, Jesus called his disciples to rest when the incessant demands of their ministry threatened their well-being. He said, 'Let us go off by ourselves to some place where we will be alone and you can rest for a while' (Mark 6:31).

Contemporary society now offers a wide range of leisure pursuits and recreational activities that provide the necessary break and opportunity to refresh yourself. Whether you relax by playing snooker or snorkelling, waltzing or wind-surfing, you probably meet with others when you are at play. Think about them and try to identify those to whom you could talk about your faith.

Turn to *Figure 2* and write down their names in the leisure balloon.

Social

The Samaritan woman was going about her daily routine and the everyday chore of water-collecting when she came across Jesus. He was tired and thirsty and simply asked for a drink. While this was a little extraordinary, because Jesus was a Jewish man and they usually had no dealings with Samaritans, especially women (John 4:5–42), having a drink at a well was an everyday occurrence.

In the conversation and events that followed she found the Saviour and subsequently introduced him to others. Those who are sensitive to the possibility of providentially arranged meetings and who are always on the lookout for opportunities to share their faith, can be greatly used by the Holy Spirit to bring others to Jesus.

Stop reading for a moment and think about the people you meet as you go about your business or follow the daily routine. Perhaps the shop assistant or window cleaner or traffic warden! Do you think any of these people might be interested to hear about Jesus? Turn again to *Figure 2* and write their names, or if they are unknown to you their jobs or descriptions, in the social balloon.

Church

The Ethiopian eunuch was earnestly seeking God. He had been to Jerusalem and the Temple precincts to worship and was travelling home reading the scroll of Isaiah. Philip was sent by the Holy Spirit to a roadside rendezvous with this God-fearing nobleman and had the joy of leading him to Jesus. His seeking was over and he found the Saviour he so diligently sought (Acts 8:26–39).

There are people who come to your church in search of God although they may not always know how to express it. Perhaps they are parents who have sent their children because they want them to have something they know they lack. There may be lonely or depressed or bereaved people who have come for solace and companionship. Whatever their need, it can be met by Jesus Christ and his people and you may be the one chosen to meet it.

Stop for a moment and think of those who come to your church and who you believe are still seeking Jesus. Turn to *Figure 2* and write their names in the church balloon.

Your network figure should now be filled in. Hopefully you have several people who can become the focus of your prayers and witness, and you have begun to realise *your potential for evangelism.*

If you have not filled in *Figure 2* as you have been reading be sure to fill it in before reading any further. If you cannot fill in all the balloons, complete as many as possible.

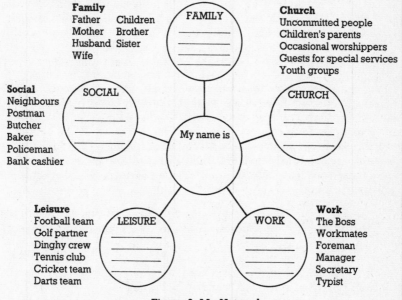

Figure 2. My Network

Evangelise your network

When you understand your network, identifying unevangelised people within it is a continuous exercise and one that should regularly challenge every Christian. Many of us are so 'spiritual' that we have moved away from people who do not share our faith in Christ and have reached that pinnacle of sanctity where we have no contact with unbelievers at all! Both by example and teaching the Lord Jesus and his apostles condemned such foolish practice (Mark 2:15–17; 1 Cor. 5:9–11).

As you attempt to evangelise your network of relationships, the quality of your Christian living and your ability to tell your personal testimony and share the Good News are obviously of great importance. Help in these areas will be found in other sections of this book and I have written practical exercises for group training in my *Tell What God Has Done* booklet (Bible Society 1982). However, you must not be immobilised or silent because of feelings of inadequacy or unworthiness, or you will never do or say anything! Many Christians never speak up for Jesus because they feel unspiritual and ignorant of the Bible. They forget that every Christian needs to be growing more like Christ and learning more about the faith from the Scriptures. They are no different from any other Christian for we all grow and learn in the school of Christ.

All evangelism follows the pattern of Christians merely being channels for what God alone can do. All you have to be is willing and available for use. When you are open toward God, with no unconfessed sin blocking the channel, the Holy Spirit is able to take your most faltering testimony and the most basic facts you share about Jesus Christ and communicate the Good News to your Listener. God the Holy Spirit is able to take your words and speak through your lips. So have confidence that God can use even you!

When you have the confidence that God wants to use *your potential for evangelism*, here are *seven steps* to take:

(i) *Pray regularly*. Pray for each person in your network and for what you know about the circumstances of their life. Pray that they will become conscious of God's love and concern for them personally. Pray about any apparent obstacles to faith such as immorality, alcoholism, or commitment to another ideology or religion. Pray for natural and spontaneous opportunities to share your faith and the sensitivity on your part to know when to speak and be silent.

(ii) *Show you care*. One of the tests of true Christian living is whether or not Christians care for other people. Jesus used very dramatic and powerful words to illustrate the practical dimensions of care: 'I was hungry and you fed me, thirsty and you gave me a drink; I was a stranger and you received me in your homes, naked and you clothed me; I was sick and you took care of me, in prison and you visited me' (Matt. 25:35–6).

Some of the people in your network may have needs as great as those described by Jesus but the vast majority will be helped by such simple things as a word of condolence or an arm around their shoulders.

There are countless words, gestures and little deeds that are tokens of your personal concern and care for others. It was the great missionary to Chinese orphans, Gladys Aylward, who said 'love is seen in what it does', so be imaginative and find an appropriate way to show you care.

(iii) *Strengthen the relationship*. We have already noted the importance of friendship in effective evangelism, so every attempt should be made to strengthen your relationships with people in your network.

This 'friendship factor' is so vital that you may need to begin by putting right what may be wrong in your relationship. If apologies are in order then be the first to apologise!

Develop the relationship by sharing experiences and doing things together such as attending a special event, having a meal, inviting them home for coffee or sharing family outings.

Allow the relationship to develop naturally by being yourself. You are not perfect, so do not pretend you are! As your friend sees you handle the problems with the help of Christ so he will begin to see the relevance of the Good News and a model of a Christian. He needs to know that all Christians are growing and though imperfect are accepted and forgiven by God.

(iv) *Tell them what Jesus Christ means to you.* The basic form of witness is a Christian's personal story illustrating his knowledge and experience of Jesus Christ. This may be very new and limited such as the brave testimony given by the man born blind (John 9:1–41), or well argued and lucid, such as Paul before Agrippa (Acts 26:1–32).

Whatever your personal testimony it should describe how you came to know Christ, whether as a child or adult, and the difference your faith makes to your life. Think of all the benefits that you enjoy as a member of God's family and share them enthusiastically. Remember that this person probably does not know what these benefits are and may only have a negative caricature of Christianity in his mind.

(v) *Introduce them to other Christians.* You are not alone as you evangelise your network, so you have all the resources of God's family to call upon. Ask other Christians to pray for the people you share the Good News with and introduce them to one another. You may find that some Christians have more in common with your contact and they would be better able to help them.

Select the context in which you introduce Christians to your network carefully. The informal gathering in a home or at a social event is far better than the formal church service. Very few churches, of whatever liturgical tradition, have the non-Christian in mind during worship, so introduce them to the church only after they express a definite interest in Jesus Christ and have formed meaningful relationships with you and other Christians.

(vi) *Expose them to Christian events and literature.* When interest in the Christian faith has been openly expressed invite people from your network to specific Christian events such as Gospel concerts, church outings and occasions, and evangelistic Bible study groups. Always be sensitive to people's reaction to these events and be ready to answer questions honestly and as fully as possible. Never be afraid to say 'I don't know', and you can always say 'I'll find out.'

If the people in your network do not have a Bible in a modern version then give them one as a gift for a special occasion. Make the gift significant and important, if not because of the occasion on which it is given, then at least in the way you give it. A suitable inscription will add to the religious and personal significance of the gift.

As you become aware of people's needs, suitable well chosen Christian literature can be very helpful. Be careful not to give too much, especially if people do not read very often and remember some people cannot read at all.

(vii) *Maintain the relationship.* Whether or not the people in your network become Christians you must maintain the relationship. Some will become Christians after a short time but others may never come to faith in Jesus Christ as far as you know.

Continue to pray for the people your life touches and build bridges for the Good News to cross. Keep on caring and strengthen the relationship for you may well be their only link with Christ.

Never stop telling them what Jesus Christ means to you and other Christians and always be ready to introduce them to other Christian people, events and literature.

As you continue to do these things so you will evangelise your network and realise *your potential for evangelism.*

3A.3

Contributing according to your gifts

How biblical evangelism emerges from the body of Christ is a crucial issue for Christians to understand. By 'body of Christ' I am referring not so much to the universal Church, although this is a legitimate use of the word, as I am to the local congregation. In the arena of the local congregation most effective evangelism takes place. It will be quite helpful, therefore, to understand as thoroughly as possible God's own design for the internal functioning of this body of Christ.

What is evangelism?

Rather than discussing the broader aspects of the ministry of the members of a local congregation, this essay focuses only on the evangelistic ministry. It thereby becomes imperative to agree on the meaning of evangelism at the outset.

I understand biblical evangelism to mean much more than doing good, or preaching the message, or getting decisions for Christ. It is nothing less than fulfilling Christ's Great Commission. The Great Commission appears in Matthew, Mark, Luke, John and Acts. It is the very last word Jesus said to his disciples when he finished his earthly ministry (see Acts 1:8). The most detailed of the accounts of the Great Commission is found in Matthew 28:19–20. There the imperative verb is to 'make disciples'. Going, baptising, teaching, and any number of other Christian activities may be evangelistic means or methodologies, but the evangelistic *goal* is nothing less than disciples of Jesus Christ.

What is a disciple of Christ? How do you know when a disciple is made?

Theologically a disciple is made when the Holy Spirit does a sovereign and supernatural work of regeneration in the heart of an unbeliever. But, in the final analysis, no human being knows for sure if and when that event takes place in other people. As Jesus said, it is only 'by their fruits' that you shall know them. What fruit do we look for? Many answers could be given to this question, but in my opinion the most acceptable fruit for measuring evangelistic results is responsible membership in a local church. True disciples are those who 'continue steadfastly in the apostles' doctrine and fellowship, and in breaking of bread and in prayers' as Luke described them in Acts 2:42. People may go to heaven without joining a local church, but from the point of view of evangelistic methodology, that is the best single indicator of whether our evangelism has been effective or not.

It is because of that I feel the best, concise, one-sentence definition of evangelism of all time is the Anglican Archbishops' definition of 1918:

> To evangelise is so to present Christ Jesus in the power of the Holy Spirit, that men and women shall come to put their trust in God through him, to accept him as their Saviour, and serve him as their King in the fellowship of his church.

What are some of the most obvious implications of accepting this definition of evangelism?

For one thing, it keeps us from falling into the trap of separating evangelism from so-called 'follow-up'. Evangelistic programmes which separate the two have built-in failure mechanisms. Evangelism itself involves seeing people, by the power of the Holy Spirit, come to two simultaneous commitments: commitment to Christ and commitment to the body of Christ. It means that Christian discipleship is faulty unless an individual has established bonds of relationship with other flesh and blood Christian people. It means that true evangelism results in church growth. As in the book of Acts, when a church is evangelistic, the Lord is 'adding to the church daily such as should be saved' (Acts 2:47).

If evangelism involves adding to the church people who are being saved, then equipping for evangelism needs to focus on the whole church. It is not sufficient to equip a person here and there for the work of evangelism. Much otherwise good evangelistic work does not result in church growth because the church itself is not equipped to assimilate the new people who are won to Christ. What I am going to say from here on, then, I am saying to groups of Christians who constitute local churches, and to individuals only to the extent that they are expected to make their personal contribution to the activities of the group as a whole.

Although church growth is complex, I believe that the major key to equipping a church for effective evangelism is *allowing the body of Christ to function as it was originally designed by God and explained in the Bible.* I have emphasised this because I believe it is the most important single sentence in this whole essay.

Our equipment

The body of Christ is much more than a human organisation. It is an organism with Christ as the head and every member functioning with one or more spiritual gifts.

(a) *What are spiritual gifts?*

The key to equipping the church, then, lies in the area of spiritual gifts. If spiritual gifts are operating as they should, the body will be properly equipped for evangelism. We must be clear, however, as to what a spiritual gift is: a spiritual gift is a special attribute given by the Holy Spirit to every member of the body of Christ according to God's grace for use within the context of the body. Notice by that definition that every member of the body of Christ – including you yourself – has one or more spiritual gifts.

Knowing this is a tremendous help. It allows you, better than anything else, to understand what God's will is for your life (see Rom. 12:1–6). It helps all the members of your church to know and appreciate where each other fits best into the total picture of your church life and activities. It allows the nominating committee to place church members according to their divine gifts rather than simply on the basis of their availability. It helps the body of Christ to become mature and to grow (see Eph. 4:13, 16).

I mentioned that spiritual gifts are given 'according to God's grace'. In fact the biblical word most used for spiritual gift is *charisma* which has as its root *charis* meaning 'grace'. In 1 Corinthians 12:11 and 12:18 we are told that the gifts are placed in the body as God sees fit. No one can order his or her own gift or gifts, nor can anyone work for a gift and receive it. God alone decides what gifts you have or do not have.

Scholars differ as to how many spiritual gifts should be included in the list. Three chapters in the Bible contain the most distinctive lists of gifts: Romans 12, 1 Corinthians 12, and Ephesians 4. Most agree that a composite of these three lists yields twenty spiritual gifts: prophecy, service, teaching, exhortation, giving, leadership, mercy, wisdom, knowledge, faith, healing, miracles, discerning of spirits, tongues, interpretation of tongues, apostle, helps, administration, evangelist, and pastor. Mention is made elsewhere in the New Testament of five more, bringing the total so far to twenty-five: celibacy, voluntary poverty, martyrdom, hospitality and missionary. Then the question arises: are there gifts in the church being used today that are not mentioned specifically in the Bible? Some would say no. My opinion, and that of many others, is that there are. Some of the most commonly mentioned are music, preaching, writing, and craftsmanship. I personally do not include those in my list, but I do feel that two others should be included: intercession and exorcism. Added to the twenty-five in the Bible, this brings my list to twenty-seven. I have no quarrel with others who have lists of nineteen, twenty, twenty-five, thirty, or what have you, but I have settled on twenty-seven.

Not only is it important to know what the spiritual gifts are, it is equally important to know what they are not. Let me mention four key areas of potential confusion:

(i) Do not confuse spiritual gifts with *natural talents*. Natural talents are God-given abilities that are distributed to human beings in general. Spiritual gifts are given only to members of the body of Christ. Sometimes God will see fit to take a person's natural talent and supernaturally transform it into a spiritual gift. Sometimes a person's spiritual gifts will have no evident relationship to their natural talents. But spiritual gifts are given specifically for the ministry of the body, not for human activities in the broad sense.

(ii) Do not confuse spiritual gifts with *fruits of the Spirit*. The fruits of the Spirit are listed in Galatians 5:22-3. Love is the chief fruit of the Spirit. In 1 Corinthians 13, the apostle Paul explains the relationship between the two. The Corinthians had all the spiritual gifts, but the gifts were worthless. Why? Because the believers did not have love, the fruit of the Spirit. The fruit of the Spirit is the indispensable foundation upon which all the gifts of the Spirit must be exercised.

(iii) Do not confuse spiritual gifts with *Christian roles*. Many of the gifts in the list above describe qualities which should characterise every Christian. For example, all Christians must have faith, not just a few. I label that ordinary kind of faith as our Christian role. But it is qualitatively different from the special gift of faith that is given to only a few members of the body selected by God. The same applies to the gift of giving. All Christians are expected to give at least ten per cent of their income to God. We all have the role of tithing. But a few are given a very special gift of giving far above what the average Christian is expected to give.

(iv) Do not confuse spiritual gifts with *counterfeit gifts*. It is a sad but true fact of life that the devil can and does counterfeit spiritual gifts. This should not discourage our use of gifts, but it should keep us on our toes. Those with the gift of discernment of spirits have a God-given ability to know the difference.

In light of what has been said, it is clear that one of the most important spiritual exercises for every church member is to discover, develop and use his or her spiritual gifts. This is the true starting point for equipping a local church for evangelism.

(b) How does one discover spiritual gifts?

Before I list the five steps, it is necessary to realise that a person needs to be emotionally mature to come to realistic terms with gift discovery. In our society, emotional maturity usually arrives between eighteen and twenty-five years of age, although earlier for some and later for others. New Christians who are already emotionally mature should discover their gifts in a period of between four and twelve months after their conversion and incorporation into the body of Christ.

The following five steps will be extremely helpful in gift discovery. While this specific outline is mine, the ideas in it are commonplace.

(i) *Explore the possibilities.* Accumulate as much knowledge as you can concerning the options. Purchase and read several books on the subject. Compare the author's opinions with your knowledge of the Scriptures and then decide on your own definitions. The more you know about the gifts, the easier it will be for you to recognise yours.

(ii) *Experiment with as many as you can.* As you experiment with gifts, pray that God will help you discover not only the gifts you have but also the gifts you do not have. For many people discovering a gift they do not have is a great source of relief from unnecessary guilt feelings, and a reasonable explanation of why they have tried hard to do some kind of Christian ministry with an obvious lack of success.

(iii) *Examine your feelings.* God, I believe, matches our gifts to our personalities and our temperaments in such a way that if you have a certain spiritual gift you will enjoy using it. Conversely, if you dislike doing a certain job in the church (after conscientiously experimenting with it) it may be a sign you do not have the gift.

(iv) *Evaluate your effectiveness.* If God has given you a certain spiritual gift, it will 'work' so to speak. You will be successful in using it (other things being equal) because the Holy Spirit is working supernaturally through you to accomplish God's purpose.

(v) *Expect confirmation from the body.* The body of Christ, like the human body, is a unit. The parts work in conjunction with each other. If you have a bona fide spiritual gift, other members of your church will affirm in one way or another that you have the gift.

The awareness of the need for spiritual gift discovery has been increasing rapidly over the past few years in our churches. Hundreds of churches have now been renewed through awakening to spiritual gifts, and many of them have experienced vigorous growth as a result. From such churches, several specific recommendations have emerged to help others enter into the same exciting experience.

(i) *Inform, motivate and encourage the congregation.* This can be done, for example, by a series of sermons, and the pastor can mention spiritual gifts from the pulpit regularly. Many have found that spiritual gifts provide a stimulating subject for adult Bible study groups. For these I recommend my book entitled *Your Spiritual Gifts Can Help Your Church Grow* (Regal Books). Church-wide reading programmes can also help. In my book I list the ten books on spiritual gifts I consider at the top of the list.

(ii) *Hold a spiritual gifts workshop.* For this you will need quality materials. A growing number of denominations are designing materials for their constituency. Some independent agencies and parachurch groups have also developed resources for this. The pastor should take leadership in such a workshop if at all possible.

(iii) *Build spiritual gifts into your regular programme.* As the weeks and months go by, more and more churches are gearing their programmes around spiritual gifts. One church I know now has a staff member with the title 'Minister of Spiritual Gifts'. Another holds spiritual gifts discovery workshops three times a year on a regular basis. Each of these churches is sustaining a growth rate of over 300 per cent per decade.

(iv) *Diagnose the health of your local body of Christ.* Some churches have tried spiritual gifts discovery and found that their evangelistic programme did not thereby become more effective. Discovering spiritual gifts is not a panacea for all church problems. Church growth is always complex. Part of equipping the local church for effective evangelism is making sure that the church is healthy in all ways. In order to evaluate this you should know the vital signs of a healthy church and you should be able to identify the major growth-inhibiting diseases. The Bible Society is one organisation that can provide help for church diagnosis.

(v) *Establish a regular, structured witnessing programme.* Evangelism takes doing. Part of equipping the local church is providing a programme that will make evangelism intentional and constant. Organisations such as Evangelism Explosion have excellent programmes that can furnish channels for ministry to those who have the gift of evangelist and to others as well (see 5A.17). My suggestion is that all church members, old and new, prayerfully go through a programme which trains them to share their faith with others. Through it those with the gift of evangelism will discover their gift and those with simply the role of witness will be better witnesses for Christ for the rest of their lives.

The most important person for equipping the local church is the pastor. This may be less than true in some very small churches, but in most medium and large churches it is a recognised fact. My advice to lay people who get excited about spiritual gifts is to pray that their pastor will share the excitement. If he or she does not, it is usually not productive to attempt to bypass the pastor in order to make changes in church life.

While the whole body must be equipped for evangelism, the gift of evangelist is the primary gift for the task. My studies have shown that in most congregations somewhere between 5 and 10 per cent of the active members will have the gift of evangelist. They need to discover their gift, be recognised by the other church members, and be given full opportunity to use their gift to win people to Christ. At the same time, all Christians have the role of witness and should be sharing their faith with others as the opportunity arises. But the 90 per cent who do not have the gift of evangelist have other important gifts they need to be using. If they do not, the new converts will not be assimilated into the body, the evangelistic effort will be curtailed, and the church will not grow.

Equipping the local church for effective evangelism is not easy. It requires motivation, dedication, and just plain hard work. But the rewards are abundant. If the angels in heaven rejoice when one soul comes to repentance, how much more should we also rejoice when our efforts open the way for the Lord to 'add daily to the church such as are being saved'?

Presence Evangelism

3B.1

The Church and where people are

The local church is the body of Christ, that is, a demonstration of the life and ministry of the Lord Jesus lived out in a particular neighbourhood. Being that Christ-like corporate servant to the neighbourhood involves (a) allowing the shape of the church to be changed by living out an alternative life-style in Christ (b) serving the neighbourhood.

1. The shape of the church

Presence evangelism only exists over the long haul; years not months; decades not years. Members of the local church will need to be prepared to

live together in a way which allows the sharing of a common life together

deliberately take time to express togetherness and sharing in family life, in work, in leisure as well as worship and service

discover ways and means to share financial and material assets

respond together to our complex society in a simpler life-style, trusting God for security.

The structures of the church will therefore be flexible in order to respond to the demands of demonstrating the life of Christ in a particular neighbourhood.

Presence ministry requires a total commitment to one another so that despite the imperfections, the inconsistencies the sin and failure we can still be bold to say, 'If you wish to see Jesus, then look at us!'

2. Serving the neighbourhood

Presence evangelism, above all, means living in the neighbourhood which the church seeks to serve. Often, especially if it is an inner city or deprived area, this will mean families, couples, singles literally moving to live in that area. Those members who do not live in the neighbourhood will need to recognise that they are committed to being involved in the neighbourhood of the church as a priority over the home neighbourhood.

'Presence' also means deliberately becoming a part of life of the neighbourhood quite apart from any particular 'ministry' or 'Christian activity'. Church members will apply for teaching posts in local schools, to work in local shops, banks, post offices, offices. Church parents will be active in parent/teacher associations, church footballers involved in the local team, and so on. If local societies and clubs meet in the neighbourhood then church members will be a part of them. Some will make it their interest to know local history; others, the places of particular interest – museums, ancient monuments etc. – others will become involved in Local Government.

The church needs to be in relationship with all the community services and caring agencies at work in the neighbourhood:

social workers, doctors, district nurses, home helps, midwives, health visitors

probation officers, the police (police liaison committees)

voluntary bodies, e.g. victim support groups, parent aid groups, playgroups, other church groups, rotary clubs

Local Government bodies, e.g. planning, environmental, health.

While relationship with the organisers and leaders is important, there is no substitute for knowing the local officers and personnel who are caring for the people whom the church knows.

All this earns the right and, over a long period of time, prepares the way for particular ministries:

(i) *Housing*. Involvement in the provision of accommodation for deprived groups by liaison with housing associations (or form your own), rehabilitation of houses, use of land, involvement in and encouragement of any schemes designed to improve the housing stock.

(ii) *Children and Family work*. Provision of playgroups and drop-in times for parents and children. Encourage activities initiated by the people.

(iii) *Young People*. Provision of drop-in centres, but more especially long-term commitment to get into friendship and involvement with families by living by and with them rather than providing activities.

(iv) *Coffee house/literature base*. This could be in church premises or in the high street.

(v) *Use of church premises*. Church buildings need to be used and adapted for the use of the neighbourhood; aim to be open all the time.

'Presence' means availability and, therefore, means spending money. A church wanting to be present needs to accept that money will have to be spent on that presence whatever form it takes. Effective presence evangelism requires:

(i) *Vision*. a specific, detailed picture towards which the church is working. The raw materials of the vision are God's word and the life of Christ within the members of the church.

(ii) *Understanding of the neighbourhood*. The neighbourhood will not write the agenda of God's purpose but it will write the agenda of 'how' that purpose is achieved. Therefore, the local church starts by defining its neighbourhood geographically and making a survey of its make-up, its needs, its culture, its community life.

(iii) *Meeting actual needs*. Once the church has a real understanding of the community it is in, its serving will be to the actual felt needs of the neighbour-hood and not to theories.

Essentially, presence evangelism enables the local church to lay down its life for the neighbourhood.

3B.2

Being where people are

Jesus went

When Jesus wanted to communicate himself to someone he did not establish himself in a place – e.g. his carpenter's shop, the Temple, Herod's Palace – and invite that someone to come to where he was.

He walked a vast distance out of his way to meet with a social outcast by a well; he called on Zaccheus; he risked an untimely death from some infectious disease when he visited the sick by the Pool of Bethesda; he acted against human common sense by going to see a madman, crossing a lake by boat so that he could deliver and heal; he went with Jairus to his home in order to awaken his daughter from the sleep of death. Jesus never set up a surgery or a centre or a crusade HQ. He did not send out his disciples to invite people to come and hear him. To have done so would have been contradictory to the nature and character of the one who had forsaken heaven to come to earth, where *we* are.

Christians say 'come'

Whilst Christians sit in back-rooms, prior to gospel meetings, praying: 'Lord send them in!' Jesus, who is living within them, is longing to take them out to where people are. Churches are convenient places for Christians to meet for worship and fellowship; the world is the place for real evangelism.

Throughout the Scriptures the pattern has been well-established: whenever God had a communication for someone, if one of his people was available (not necessarily always willing!), God would command his chosen one to go. Moses – go to Egypt; Jonah – go to Nineveh! To Gideon, Joshua, Elijah, Elisha, Jeremiah, Abraham, the Lord said 'Go!'

Then Jesus, the Word of God, spoke to his disciples, saying: 'Go – everywhere, communicating me to everyone.' I obey this great commission only when I allow Christ to lead me out to where people are.

Sadly, it has become an established pattern for Christians to transfer the responsibility for effective communication to those outside the church: 'Please come to see our monthly film,' or 'We have a world famous speaker we'd like you to come and hear,' or 'Will you come to our special event,' or 'Here, take this piece of literature, thank you, would you please read it?' On each such occasion the outsider is made responsible for whether or not he or she ever hears or reads the gospel; if they attend the meeting or the event they hear, if they peruse the leaflet they read, otherwise they are forsaken in a condition where communication has not taken place. Even now too many Christians are removing the *go* from the gospel and the *reach* from preach.

Jesus says 'Go'

I believe it is a matter of getting concepts right and evangelism is not me trying to convert the world for Jesus, rather it is me allowing the Jesus who lives within me to take me wherever he wishes me to go, there permitting him to communicate himself by loving deeds, gentle words and demonstrations of the Truth he is, to whomsoever he chooses. He said, 'As my Father sent me so send I you.'

(a) *At home*

When Jesus is leading me out it will be *first in Jerusalem* – Jesus communicating himself to people where they are beginning where I am! I am in the house where I believe Jesus wants me to live, so I can expect him to communicate himself through me to my own family.

(b) *Next door*

I am in the school or the job or house where Jesus wants me to be, so I can expect him to lead me to the next desk, the next bench or house. Jesus will be leading me so that he can speak to or love the person who is right next to me, and then the person next door but one. Going into all the world means going into all the world I have, however small and restricted it might at times appear to be; no matter how vast the distances within it.

Once I accept the principle it is a matter of faith; trusting Jesus to lead me to the people around me, trusting Jesus to communicate to them in whatever ways he chooses. Given the smallest amount of my faith Jesus will shift mountains of hesitancy and fear in order to reach the person he loves.

3B.3

The art of sensitive listening

There are many thousands of people in the world whose great longing is to find someone who will *listen* to them. But real listening is a task which requires concentration and discipline; so most people prefer to talk, which is a much less demanding assignment. Also, many of us are basically far more interested in ourselves than in other people and so we prefer to hold the floor. Like James Thurber, we do not listen to anyone; we just wait for them to stop speaking so that we can start.

The listeners of the world are valuable and wise people like the owl.

> A wise old owl sat in an oak
> The more he saw the less he spoke
> The less he spoke the more he heard
> Why aren't we like that wise old bird!

We can learn a great deal from thinking about the way Jesus himself listened to people when he wanted to persuade, confront, or comfort them with news or claims of our kingdom of God. We need to learn from him so that our own presentation can be modelled on his. No two encounters were the same for him.

He always saw the person and the context. One may come at night when no one would see him; one man was good, well set up and conscientious with no obvious need for repentance; one woman came weeping and desperate; one man's spiritual and emotional needs were showing themselves in his physical illness; one was a scoffer who had no intention of being convinced; one woman was trying to cover up her embarrassment about her personal life-style by religious talk. Jesus saw the human being in front of him and also beyond the surface to the social background, the emotional hunger, and the personal problems which were all part of the spiritual need for regeneration. This understanding coloured the way in which he presented his message, which, though always the same, often sounded quite different. Why was his perception so good?

Basic principles of listening

These basics can apply in any light chat between friends but they are essential for a person who is engaged in a conversation with a purpose.

(i) *Give yourself wholeheartedly to the task of taking in what the other person is saying.* The conversation may last for five minutes or an hour, but the degree of commitment is the same. You cannot be free to 'hear' what is said if half your mind is somewhere else. What is more, a sensitive speaker will detect very quickly if your attention is wandering and will soon stop saying anything of consequence. This first rubric is difficult. It involves unselfishness, flexibility, and adaptability.

(ii) *Be prepared to give priority, for the moment, to what he is saying.* You may think you have 'the answer' or some important piece of information to pass on, but you *must* wait. There is no value in giving the answer until you know what the question is. Words of wisdom become useless if they are said in the wrong place or at the wrong time or to the wrong person. This applies particularly to an evangelistic enterprise. We have to hear and understand the personal attitudes or needs of the other person so that we can deliver our message in a way which is relevant and appropriate. We have to earn the right to speak!

(iii) *Listening means just that!* It means not interrupting and butting in. It means controlling our desire to speak. It means waiting until we have heard the full story. In short, it means that we are seeking 'not so much to be understood as to understand' as St Francis of Assisi describes it. This means that we do not at once protest or contradict or even agree with what is being said, until we have heard the context. Otherwise this conversation can easily degenerate into an argument.

(iv) *It means not jumping to conclusions about how the person may be reacting.* We may have been led to make that assumption because we have met it before, or we might ourselves have reacted that way. But unless we make sure that we know accurately how the person speaking is actually reacting, we cannot be listening properly, and we may be in danger of missing the point.

(v) *It means understanding precisely what the speaker means.* A subsequent sentence may explain this, but if not, a short question may be needed to clarify. For instance, the word 'guilty' may signify a dozen things including a generalised feeling of discomfort when no real guilt exists. Which of the meanings does the speaker have in mind? That affects quite extensively the response the listener may make!

(vi) *Questions have a a place* in the listening process provided they are few and purposeful. Their main value is in helping the person to reflect on what he is saying or in elaborating its meaning. If a conversation turns into a series of questions and answers, it has largely ceased to be a spontaneous and free conversation. It has become more of an 'examination' with a different outcome.

(vii) *Recognise non-verbal communication.* Words are often an inadequate medium of expression. They are limited and often only tell part of a story, particularly if the speaker is not articulate. So the listener is using his second pair of ears (namely his eyes) to observe the expressions and the language of the speaker's face, hands, and general demeanour. They will often reinforce, contradict or amplify in some way what is being said. The listener must learn to be sensitive to atmosphere, not just words.

We must not bombard people with the gospel in an arrogant way, forcing upon them something they do not understand. Many a good message has been ruined by an inept messenger! We *ourselves* must commend the gospel by our respect, courtesy, patience and care for the other person, and the attention we give to him as a total person – not a scalp to be hunted. We also have to respect his right to make his own response without manipulation or pressure. This is often difficult when we really care.

Listening is a complex operation and essential to effective communication. We can all learn to do it better.

He who answers before listening – that is his shame and his folly (Prov. 18:13).

3B.4

Introduction – Saying no to your local church

As Christians, we all need to be members of a local fellowship. But it is possible for that local fellowship to absorb *all* our time, energy and effort to such an extent that we've no time left for bridge-building and outreach to our neighbours, friends and communities.

We could find, for example, that we go to the fellowship home groups, the fellowship Bible groups and mid-week meetings, the fellowship praise groups, prayer groups and social groups. When we have a bit of spare time, we drink coffee with members of the fellowship, go out with members of the fellowship, play squash or garden with members of the fellowship, and even go on the fellowship holiday! It's nice this way, and we're spared the stress of bridgebuiling and outreach.

But we must allow time to turn outwards, and here are a few suggestions as to how it can be done. This is in no way a comprehensive list, and you might not find exactly what you are looking for, but don't let that blind you to the principle. Sometimes it's necessary to say no to some of the activities of the local fellowship, in order to say yes to the world.

3B.4a

Pubs

There are tremendous advantages in using pubs and clubs as evangelistic agencies, but before you start be warned:

(i) Your local fellowship might not like it! Often, resistance to a pub ministry can come from within the local fellowship of which you're a member. This usually stems from a misunderstanding of what a pub ministry is trying to do, but there can be deeper reasons. Some feel that pubs are basically evil places, from which Christians should withdraw. Others are strongly teetotal, and some have never been near a pub at all, and assume that therefore they must be 'bad' places. Don't be put off though. Christ wasn't ashamed to be seen where people gathered, and we will answer to him alone in the end.

(ii) Try to avoid carrying on a pub ministry *apart* from your local fellowship. It can be done, but it's so much more effective if it's part of the local work.

(iii) Pubs can be frightening places to work in. The environment is beyond your control, and without much prayer, can get out of control.

Why bother with pubs and clubs anyway?

There are tremendous advantages in bothering with pubs and clubs.

(i) *Pubs are where many men can be found.* As a Christian body, we've been very unsuccessful in reaching men. But we know where they are to be found – and if they won't come to us, the solution seems rather obvious, doesn't it?

(ii) *It's their ground.* Evangelising in a pub is very much working on 'their ground', not ours. That puts the church at a disadvantage, and that's a great advantage! As the 'guest' in the arrangement, I always feel much more freedom than when I'm the 'host'.

(iii) *It shows acceptance.* By using the pubs, we show that the church is prepared to move outside its building. This is a tremendous witness to the non-Christian community, who are quick to accuse us of being a 'holy huddle'. It also helps people feel that they are not 'beyond' the church. Let's face it, we have sometimes given that impression, haven't we?

(iv) *It's informal.* The atmosphere in the pub is informal – ideal for gossiping the gospel, and a good place to invite non-Christian men to.

There are those who are apprehensive about pub work because they feel it is encouraging men to drink. But in my experience Christian pub work has the opposite effect. Men drink in the pub often because that's the only way they can stay there. But when the church holds pub nights, the main purpose is friendship together – and we don't need to drink to keep it going! The result is that even the heavy drinkers don't need to keep drinking to keep the friendship going.

How pub ministries work

I know of two effective ways of carrying out a pub ministry, and there are certainly others.

(a) *The informal approach*

This ministry depends on ordinary people being prepared to share their faith. A group is trained, using *Breakthrough*, *Evangelism Explosion* or something similar, to share Jesus. Then members of the group go to a pub, sit beside someone, and get chatting. I know it sounds a bit vague, but it works! It might be polite to check with the publican first, and to make it clear what you want to do, and who you are. Incidentally, a word about publicans. They're not so anti-church as you might be lead to think. They're business people, and they'll hire you rooms etc., in the normal way, but they're often quite willing to give you a helping hand. Maybe the gap between the church and the pub isn't as wide in their eyes as it is in ours.

(b) *The regular meeting approach*

This requires more organisation. First, find a few men who will share the vision with you, and then:

Book a room in the pub, regularly over a year.

Sort out an interesting secular programme. Surprised? But a good sound spiritual programme won't get the sort of men you want, will it? Look for people with local interests, hobbies, interesting jobs, holiday slides, singers, etc. The nationalised industries – water, gas, coal – have good films for free, and they will gladly lend them.

Use these meetings to build up your regular support. It's most important to get a good base.

Programme in your evangelistic guest nights, as and when you feel it's right. A word of caution here. Make sure your speaker has a good approach to men, and can cope with the dynamics of a pub. After he's finished, allow plenty of time for chat afterwards. Do this regularly.

Back up

There are a few other events/happenings you can use to strengthen the pub work, and also begin to build a bridge the other way – *from* the pub, to the church fellowship.

(a) *Men's suppers*

Not all men go to a pub, and some won't come near. So now and again have a church-based men's night. A supper (or whatever goes in your area) and a speaker can reach those non-pub men, and will also draw some of your pub men into the church premises. They will be more prepared to come to your premises now that you've broken the ice and gone to theirs!

(b) *Away days*

Look for opportunities to run trips out for men. Try and make sure they interest men. Recently, one pub group ran a trip to a reservoir and looked around all the workings. There are many other such possibilities, and they all cement friendships – and form new ones – as well as shifting the ground away from the pub.

My place?

Pub ministries depend on Christian men being prepared to take the opportunity to reach non-Christian men in the secular environment of the pub. Pub ministries stand or fall on this commitment, or lack of it. You'll have to convince Christian men of this truth. Encourage them to believe that by supporting this ministry they are fulfilling the great commission of Matthew 28 as much as if they were preaching an evangelistic sermon, or sharing the gospel in someone's front room.

I started with a word of warning, so I'll finish with one. Pub ministries take a long time to show results. Don't expect to see your fellowship suddenly full of newly converted men after six months. If you're patient, and work away at the task, you will see results.

3B.4b

TV meetings

It is presently estimated that 1,600,000 people in the United Kingdom own a video cassette recorder, which would mean that there is a set in 8 per cent of the nation's homes.

By the end of 1984 the figures are expected to be 3,600,000 (18 per cent) and by 1986 to have jumped to 6,000,000 (30 per cent). At today's rate this would also mean that 100 million video cassette tapes would be borrowed in that year alone!

Even allowing for some fluctuations in the figures, the message is loud and clear: the video revolution is well and truly upon us and will significantly shape popular communication from now on.

How to harness this medium

(i) Collect as much information as to available material for sale or hire and classify it in sections. Most suppliers advertise in the Christian periodicals on a regular basis.

(ii) Start a video library in your church. It is much better for the local church to be involved in this, as the material can be expensive for an individual to purchase or rent.

(iii) It may be possible for a group of local churches to start a joint video library and therefore minimise the expense.

(iv) Once a video library has been established, ways and means must be devised to bring tapes into the homes of the people, and this can be done in various ways as follows:

advertise free video films in the local press with titles and short summary of content. Available for free loan for forty-eight hours ... A suitably designed leaflet could also be delivered to local homes or else used by Christians to pass on to their friends that they know have video recorders. Why not embark on a door to door visitation programme in which video film could be offered for forty-eight hours free of charge?

suitable evangelistic literature should also be made available with the films

the value of this approach is that people can watch in the privacy of their own homes and at a time suitable to them.

(v) Why not set up TV sets and video recorders in the church lounge on certain days and invite the old folk for lunch and the chance to see a video film? The same approach could be used in the mornings and young mothers could be invited to watch a screening. Créche for small children and coffee provided.

(vi) A local church could arrange a video crusade or mission with the same video being screened in say twenty Christian homes during the week and culminating in an invitation to a special guest service at the end of the week, or better still an invitation to a buffet supper and an after supper speaker.

(vii) Let individuals use the church resource material for screening in their own homes and then inviting a few friends and neighbours in.

(viii) What about contacting schools/youth clubs/working mens' clubs/pubs Old Peoples Homes/Prisons/Remand Centres and saying that you have the following video films available for free hire.

(ix) The best videos are those specially prepared for the medium, and not those that are just films of live events. You need a video that doesn't allow the viewer to be just a spectator but rather one where the speaker is actually teaching him.

(x) Before using a video for evangelism please make sure that you have viewed it and feel happy with its content and presentation.

(xi) One of the dangers in using this modern means of communication is that you can even unconsciously think that of itself it will produce conviction of sin and the miracle of the new birth in a person's life – it won't. Make sure that you pray much about its use – in fact maybe you should pray more!

3B.4c

School gate

Very few people these days live in communities where everybody knows everybody else. Those who live in the urban sprawl, high-rise apartments, or who escape each evening from the city into the country, like to keep themselves to themselves. The fact that the majority of people work in one place, live in another and find their recreation and entertainment somewhere else, breaks up any sense of community. Rather, we live in networks of relationships which are different with each individual, even within the same family. Our frequent moves in search of jobs or suitable housing removes us from relatives and friends. The resulting sense of isolation and loneliness is often most severely felt by young mothers at home with small children.

In such circumstances the Christian witness must consider the evangelistic potential of any brief, regular occasions for social contact. Now that the supermarket has largely replaced the corner shop, there is no longer the occasion for chit-chat while standing in a queue. Some mums find opportunity to meet people through coffee-chats, women's meetings, keep fit and 'popmobility' groups. There is one other place which is of strategic importance – the school gate.

In his book *Good News To Share*, Gavin Reid has aptly described the school gate as the twentieth-century equivalent of the village well. It's the place where women congregate once or twice a day with time on their hands while they await the appearance of their offspring. So if you are in the habit of collecting an infant and live within easy walking distance from the school gate, set out that little bit earlier and leave the car at home! The daily walks not only provide fresh air and exercise, but the chance to walk to and from with other mums and to chat at the gate. As it is a daily encounter during term time, friendly relationships can be established and trust built up.

During the course of conversation common problems are likely to crop up because all of the mums are struggling to bring up a family within a similar age bracket. The following topics emerged as we chatted together:

How do we bring up our children to face the world of today and tomorrow?

Coping with the aftermath of a still-birth and understanding those who have been through that tragic experience.

Our responsibilities towards elderly relatives when they become increasingly dependent upon us, sometimes creating a conflict of loyalty between them and husband and children.

Finding fulfilment in our work

Tension in the family.

A step further

Time for conversation is often all too brief, being interrupted by excited children with their demands for attention. Why not take the initiative to suggest a get-together one evening, or some other suitable time of day, to exchange views and gather ideas to help cope more adequately with the problems?

Rather than act in isolation, it is preferable to discuss the possibilities with two or three other Christian mums. In this way you can pray together for the Lord's guidance, help each other out with the practical arrangements and provide a range of Christian experience to draw from in the meetings. We have had meetings in our home on all of the topics I've mentioned. Each drew a living-room capacity crowd, because we were talking about issues which we all considered to be important.

The way to start is to arrange a one-off meeting rather than a series. The prospect of a long-term commitment will put many people off. So experiment with one to see how things go; then at the end of the meeting you can sound out opinion to see if those present would like to meet again.

Topics such as those already mentioned provide an opportunity for everybody to make a contribution. Both Christians and non-Christians can speak from their own experience, without creating an 'us' and 'them' atmosphere. Down-to-earth themes which are of common interest provide the occasion for Christians to demonstrate the relevance of their faith in Christ and to testify to the strength and guidance which he had given to enable them to cope.

From our limited experience we would emphasise three practical points:

(i) Ensure that the meeting ends at the stated time, so that those who need to go can leave without embarrassment. A clear end to the meeting also provides an opportunity for those who so desire to stay on and talk further. It is what happens afterwards which is often the most significant part of the occasion.

(ii) Realise that people seldom come to Christ at the first meeting or even during a subsequent meeting. Be prepared to run a series if the demand is sustained, and pray for occasions to discover how they felt about the programme during the days that follow. It took us two years to progress from occasional meetings on topics on general interest, to simple Bible studies on a regular basis. Now two groups are going strong, one for women and the other for couples.

(iii) Think of ways to involve husbands who usually will not come out for a meeting but will for a meal!

A great deal can come out of a casual chat at the school gate. Now the opportunity has passed for us as our youngest is old enough to go to school on her own. We wish we had started sooner.

3B.4d

Parent-Teacher Associations

The majority of schools in this country no longer operate as totally self-contained units. The cuts in education grants and the need for close liaison between teachers and parents have ensured the emergence of a vast number of Parent-Teacher Associations or 'Friends' of various schools.

Their main mandate is supportive. To raise funds for additional materials and to improve school-parent relationships. However, many such groups are short of personnel and will welcome the support of parents who offer themselves for election to the PTA or Friends Committee at an Annual General Meeting.

The results of such involvement from Christian parents can be enormous:

(i) *By developing friendship.* The PTA produces a wealth of new relationships with non-Christians. The ongoing contact at the school gate can produce great opportunities for personal witness.

(ii) *By raising a Christian voice.* For example a local PTA has launched a campaign against the local adult video network which operates opposite the school. This initiative has been taken by largely non-Christian parents concerned over the issue. Christian involvement in the PTA has helped to stimulate concern for such matters.

(iii) *By demonstrating Christian participation.* I'll never forget the hush when I chaired my first PTA meeting, asked everyone to explain what their employment was, and then shared my own! Involvement in PTAs has brought an increased awareness among non-Christians of the nature of biblical Christianity.

This is not meant to imply that such involvement is problem-free. Far from it. Time and again one will have to consider the rights and wrongs of involvement in this or that particular project. However, many have discovered that by exercising an ongoing series of checks with the Lord, progress has been made. Sometimes our reasons for declining to participate in one project or another can lead to a really fruitful discussion.

3B.4e

Home meetings

1. Why evangelise in a home?

The majority of the population do not attend church, or for that matter have any idea what goes on in a church. Crossing the threshold of a religious building is a great psychological barrier. But all unconverted people are familiar with a home and the majority drink tea or coffee and eat! So the house meeting has the inbuilt advantage of being a normal familiar setting.

There is of course strong biblical warrant for using a home because Jesus often operated and ministered in homes. Matthew, when he was converted, invited his friends for a meal and Jesus came and spoke. In the New Testament Paul urged all Christians to be 'given to hospitality'.

2. Who can run one and when?

Literally anybody – and in any size and kind of home. Your home will be suitable for your friends. If you have a few seats, can make a cup of tea or coffee and open a packet of biscuits then you can start. And by the way, house meetings can be run at any time during the day.

3. Who shall we invite and how?

Use a personal invitation card on which you can write the name of the person you are inviting and say that there will be a speaker or whatever after coffee and refreshments. It causes problems if you get people into your home on false pretences.

Make your card an RSVP as this gives it a sense of value.

Invite people you know. Go after near neighbours, friends, unconverted relatives and work colleagues. The best house meetings are always those where the folk being invited know the householder.

Don't try and invite neighbours to another house the other side of town!

4. What about content?

(i) It can take the form of a simple Bible study that is relevant to the folk coming – followed by discussion.

(ii) A mature Christian or visiting evangelist can speak on a set subject e.g. 'Relevance of Christianity for Today'.

(iii) You could have a general discussion on some topical issue that has a very definite Christian application. In this situation it is always wise to have someone in the group who can make sure that the conversation is directed along the right lines and that a positive conclusion is arrived at.

(iv) A film or filmstrip could be screened. This could be followed by someone presenting an application of the message in the film or by a discussion of the film.

(v) Play a short taped message (ten minutes) that has been specially prepared for this purpose. Ask the group for questions. Write them down and then work your way through them in discussion.

(vi) Invite a person to simply share their testimony as to how they found Christ and what he means to them today.

(vii) Always give people an opportunity to ask questions.

5. Practical points to note

(i) Don't invite all your Christian friends to come to make up the numbers or to give you more courage. The best house meetings are always those where the non-Christians outnumber the believers.

(ii) The few Christian friends that are invited should not come complete with large Bibles!

(iii) Don't invite known members of religious sects who could be troublesome by trying to take over the meeting.

(iv) If young mums are invited and they bring their children (mornings) then try and arrange a créche in another room.

(v) As folk arrive do introduce them to each other.

(vi) Serve coffe/tea/refreshments first, as this helps people to relax. By all means serve another cup later on.

(vii) Don't argue with anyone!

(viii) Don't deliberately raise a controversial subject e.g. 'CND and the Christian Church'.

(ix) Be positive and not negative in condemning other religions or sects. Always seek to show the positive answer in the Christian gospel.

(x) Allow the speaker or the leader of the meeting to lead. That's what he's there for.

(xi) Have some evangelistic literature available after the meeting.

(xii) Follow up on a person-to-person basis all who took relevant evangelistic literature and who asked pertinent and searching questions.

3B.4f

Local media

1. Your local church now

Try answering the following questions for your local church:

(i) Do you have a complete up-to-date list of every local newspaper (including the growing number of free papers), local radio stations, television stations, hospital radio stations, news agencies and freelance journalists in your area? Do you know the editors, news editors, religious producers and any journalists who are Christians?

(ii) Have you made contact with them? Do you keep in regular touch with them and provide them with a regular supply of news from your church, including the church magazine?

(iii) Have you invited any of them to speak at a church meeting about their work in relation to the church?

(iv) At whom is your church magazine aimed and what is its objective? Is it fulfilling that objective? Is it reaching out to the community at large? What is the response?

(v) Do you have a press or public relations officer? If not, have you ever thought of appointing one?

(vi) Has your church analysed and discussed within the past two years the ways you communicate with each other within your church?

(vii) If your church has made plans for the future and is seeking to grow, what plans have you made in the area of publicity – both internally and externally?

(viii) What publicity material do you have for new members of your church?

(ix) Has your church prayed about, considered and discussed outlets through the mass media for evangelistic outreach within your local community?

(x) Has your church considered encouraging members to write letters, sharing a Christian viewpoint on topics of interest, to the local and national media?

Possible action

After answering these questions you may find it helpful to call together a meeting of church members who have either a gift for or an interest in the media. If you are not the minister of your church, make sure you talk the idea through with him; he needs to be behind what you are attempting. Perhaps the ten questions mentioned above could form the basis of a discussion. Do, however, ask yourself the most important question – 'Is my church worth publicising?'

2. Church public relations

At an individual level if you become involved with the local media you in fact become the church public relations officer. Done well, good public relations can achieve:

● an increased respect by your local community to the work and worth of your church

● an increased recognition that God is at work and Jesus Christ is alive

● newspapers, radio and sometimes television, approaching you for stories

● increased church morale and understanding of public attitudes

● more people enquiring about the Christian faith.

3. Research

If you are still serious about getting involved you will need to prepare a comprehensive list of outlets and contacts covering the area of your local church. For national outlets see Brads Directory of Media Information. Most public libraries should have one.

(a) Newspapers

(i) All the local daily, evening and weekly newspapers circulated in your area. Their addresses, telephone numbers, names of editors, news editors (or chief reporters), and any known Christians on the reporting staff.

(ii) Free newspapers covering your area, addresses, telephone numbers and names of editors.

(iii) News agencies (these distribute news on a much wider basis and are invaluable contacts – especially for help and advice if you have a good story.) These can be obtained from the Yellow Pages telephone directory. Note name of contact.

(iv) Ask around for freelance journalists or writers, particularly those who handle religious news stories.

(v) There are a number of Christian papers and magazines which will be circulating in your area, such as the Church Times, Church of England Newspaper, Methodist Recorder, Baptist Times, Catholic Herald, Buzz, Family, Today, Christian Woman and very many more. Find out the addresses and telephone numbers of all of these publications, depending on your denominational bias. They are glad to receive stories.

(vi) Really good stories, which hold a much wider news value, can be sent to the Press Association, Fleet Street, London EC4. They serve all major media in the country.

(b) Radio

(i) Find out which local radio stations cover your area. Note their address and telephone number and names of the news editor and religious producer. Also list the type of religious programmes they put out.

(ii) Make a list of the national radio religious programmes, such as 'Sunday' on Radio 4. Listen to them and make a note of the producers' names as they are pleased to hear of good stories which fit into their programme format.

(c) Television

(i) Find out the local television stations which cover your area. Note address and telephone number and the name of the news editor and religious producer.

(ii) Look out for regular religious programmes of a magazine format on television. e.g. BBC's 'Sunday Night'. Make a note of the producers' names as they are pleased to hear of exceptional stories.

(d) Other outlets

(i) Find out whether your local hospital has a radio service. If so, enquire who is responsible for the religious output. They are always grateful for contributions.

(ii) Most denominations have regional or area magazines. Find out the details of the one serving your church and establish a contact for supplying information about your church.

Response

If you start all or any of these ideas you will get a response. You may be involved with your church magazine, or contribute to a local radio station or even have a column in the local paper. What you say must cause people to respond and you must decide how to handle these queries. Can you do it yourself? Do you need some trained ministers or lay folk to help? Do you need to organise a team of counsellors?

Further details of workshops and more specialist training and detailed workbooks can be obtained from Christian Communication, 11 Faringdon Road, Swindon, Wilts.

3B.4g

Vagrants

Vagrants is the nice name given to people who used to be called 'tramps'. These nomadic people know no boundaries either geographically or culturally. They can be found in derelict buildings, park benches, London's tube stations and railway stations and waiting rooms. They have no sense of time, decency or hygiene. We could run out of adjectives trying to describe them, but we must never forget that they are people. This means that they are made of the same material as anybody else, having a spirit, a mind and a body.

Most of them are people who have either lost their way or have lost hope altogether. Preaching at them, saying prayers over them, or giving them tracts is not the answer. Even dishing out soup and tea can only be perpetuating their problems. What they need is a group of understanding and caring people, who are prepared to give time, effort and practical resources, excluding money, in order to find out the causes as well as the effects. It is essential to find out who the person is, how long they have been in that condition and also to extract some of the reasons behind their profile.

Most have hit rock-bottom and have no hope of changing their situation because they have literally given up. Trying to offer a vagarant or tramp a meal and/or a bed is simply not enough. In order to help people like this, there has to be commitment and a plan of action that has content and meaning to it.

Any work amongst this strange society is not to be undertaken by novices, because they will be taken in and the problems of the individual will only be perpetuated and add to the long list of do-gooders that he or she could enumerate if given the time and opportunity.

Most of them cannot read, so giving them tracts is a sheer waste of time and only adding to the wastepaper industry. Like other gypsies, they cannot read, or write, but they certainly know how to count. The desperate need is practical evangelism and seen in this context, accommodation addresses that offer more than just a 'crash pad' accommodation programme and assessment 'drop in' centre.

How do we help the 'drifter' in practical terms?

(i) Find out his name.

(ii) Obtain any home address or town and discover whether he or she is a missing person.

(iii) If possible, ascertain whether the person is involved in any criminal activity, because harbouring such a person would only implicate you!

(iv) Find out whether the person really wants to change his or her lifestyle.

(v) Have some addresses to which the person can be referred to if they are determined and motivated to change.

(vi) Share in simple terms how important it is for him or her to realise how much God loves them.

(vii) Cut out pious platitudes, evangelical cliches and terminologies which will mean nothing to the hearer.

(viii) Spend time and, if you cannot do this yourself, arrange for somebody else who can spend some time in getting alongside the person.

(ix) Don't offer them junk food, but lift their sights regarding their food intake and, if possible, find out where they can get cleaned up physically. This means an enormous difference to the individual that somebody literally cares.

(x) Don't give them money as they will only go out and squander it. Rather take them for a meal or have a sandwich with them rather than giving it to them and then passing on.

(xi) Give the person your absolute attention and respect and, that way, you will receive it back.

Helpful tips

(i) If you are taking them to a meeting, then don't ask them to turn up at some address, get somebody to go and find them and bring them to the meeting, or church, etc.

(ii) Have a list of special addresses of people who specialise in helping the vagrant. If you can find out more than ten addresses, you have really achieved something!

(iii) If they are stoned out of their head either from the influence of drugs or drink, it is most unlikely that you will get anywhere with them until they are sober.

(iv) Be absolutely certain that God has led you to this person or this person has been led to you and pursue the matter until you are convinced that you cannot do something for them and with them.

(v) Emphasise to them that, in spite of their guilt, they can be forgiven and encourage them to forgive themselves as well as to accept God's forgiveness through Christ.

(vi) Never give your home address or telephone number or the address of your pastor or minister or priest without telling them. This is unfair either to your family or to your minister and his family, because these people have the habit of turning up at the most unexpected and inconvenient time, and often when you are not there. This creates problems, which, I hope, are obvious.

(vii) Never forget, that a need does not necessarily constitute a call, therefore be absolutely sure that you are using your time wisely and effectively with the vagrant.

(viii) Never argue with them, but show compassion and love and concern and, if the person is not prepared to listen to you, then bid him or her goodbye with a friendly gesture and depart. Having had experience of many tramps over the years, and especially being involved with drug addicts for eighteen years, I am aware that there are fundamental underlying causes behind the social diseases of vagrancy. They are spiritual, emotional, social, psychological and biochemical.

We in the Christian Church must learn to translate biblical psychology into practical and down-to-earth Christianity, where we wear our Christianity on our sleeve, are prepared to get our hands dirty, and are always faithful to our Lord in sharing the truths of his liberating gospel with these desperate people.

The therapy of the Holy Spirit is available to people who need it and want it. Vagrants are not hopeless individuals. They are people who have become hopeless about their situation.

Communication

3C.1

Principles and Practices of Communication

We are all in the business of communicating and in evangelism the problem is even more acute.

Let us try to understand this by looking at a model on communication. Keep one eye on the diagram and the other on the reading matter, and follow this discussion through. If I have a 'message', for example, 'Jesus is my Saviour', this relatively simple message needs to be communicated through who I am: my culture, social class, education, motives, attitudes, environment, experiences, etc.

In all these areas I have consciously or unconsciously made certain assumptions about my own understanding of what is in my mind when I say 'Jesus is my Saviour'. In other words, I think I understand what I mean when I communicate my message.

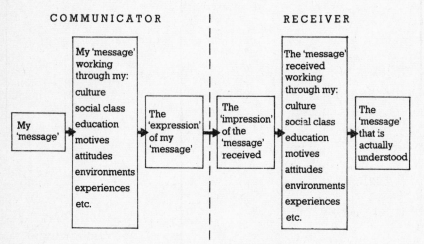

The Process of Communication

I must now attempt to 'express' my message to the 'receiver'. This may be done verbally, by action, by sight or by any other of our five senses. The message in the mind is no good to the 'receiver' unless it can be expressed in some form. Moving on now to the 'receiver' what does he see or hear, what is the impression received? Naturally this is going to be coloured by the culture, social class, education, motives, attitudes, environment, experiences, etc. of the 'receiver'.

If these characteristics are similar to those of the communicator then the greater the chances of effective communication. Finally in this process, that which is actually understood in the mind of the 'receiver' is often different from the message in the mind of the 'communicator'. May I give you an example: a musician friend of mine asked a group of twelve-year-olds the whereabouts in the Bible of Adam and Eve. The response was spontaneous and enthusiastic, 'The book of Guiness sir'.

Communication by its very nature demands a response. So much of our communication these days is done from a distance. Someone speaks and we listen. The days are gone when we can expect people to fill the pews to hear a great or less famous preacher 'sock' it to them. In an age when our education system teaches young children to ask questions, we must be aware that we must allow more time for them to do this in an atmosphere that allows a relaxed exchange of views.

Christian communication by its very nature should be 'enthusiastic'

One of the derivations of the word 'enthusiasm' comes from the Greek, meaning 'inspired by God'. Whether our subject is heavy or light there must be a real conviction and belief in its expression. In the last analysis the 'receiver' will be asking, is this person giving this message genuine – does he really believe what he is saying?

Effective communication must be visual and active

Recently a missionary society suggested these figures in regard to the effectiveness of our communication.

Message received by	Information remembered after:	
	3 hours	3 days
Hearing only	70%	10%
Seeing only	72%	20%
Hearing and seeing	85%	65%

While these figures have no substantiation, they act as a pointer to a truth which many teachers and communicators have known for years, and which they have used to tremendous advantage.

Communication in the Old Testament

The religious historical stories

In the books of Ruth, Jonah, Esther and the Song of Solomon we find historical stories entertaining in themselves and yet containing at the same time spiritual truth about the covenant grace of God. Consider the drama of Jonah in the great fish, the beautiful romance between Ruth and Boaz, the collection of love poems and songs between a man and a woman in the Song of Solomon, and the intriguing account of Esther and Mordecai as they planned to save the Jews from extermination.

The Psalms

In the Psalms we have the most famous poetry in the world. Written by a number of poets expressing utmost despair on the one hand and the glorious majesty of God at the other end of the spectrum.

The visual symbols of Jeremiah

Let us look at just one example of dramatic symbolism in the Old Testament. Jeremiah demonstrated God's message to his people through every explicit visual aids:

the linen shorts and the wine jars (Jer. 13)

the iron pen (Jer. 17)

the potter and his clay (Jer. 18)

the smashed clay jar (Jer. 19)

the wooden and iron yoke (Jer. 27–8)

the buying of the field at Anathoth (Jer. 32)

The vivid demonstration of God's word through drama was very much a part of the message of God.

Communication in the New Testament

The communication of Paul

Notice the varying styles of Paul in his writings to the churches – compare Romans with Corinthians, or Philemon with Galatians, or Timothy with Ephesians. Paul used different approaches to different situations.

Paul's preaching varied between races and countries – compare his sermon in the synagogue at Antioch (Acts 13) and his preaching to the Athenians (Acts 17). It is important to note that Paul quoted their own poets. Epimenides the Cretan and Aratus a Cilician. Paul spoke the language of the culture: 'So I became all things to all men, that I may save some of them by whatever means are possible.' Paul's intention was not to express a logical watertight system, but to use all possible means of declaring the message of Jesus crucified, buried, resurrected and glorified.

The place of the Holy Spirit in our communicating

Without fervent prayer and belief in the Holy Spirit to convict and convince, then all our efforts to communicate are worthless. However, I would refute the idea that because we are relying on the Holy Spirit we do not need to prepare our communication very carefully. Sometimes God does give us a message on the spur of the moment but generally God gives 'fruit' from our hard work and study. Poor preparation leads to rigidity and inflexibility in a poor process of communication of the most boring kind. I think too many of us are well aware of the results of this in our presentation of the gospel.

Jesus – communicator par excellence

Jesus attracted the people not only because he performed incredible miracles but also because of his communicating power. He was always using parables, drama, and picture and object lessons.

Notice a number of aspects to Jesus' approach:

(i) *Jesus was authoritative.* He had understanding, depth and background information – historical and biblical (Matt. 12:38–42).

(ii) *Jesus was visual.* He used objects and pictures that were familiar to the people (Luke 21:29–32; Mark 4:21–3).

(iii) *Jesus was simple.* Making in-depth statements in an easily understandable manner, for example speeches on Light, Bread, The Good Shepherd, the Vine (John 6:35; 8:12; 15:1).

(iv) *Jesus did not always give answers.* He expressed many of his teachings in parables so that '. . . they look, but do not see, and they listen but do not hear or understand' (Matt. 13:13). We must not always express the whole counsel of God: we must trust the Holy Spirit more to give understanding.

(v) *Jesus used humour.* Examples: the illustration of the speck in your brother's eye compared with the plank in your own eye (Matt. 7:3–5); forgiving someone 490 times (Matt. 18:21–2)!

(vi) *Jesus used poetry.* Consider the freshness of the message of the Beatitudes (Matt. 5).

(vii) *Jesus used argument.* Jesus was not afraid of debating and arguing his case with others, for example Sabbath controversy (Matt. 12:1–32).

Jesus communicated the Good News through a variety of styles and methods, each one of them sensitive to the needs of the particular community and individuals he was addressing.

The Trinity in its essence expresses the creativity of our almighty God. We live in a world in which our Lord Jesus Christ expressed his life, death and resurrection in a most dramatic fashion. Our communication cannot be anything less than the fullness of his creativity working through our humanity.

3C.2

Music

Music and its role in our society

To see the relevance of music within evangelism it is first necessary to consider its role within society. In the sixties rock music was seen by many musicians and music fans alike as a force that could change the world. Rock music and the rather vague sentiments that were being expressed at the time were seen as having a revolutionary effect. But the sixties came and went without the expected changes, and people began to get music back into perspective and to even feel a little bit embarrassed about the grandiose claims that permeated many a book on contemporary music at the time!

Naturally, music has a major effect on everyone's life in some way or another, and most young people for some section of their life are influenced by the attitude and style of the groups that they and their peer group favour. It may not be a life-changing force but it can have a very significant effect. Pop music reflects the values and attitudes of the society in which we live. On the whole it adopts those values – though occasionally it rebels as happened in the punk movement. Rock music likes to think it is rebellious, though in reality the attitudes are normally fairly predictable and mirror what can be read in the daily press or seen on TV.

Without claiming too much for it, it is nevertheless an important form of communication that influences either consciously or sub-consciously, and in approaching the use of music in evangelism we need to recognise its strengths and its limitations. The response to music is on several levels and certainly one is emotional. It is not such a logical way of communicating as a spoken explanation of the gospel, and therefore on both these counts it is probably not the medium for expecting or calling for decisive and immediate responses.

The other side of the coin is its strength, its ability to open people up to new possibilities, to break down barriers, to put a spotlight on a subject or situation and make people look at it in a new way. Music is an art form and it should not be turned into propaganda or manipulation. People have sometimes used it as an excuse to say nothing, forgetting that is *is* a form of communication and like it or not we say something about ourselves and our beliefs or lack of them in everything we perform.

The role of music

In the society in which we live many people are so far away from the concept that there really is a God, that they are not ready to hear a talk bringing them to a point of commitment. It is at this point that music can have such a vital role – building bridges and leading people from nowhere in terms of belief to somewhere, to the possibility of recognising that there might be a God.

(i) *To challenge preconceptions.* It may be seen as the first positive step in a predominantly post-Christian society. It has often been described in this context as 'creating doubt in the mind of the ardent non-believer'. Most people think they know about 'religion' and that they do not want it. Music can be one way of challenging their preconceptions.

(ii) *To introduce a Christian viewpoint.* Music can then build on top of this, by introducing certain Christian principles, by observing the world through the eyes of a Christian and by introducing the audience to Jesus in songs and chatter. In this context its strength can sometimes be in not saying too much. A song can be very like a parable – putting a spotlight on a situation – giving clues, but not giving it all away. The parable had a story, the song has the tune – both therefore stick – or can stick, in people's minds after the event to be chewed over later.

On a personal note, it is interesting how often people come to me and say, 'It was so and so concert that started me thinking and now a year or two years later, I'm a Christian.' Music can be a very valuable first link in a chain. Of course, it can be more than that – but that I see as one of its most important roles.

How to use music in evangelism

(a) The concert

The strength of any event is if it is *not* done in isolation. For instance, concerts are often most valuable as the prelude to a Mission. Many universities, colleges and parishes use them in this way, or in the context of an ongoing work. As a piece of entertainment and communication they are of value in themselves, but this value is multiplied if they are not in a vacuum.

When sending out guideline notes to concert organisers I summarise the aim as 'to entertain, to stimulate thought and to share my beliefs about Jesus Christ'. I then add the comment that my songs 'are not so much preaching, but more a reflection of what I am and the way I see things as a Christian'.

In booking an artiste or a band it is good to find out their *aim* and what they hope to achieve. Artistes and bands have different emphases in terms of the message, and *it is as well to check that organiser and performer are heading in the same direction with the same expectation.*

(i) *The music.* Careful analysis needs to be made at this point. Churches are tempted to put on a concert 'for our young people'. Then they book an artiste or group that the leader likes who may not be suitable musically for young people at all. It is not hard to do research in this area – a weekend spent at the Greenbelt Festival will give an indication of the range of music that is available.

It is a big mistake to assume that music is just for young people. What curious quirk of age is it that stops people liking music and when does it occur? The truth is it does not occur though people's tastes often get determined in younger years, i.e. the people who grew up in the sixties still like that style of rock music and turn up in their hordes to Eric Clapton concerts, etc.

In terms of evangelism this means that music can be used in a much wider context than just the youth club or college or university circuit. More of this later – sufficient to say at this point that the style of music needs to suit the audience who will be there. Unnecessary tensions can be caused by putting the wrong band together with the wrong audience.

(ii) *Venue.* Some halls or churches militate against concerts because of acoustics, size or lack of warm atmosphere. In fact it is amazing what can be done with simple lighting. Nevertheless, it can be an advantage to hire a local theatre or hall and provide a 'neutral' setting into which to invite people. Churches or even cathedrals can be good settings – some shy away from ever using this kind of venue, but it can have its own advantage in breaking down the barrier of crossing the church threshold, and that can be important in a long-term way. On the other hand, some styles of music seem to work better in that atmosphere than others. To put a heavy metal band into that context is incongruous to say the least!

Perhaps the key factor is warmth and friendliness of atmosphere and the requirements to achieve this will differ according to who the concert is aimed at and the style of music.

(b) Alternative contexts for using music

The concert is an event staged on our own terms. Obviously evangelism does not only occur in this context. There are groups and performers who will appear in pubs, clubs, prisons, schools and wherever the opportunity occurs. Teams are sometimes formed who specialise in this sort of evangelism.

(i) *Schools.* This is an area that requires particular sensitivity. Many schools are open to performers coming in and reflecting their Christian views in music, but most would, quite rightly, resent any pressurizing or high-powered evangelism. This is very much the area of opening people up to possibilities and provoking thought. There are artistes who specialise in this area, and this is valuable because getting the wrong person in can harm any work that has been going on, and leave a legacy that can take years to overcome.

If there is a special mission in a church or area, a musician or group of musicians linked with the event are often welcome in assemblies, RE classes, lunch time concerts or after school concerts. It will probably only be possible if relations are good with local schools, and again it is important to weigh up the artiste's ability and experience in this area. After all, you remain after the performer has moved on!

(ii) *Senior citizens*. It goes without saying that youth clubs are an area for using music in an evangelistic context – though the style of music may differ from area to area. However, one area that is often overlooked is the older age range. I have played to pensioner's groups with delightful responses. This often neglected area is wide open to these possibilities as any other and sharing one's faith in the context of music is often very much appreciated.

(iii) *Barbecue or home based event*. Many events of a genuinely evangelistic nature simply take a little initiative. For instance, I have known several groups aiming primarily at *young marrieds* that organise barbecues (in summer) or mulled wine and mince pie events at Christmas. They are paying events which have a piece of thought provoking informal entertainment as the focal point. Music is obviously one of the ingredients that can work well in this context. Performers need to be versatile for this sort of situation; it is almost a cabaret spot and not everyone can operate in this way. Also, because they are the sort of events that are usually held in someone's house, they are not ideal for a rock band! Solo performers or acoustic duos can be very effective perhaps working in conjunction with a poet.

(iv) *Dinner and cabaret situations*. Dinners are an ideal, unthreatening situation in which people can relax and listen to speakers or music. I have sung at dinners that range from those organised in the local church hall through to the smartest hotels. 'Christians In Sport' have used this method most effectively in recent years. Again, it is often close to a cabaret situation so it needs to be entertaining in presentation.

Probably the key to the success of all these kinds of events is versatility in both performer and organiser. It is surprising what can be done with a bit of vision and good organisation.

(v) *The evangelistic meeting*. I have so far discussed music in isolation, but of course it is regularly used in evangelistic campaigns and in church iself. There are different views on the best way to use music in these contexts.

In the context of the local church service, obviously the music will be predominantly of a worship nature, but it can be very powerful to include a song that highlights a subject that is about to be spoken on, or a passage that has been read from the Bible.

Family services are obviously an ideal context for music, whether it is worship, or what I call the 'spotlight' songs.

In an evening of mission a singer can work in well with a speaker to illustrate a theme. The tendency now is to have celebratory evangelism – which means using worship songs for the audience. This appears to be more logical within a local church context than in a bigger event. However, it is most important to consider what a person who is not a Christian is supposed to do during these 'praise' sessions. The time might be better served with songs that would challenge his thinking and preconceptions – songs that comment on life through the eyes of a Christian – thus allowing music to work in its role of opening up new possibilities.

(vi) *Audio-visuals/video*. One of the most successful evangelistic projects that I've been involved with was called *The Champion*. It was a series of six songs on the life of Jesus from his entry into Jerusalem through to his resurrection and ascension. It is illustrated with superb cartoons that capture humour, sorrow, majesty and suffering. The filmstrip (and now video) has been used in innumerable contexts and among all sorts of ages. The linking of music with the visual, which is happening more and more in this video age makes a quality of music – in a good visual setting – readily accessible be it for a front room, a school RE period or a church service.

God the creator has blessed us with many creative gifts. Music is one such gift – it can be used in an infinite variety of ways and in an infinite variety of settings. Music can break across barriers of race, sex and age. It can be in a myriad of different styles and presentations. It can be subtle in message or blatant. But if it is to be used to carry the Christian message. It must be marked by truth. Gospel music must not be an anaesthetic to lull people into the kingdom. It is not sugar to sweeten the pill. It is not a mallet to beat people over the head. It is an art form that must be used wisely and truthfully and to the glory of the creator.

3C.3

Drama

Introduction

Many actors and actresses admit to having recurrent nightmares about performing . . . a breathless colleague, with a wild appearance, rushes up, thrusts a clown costume upon them and pushes them on stage, whispering frantically, 'You're on! It's the neurosurgeon sketch!' 'But I've never . . .' 'Go on!' 'But I don't . . .' Too late; the lights come up and the neurosurgeon sketch must be improvised in front of the board of the National Theatre . . . the costume doesn't fit.

The point of this is to emphasise, at a time when the use of drama in Christian outreach is fast becoming 'vogue', that done casually, without proper rehearsal, it does indeed become a nightmare, both for the actors and the audience. When we are talking about performances which are given in connection with evangelism – that is, primarily for those outside the rather more indulgent context of the 'church family' – we must be careful to apply high artistic standards to match our spiritual integrity. It is obviously counter-productive if a sceptical audience spends all its time criticising our theatrical ineptitude, when we want them to listen to our message.

Learning the skills

The first thing to establish is our attitude: if we treat drama as 'a bit of fun' or as a 'gimmick' to sugar the evangelistic pill, it will remain just that – trivial; but if we give it respect as a means of communication, approaching it in a humble and workman-like way, prayerfully and creatively, then drama can affect people as deeply as any sermon and often more memorably because of its visual power. Drama is about people and their emotions; in the hands of those who know him, it can also give insight into the actions and feelings of God.

'Are all evangelists?' 'Are all teachers?' 'Do all play the guitar?' As St Paul implies in teaching about different gifts within the church, so we must also assume that not everyone can act, but that those within whom God has put this gift should work hard to develop it. The practical suggestions given in this article go hand in hand with a firm encouragement to anyone wishing to use drama in preaching the gospel that they learn the skills and the craft of the actor (how to project the voice, how to move well, how to create and sustain a character, how to deliver a comic line and so on). A good actor, like a good pianist, is not born overnight.

For those seeking this kind of detailed help I suggest reading these books for starters: *Voice and the Actor* by Cicely Berry, *An Actor Prepares* by Constantin Stanislavski, *One Hundred Plus Ideas for Drama* by Anna Scher and Charles Verall, and *Improvisation Games* by Viola Spolin. You won't find these in your religious bookstore, but they are all basic resource books on technique and workshop ideas – just four titles from many which a local drama group might use to help improve their skills. The danger if they do not, is that they may find that their audience, conditioned and in many ways educated by the dramatic medium of television, remains unmoved. Let us realise the importance of visual communication today, but let us learn to do it *well*.

Various ways in which drama can assist evangelism

(a) Teaching the Bible

Widespread ignorance of the main stories and teaching in the bible has often made evangelism more difficult. Drama can help to re-open what for most people these days is a closed book. It is interesting to see how much the whole English dramatic tradition owes to the vision of the church in the Middle Ages. The great mystery play cycles show how vital theatre was in teaching people the biblical background to the life of Christ, since most of them could not read for themselves. Today, as video stores overtake book-shops and illiteracy increases, it is arguable that our own society is entering a similar situation. The Bible is a storehouse of material which is ripe for dramatisation. It deals with so many incidents describing the natural interaction of God with the lives of ordinary men and women, that, when presented in dramatic form, it can vividly recreate the basic spiritual awareness and expectancy on which the preaching of the gospel depends.

(b) Helping the preacher

The predominance of television in many people's lives has drastically reduced the number of occasions where they are prepared to listen to one voice for any length of time. They are used to receiving information with word and picture coming simultaneously. It has also reduced their span of attention. When 'the Word became flesh' in Jesus, God was acknowledging man's need to see and to experience as well as to listen. In a similar way, drama can help to 'flesh out' the gospel.

At the last supper, when Jesus played the part of the servant and washed the disciples' feet, he was, if you like, performing a play. The point was unforgettable. There was still a need for some explanation afterwards, but the shocking experience of the master playing the servant was the heart of the communication and made the teaching about serving one another so easy to draw out. It is precisely in arresting the attention, in involving people, in giving them an unexpected jolt, that drama can aid the presentation of the gospel so greatly. Short pieces of drama can break up a lengthy talk and create a marvellously attentive atmosphere on which a sensitive preacher can build.

(c) Presenting the gospel

We have to beware of suggesting that a person can come to Christ entirely through the performance of a play. Drama is, to use a biblical metaphor, primarily a medium for sowing rather than reaping. People come to Christ through the direct intervention of the Holy Spirit and through the witness of Christians testifying to the reality of God in their lives. Plays and sketches, though dealing with truth, are essentially 'unreal'; we pretend that the characters and events portrayed are real, though we know they are only being acted out. Thus it is possible to present the message of good news through drama but it will still be necessary for a member of the audience, to whom the performance has spoken, to say to one of the cast, 'I understand all that you are saying, but is it actually true in your own life?' – like the man who said to Jesus, 'Lord, I believe, help my unbelief.'

When using drama in evangelism it is vital to make time and opportunity to talk personally with people afterwards. The play may be an important step along the road but the witness of the individual Christian is crucial. Zacchaeus responded joyfully to the spectacle of the crowd and the presence of Jesus on the street though his real change of heart came later after talking to Jesus in the quiet of his own home.

(d) *Reflecting ourselves*

In his second letter to Timothy, Paul talks about Jesus bringing *life to light* through the gospel. In the same way, drama can bring human life under the spotlight; it can examine our relationship, expose our sins and follies and show us our need for God. An audience will learn a lot from seeing themselves on stage – it may be funny, it may be sobering, but it should never be boring. In this way, a sketch which is truthful about the way people behave at home, in the office, at a cocktail party, in the dole queue (without being obviously 'religious' or biblical), can be an excellent preparation for the gospel. A truly religious understanding of life will include every aspect, not just the spiritual side.

(e) *Inspiring worship*

Drama can be used very effectively within the context of worship; not that everyone watching is directly involved in worship (as with praying and singing) during the performance, but through the performance they can be inspired to deeper worship by, for example, understanding more about the nature of God, seeing Christian faith in action or being challenged about their failures. In a church service, drama could replace one of the Scripture readings or come just before the sermon. If sightlines are a problem, then it is worth building a small stage in the chancel area, which can be easily removed during the singing of a hymn so as not to get in the way of other things.

(f) *Relaxing an audience*

Many people come to evangelistic meetings rather nervously because they suspect they are going to be got at. Drama is an invaluable way of helping them to relax; it is, after all, entertainment; it does not 'buttonhole' and speaks about specific things in a general way. Sometimes, in the context of a mission, it is a good idea to devote several evenings entirely to the performance of a play or a series of sketches, as there will always be those who prefer the more 'open-ended' communication of theatre to listening to a speaker. If the play is good, they may come and hear the speaker on another evening! Whenever theatre and a speaker are combined, the audience should be made aware of this from the start – perhaps introduce the speaker early on so that they know who he is when he gets up.

The creative process: a few guidelines

There is only a little space here to mention a few suggestions in note form towards producing drama. Please supplement these by referring to the material under 'Street Happenings' (section 5A.9) and bear in mind that much of this concerns short sketches rather than full-length plays.

(a) General planning

(i) Do this well in advance to give time for writing, rehearsal and administration (an amateur group might take three weeks to produce one sketch). For a large production there is a useful check list on pp. 125–130 in *Lightning Sketches* (Hodder and Stoughton). Clear all copyright/licence restrictions when using other people's material.

(ii) *Check the stage area.* Make sure that the space used for the rehearsal is the same as for the performance. Remove unnecessary clutter and see that the background is not visually distracting (plain-coloured or black flats/drapes may be best). Choose costumes which will stand out well against this.

(iii) *Know your audience.* The key to good communication is vital when doing performances in schools where the age differences are so marked.

(b) Writing

(i) A script produced by *one writer* or by a partnership, will always be better than one written by a committee. Be prepared for helpful changes which may emerge during rehearsals.

(ii) Look for *lighter touches* even within a serious piece. Be entertaining, in the broadest sense, and above all, *think dramatically*; avoid ideological discussions where nothing is happening or, at least, create interesting situations from which those discussions arise.

(iii) *Keep in touch* with current affairs through the newspapers. Many good ideas for sketches are prompted by up-to-date stories and articles. Try and approach your subject through the mind of the unbeliever.

(iv) *Translating the Bible* is sometimes necessary to sharpen its relevance to modern life. For instance, the truth contained in the parables is eternal, though the details surrounding it may have to change. If Jesus said that the kingdom of heaven is like 'this' (first century Palestine), we may have to say that 'this' is like *this* (sometime from Britain in the 1980s). I saw one sketch where the four types of seed in the parable of the sower were four crates of strawberries entering a jam factory in Liverpool.

(c) Directing

(i) Choose *one person* to direct and stick by his or her decisions. The director must maintain discipline and help the actors to find motivation for every line and every move. The director's job is to focus the audience's attention throughout the performance on what is important, moment by moment.

(ii) Block the moves for the cast very carefully; cut out anything sloppy or distracting and shape the whole piece towards its climax, giving particular attention to the beginning and to the end. (It sounds obvious but these moments are often the weakest.) The director may have to find things for the actors to be doing when nothing is suggested by the text. This action should always be complementary and never 'upstaging'.

(d) Performing

(i) While all performances should be rehearsed with great *precision*, they should never feel mechanical to an audience. Make each performance fresh by thinking clearly about who you are and what you are doing; listen to the other actors and react in a genuine way to their speeches and actions.

(ii) Pick up *cues* quickly (as a general rule).

(iii) Everything that happens on stage should be *deliberate* even though it may appear (deliberately) casual.

(iv) *Music*. Dangerous gaps between sketches can be filled with a good, up-tempo soundtrack or live band to stop the show sagging. Try and provide background music (and refreshments!) during an interval.

Handled with skill, theatre is a wonderful means of communicating to people. As a church we cannot afford to ignore drama in our overall mission. We need to encourage actors and commission writers to produce plays, films and television programmes to compete with the other dominant voices in our society, so that 'in many and various ways' we can proclaim the good news to our generation.

Useful books

Time to Act, Paul Burbridge and Murray Watts (Hodder and Stoughton)
Lightning Sketches, Paul Burbridge and Murray Watts (Hodder and Stoughton)
Using the Bible in Drama, Steve and Janet Stickley and Jim Belben (Bible Society)

3C.4

Literature

In a day when the written word has in many ways taken second place to other more visual but less demanding forms of communication, the church is in danger of neglecting one of its most accessible and effective means of evangelism. We are surrounded by an abundant supply of attractive, relevant Christian literature, and yet in our personal and church life there seems little enthusiasm or commitment to get it into the hands of those for whom it was produced.

How can we become more personally motivated to play our part in seeing an increasing flow of good Christian literature throughout our land? Certainly one place to start is experiencing for ourselves, perhaps for the first time, the joy of good reading, with the stimulus it brings to emotions, intellect and imagination. And then to realise just how widely our great God can work through the written word, which by its very nature can speak time and time again in situations where there is no chance of human intervention.

Ways of using Christian literature

The following are not just abstract ideas but practical suggestions that have already been tried and proved by Christians around the country.

(a) Personal uses of literature

(i) The writing of *personal letters*[1] must be one of the simplest but most effective uses of the written word in evangelism to relatives, friends, new contacts, etc.

(ii) Letters to your *local newspaper* from a Christian viewpoint will be well received if they are relevant, brief and not preachy. If there is no regular religious feature, why not find a Christian with a gift for writing to supply one?

(ii) Everyone reads the local *postcard ads* – so why not place an attractive one in your local newsagents inviting readers to your church or offering spiritual help?

(iv) *Attractive Christian greetings cards* for almost any occasion are available in your local Christian bookshop. Sensitively designed Scripture folders[2] for times of special personal need like bereavement, marriage, new baby, moving house, etc, can be very useful.

(v) Colourful *posters* are a way of communicating a few words of Scripture to a lot of people.

(vi) The gift of a tasteful *tract or booklet* can enhance any human contact you have, and people are still being converted through picking up literature like this in the strangest places.

(vii) When you have read your Christian *monthly magazine*, donate them to your dentist's or doctor's waiting room.

(viii) The *personal loan*, or gift, of a Christian book that you have read and enjoyed can bear fruit in many more lives than you might anticipate. If your home is used a lot for hospitality or church activities, you might even consider a small shelf of books for sale, supplied by your church bookstall or local Christian bookshop.

(ix) Hold a *book party* to which you invite friends and neighbours – again your local Christian bookshop can help with advice and supplies.

(x) Perhaps you can afford to donate some Christian books to your *local library* or local school(s).

(xi) Personal membership of organisations like the *Gideons*[3] will get you involved in distribution of the Scriptures in many different places.

Church-based literature distribution

Having become excited yourself about the potential of Christian literature, you will want to make your local church fellowship more aware of the resources and opportunities available. Here are some practical ways to go about this:

(i) Ensure that your church has an attractive and well-stocked *bookstall*. One person registered as a church book agent with the Publishers' Association[4] will be able to buy supplies at a discount from up to three Christian bookshops. There is a good amount of advice available on setting up and operating a church bookstall,[5] but it is always personal enthusiasm that ensures success in this ministry. Recommendations from the pulpit and book reviews in the church magazine will help greatly.

(ii) The ministry of the church bookstall should not be confined to the inside of the church – take it out to *where the people are*. House groups, schools, special sales, local markets – all can be fruitful sources for both sales and evangelistic witness.

(iii) A *church library* will overcome the objections of those who feel books are too expensive – but an enthusiastic and committed librarian is a must.

(iv) If your church is to be serious about using literature widely, a *literature budget* is necessary. This can be used to support the bookstall and to purchase evangelistic literature. If necessary, include a book allowance for your pastor to encourage him to be more enthusiastic about Christian literature.

(v) One large church used its literature budget to supply *free literature packs* to its members – a selection of tracts, booklets, special occasion folders and a Gospel in a clear plastic pocket. Supplies of each item were readily available to replenish the packs, and through this many church members gave away Christian literature for the first time.

(vi) Do you have helpful literature available for visitors to your *regular Sunday services*?

(vii) *Door-to-door visitation* should never be attempted without each visitor having a range of free literature with which they are familiar and happy to enthusiastically give away to each contact. Evangelistic papers like *Challenge*[6] and *Release*[7] give opportunities to visit interested contacts regularly.

(viii) *Mass tract distribution* on special occasions – carnivals, fairs, etc., – can often receive more support from church members than might be imagined. Designing and printing your own tract for that particular occasion can increase interest and participation.

(ix) Sensitively chosen literature can greatly enhance *hospital visitation*, in which most church fellowships are involved to some extent. Hospital patients have time to think and read, and God can speak through the right kind of literature.

(x) Another group of people who can be very effectively reached and helped through literature is those in *prisons* or other similar institutions. Again, care needs to be taken in choosing the right kind of literature and in presenting it out of an attitude of care and concern. Always work through the Chaplain or Prison Christian Fellowship.[8]

(xi) Many young people cannot afford to buy a lot of Christian literature – so for their own reading and for giving to their friends, *inexpensive magazine books* or bookazines,[9] as they are called, are the answer.

(xii) Finally, if you need still more ideas or help, your *local Christian bookshop* should be more than willing to oblige. If you don't have one, then is it possible that your church buildings are in such a location that with some imaginative reconstruction you could actually open one yourselves? Plenty of help and advice can be obtained from the specialist literature organisations listed at the end of the chapter.

Jesus made very clear 2,000 years ago the principle of responsibility for the resources that God has entrusted to us: 'From everyone who has been given much, much will be demanded' (Luke 12:48). Today we have resources in the area of Christian literature that many of us are hardly aware of. As we consider the many methods of evangelism offered in this manual, let us see how the use of the written word can complement each one of these, and how literature in itself can form the basis of much effective personal and church-based evangelism.

Notes

1 See the appropriate chapter in *Effective Evangelism*, J Oswald Sanders (STL Books, 1982).
2 Samples available from CPO, Ivy Arch Road, Worthing, West Sussex BN14 8BU.
3 The Gideons International, Western House, George Street, Lutterworth, Leicestershire LE17 4EE.
4 The Publishers Association, 19 Bedford Square, London WC1.
5 The Bookstalls' Newsletter, 11 Thorpe Chase, Ripon, North Yorkshire HG4 1UA.
6 Challenge Literature Fellowship, Revenue Buildings, Chapel Road, Worthing, West Sussex BN11 1BQ.

7 Bethel Publications, 142 Dantzic Street, Manchester M4 4DN.
8 Prison Christian Fellowship, Whitefield House, 186 Kennington Park Road, London SE11 4BT.
9 STL Bookazines, PO Box 48, Bromley, Kent BR1 1BY.

Useful addresses

The Bible Society, 146 Queen Victoria Street, London EC4V 4BX
CBC (Christian Bookseller's Convention), 27 Camden Road, London NW1 9NL
CLC (Christian Literature Crusade), The Dean, Alresford, Hants.
SGM (Scripture Gift Mission), Radstock House, 3 Eccleston Street, London SW1W 9LZ
STL (Send The Light), PO Box 48, Bromley, Kent BR1 1BX
SU (Scripture Union), 130 City Road, London EC1V 2NJ

Useful books

Literature Evangelism, George Verwer, (STL Books, 1977)

Managing the Church Bookstall, Religious Book Foundation (Hodder & Stoughton, 1980)

An Unfading Vision – The Adventure of Books, Edward England (Hodder & Stoughton, 1982)

3C.5

Radio and TV

It is possible in the USA to switch on the radio or the television set and to hear a directly evangelistic message. That is to say a relay of a church service containing a powerful evangelistic sermon or a programme which may look like a light entertainment show but which is aiming specifically to evangelise. Indeed, several whole channels in various cities and states are devoted exclusively to such programmes.

In some 'evangelistic' shows a preacher may even invite the viewers or listeners to express a personal commitment to Christ by touching the radio or TV set and praying with him on the spot. He is certainly likely to offer to send much free literature to anyone willing to write in. Christian 'stars' and others are to be seen and heard giving explicit testimonies of their conversion. Chat show hosts on Christian shows might even invite people to 'phone-in with prayer requests when prayers will be conducted 'live' over the air.

It is even possible to 'advertise' Christianity, faith, church-going and other religious elements during commercial break slots in ordinary secular programmes. The possibilities for initiative in Christian evangelism through radio or television seem limitless.

But the American system has drawbacks. First most of the broadcasts have to be paid for. So the system favours the rich. Secondly, because broadcasting time is available to anyone who can pay for it virtually irrespective of their motivation for making programmes, opportunities for broadcasting are equally available to those with philosophies alien to Christianity. There is certainly no guarantee of programme quality.

In Great Britain the system is different. Most of our broadcasting is governed by two bodies. The BBC looks after all BBC radio and TV stations and programmes whilst the Independent Broadcasting Authority monitors and to some extent controls all the independent companies which go to make up ITV, Independent Local Radio and the board of Channel Four. It is not possible to buy programme time on radio or television administered by either organisation. Furthermore, the IBA's code of advertising specifically excludes commercials of a religious nature. The power to decide on programming lies less in the hands of those who hold the purse strings and more with those employed to make the programmes. The broadcasting organisations have hierarchical structures so there is of course monitoring and discussion of programme structure. However nearly all responsibility lies with those who are the 'professional broadcasters'. One politician was moved to remark that broadcastings were too important to be left to the broadcasters! At the time of writing we are waiting to hear the exact constitution of Britain's first cable television networks. We know that they will be organised differently to both the BBC and the IBA. It is possible that they will lead to changes in some of our broadcasting styles and eventually to the systems.

Criticisms of the system

Some Christians would like to see a system similar to the American one available over here. They would like to be able to buy broadcasting time and transmit gospel programmes having the freedom to make such programmes in their own way.

Others are critical of our radio and television for their refusal to be generally involved in the processes of evangelism.

Few would deny the media's power in the communication of ideas to a vast audience. However, some Christians would point to the general promotion of non-Christian ideas. At the same time they notice that Christianity is often ignored completely or portrayed in confusing, highly intellectual or irrelevant ways.

Broadcasting and evangelism

It is quite correct to assume that the BBC and IBA have no committed interest in the process of evangelism. I think it would be equally true to say that Christianity *is* often given inadequate treatment by many programmes and that unchristian ideas are made to seem more attractive. I am thinking here not particularly of religious programmes, but the popular shows enjoyed by most people, including drama, comedy and light entertainment. Philosophies are often transmitted through those programmes in a far more effective way than through those serious programmes which discuss such philosophies directly.

More people are likely to watch and be influenced by a soap opera than by a serious discussion. That is why some people would like to see the Christian equivalent of soap opera on our television screens and why some of the American 'razmataz' seems attractive. However, there is little likelihood of such programming on our screens at present.

Instead it *is* common to see a vicar caricatured as a fuddy-duddy 'has been' with his head firmly in the clouds. However, it is almost unheard of to see a character in a soap opera or drama with a real and living Christian faith. It is rare to see or hear a programme which sets out to explain in simple language the Christian message, yet it is common to see and hear horoscopes put over in an appealing and committed way.

For those who long to see evangelism conducted on our television and radio in the same way as it is conducted in some of our churches, the future is bleak. Some people argue that the broadcasting media have been responsible for helping to lower our moral standards and even for eroding our national faith in God.

In favour of our system

If all the above makes you feel negative towards the British system of broadcasting, think about it a little further. First, the particular controls we currently experience on our broadcasting mean that we are able to enjoy a system free from some of the worst excesses of commercialism. We gain a standard of public service second to none in the world. Some of the quality programmes made by both BBC and IBA simply would not get made in the USA or anywhere else where commercial pressures predominate and rule. Broadcasters in other countries know this and look to Britain for the lead. Also, our system throws out an acceptable challenge to all Christians: if broadcasting reflects our society, then it will reflect our Christian faith as we become involved in that society. We need to become involved so that the Christian message can become relevant and clearly communicated in a language that our fellow citizens can understand.

A preacher in a church pulpit – or an evangelist in a tent – is communicating to a captive audience who are expecting to hear something about Christianity. He can afford to use language and thought patterns not commonly used in the 'outside world'. To some extent he can afford to use illustrations relevant to people who share a common interest: the search for Christian truth and meaning. Not so the broadcaster. He or she needs to address a wide audience with diverse interests and backgrounds. At any moment the audience has the option to switch off or re-tune their set.

A positive approach

I believe that if we are to consider the possibilities for evangelism through our public broadcast media we have to sit back and take a cool look at the situation. We need to stop listing the negatives which undoubtedly do exist, and start assessing our standing as Christians within our society. We ought not to be afraid of the best that broadcasting can offer and we ought to be glad to live in a country where the broadcasting system gives so many possibilities.

We ought to see broadcasting as part of the communication of God's goodness in God's world. We need to develop a Christian view of broadcasting. That can't mean simply stating one message over and over again. It means looking with the mind of Christ at the whole spectrum of programmes. There is no need to see everything expressed in 'religious' terms.

So news becomes valuable simply because it is news, entertainment because it entertains in purity, and so on.

I think the dangers of taking a narrow Christian view of the media are shown in one particular radio station I heard overseas. The station would end an ordinary news bulletin by saying 'Now, here's the Good News . . .' and proceed with a biblical text such as John 3:16. To my mind this is a distortion of the word 'news'. The attempt to communicate the facts of news in an unbiased way has its own integrity. There is no need to distort the news concept in order to make a 'cheap plug'. Christians have a responsibility to lead society in integrity.

The wrong approach

My view is that radio and television are not necessarily the best media for the sort of straight evangelistic communication that is appropriate in a pulpit. Rather, there is a challenge to communicate a dynamic Christian relevance in the context of everyday life.

Radio, for example, thrives on ideas. It discusses, challenges and questions. It is a great market place for ideas and Christians can be fully involved in that market place if they are prepared to accept the rules of the market. As a producer, I have sometimes had Christians approach me keen to see an explicit promotion of the gospel broadcast in a programme. They sometimes suggest that we could achieve evangelistic perfection if we could only put the right person on the air. In fact they are often keen to hear words and thoughts that *they* relate to as Christians. They often think that one programme will change the world. They fail to see that broadcasting is involved in the dynamic process of life.

There is one quite justifiable Christian argument that if a message is perceived by only one person in a million, then the exercise of preaching to the million has been worthwhile. However, the broadcasting authorities can hardly be expected to take the same view when it comes to their programmes. They must be concerned for a mass audience.

The changing society

Society is always changing and so are many of its ideas and theories. Broadcasting at its best is involved in these changes. A dilemma for the evangelist lies in the fact that his message by its very nature, is old fashioned: Jesus, the same yesterday, today and for ever. The evangelist has to make his message relevant. There is relevance when modern people perceive the old fashioned faith. In turn, there is relevance in people steadfast within the old fashioned faith perceiving modern society. Either way there is a call for Christians to be actively *involved* in the changing society – both as part of it and as observers with a particular perspective.

During the middle of this century evangelicals developed a negative approach to the arts and electronic media. Such things were considered alien to the faithful. Christians were discouraged from becoming actively involved in such areas. It was even frowned upon by some to attend the cinema!

At the same time the world was experiencing a tremendous explosion in electronic media and associated skills. Not surprisingly, therefore, evangelical Christian communication was left standing whilst the world's 'message machine' became increasingly powerful.

Christians in the media

Thank God, the situation has changed considerably in recent years. There is more encouragement for young Christian people to develop gifts of communication and in the arts. There is no question that the great priority for evangelism through the media is to make sure that there are Christians working in the field. They need to be supported by prayer and to be challenged and sharpened by sympathetic Christian encouragement.

We need not be scared of our media. We need to have an understanding of it.

Start by listening and watching the media around you. Try and assess the philosophies current in the programmes you see and hear and work out how Christians can communicate an effective alternative. Listen to your local radio station. What contribution are you and your fellow Christians making to your locality? Are the local media aware of these contributions? What steps are you taking to make sure they are aware? Local radio is often a good starting point for those interested in becoming involved in making programmes. For Christians the religious programmes producer can often be a good point of first contact. Addresses and telephone numbers can be found in the BBC Yearbook and the IBA book TV and Radio published each year. You will find copies at your local library.

Reaching People
bearing in mind their age

4A.1

Children

One of the most exciting things for those working amongst this age group is that, in the majority of countries of the world, with little difficulty, a crowd of children can be gathered together to hear about Jesus. The problems we face are (a) finding acceptance with non-Christian parents (b) integrating a child from a non-Christian background into the life of the church.

The Bible has much to say about children and God, but nothing about all the methods we now use to reach them. In Old Testament times the main responsibility was placed upon the shoulders of the father (Ps. 78:1-7) aided by mother (Prov. 1:8) and supplemented by united worship and reading of the law (Neh. 8:1-12). In New Testament days, apart from home instruction (2 Tim. 3:15) children undoubtedly also benefited from the teaching of the apostles within the churches and the reading of the epistles, since they are mentioned in Ephesians and Colossians.

It was Robert Raikes who, over 200 years ago, saw in ragged, unruly children playing in the streets on the Sabbath, a group who were not being included in Christ's command to preach the gospel to *all* creation. He laid the foundation for our present Sunday school, which sometimes supplements, but more often is the sole source of the child's knowledge of God and the Bible. Sunday school has traditionally become acceptable to non-committed parents, thus largely overcoming one of our problems.

1. Additional methods of reaching children

(a) Mid week meetings/clubs

Advantages. Even non-Sunday school children can be attracted by a varied and possibly less formal approach. The time and programme is flexible.

Aims. To teach those with no Sunday school background and to evangelise.

Avoid. Indiscipline (dividing large numbers into teams with leaders is helpful).

Advice. Have one main leader who is respected by all. Publicise well. Plan a fast moving, action packed programme involving as many workers as possible – an excellent training ground for future leaders. It is better to have three ten-week terms each year than grow stale.

(b) Missions

Advantages. Provides every opportunity, annually or every two or three years to make an 'all out' effort. Unites, involves and encourages church workers. Children love missions.

Aims. Could be (a) to reap (b) to restore interest (c) to recruit

Avoid. Unwise pressure, e.g. open appeals.

Advice. Length, eight to ten days is ideal. Choose an evangelist who is able to teach the Bible, which the Holy Spirit can use, as well as being a man with the gift of 'drawing in the net'.

(c) Holiday clubs

Advantages. More time, consecutive daily teaching, popular with parents, caters for child socially as well as spiritually through a combination of worship, evangelism, games and handicrafts.

Aims. To teach and evangelise.

Avoid. Confusion. Detailed planning is essential.

Advice. Good leadership, sufficient help, suitable system (ready made ones are available).

(d) Home Bible clubs

Advantages. Reaches neighbourhood children, enabling personal family links. People who are not available for other meetings, may undertake this work.

Avoid. Commitments made to 'please' the leader.

Advice. Balanced teaching programme. Best time after school or early evening.

(e) Camps

Advantages/Aims. Enables child to experience Christian 'family' life through the attitudes and actions of leaders, and to receive consecutive Bible teaching. An excellent tool of evangelism.

Avoid. Poor discipline, lack of preparation and planning, insufficient or unsuitable helpers, too much free time (children don't know how to use it wisely).

Advice. A wise, experienced leader is essential, along with a programme which will endeavour to excite, interest, instruct and absorb the child throughout the day. Children have individual preferences, but nurture a family spirit where all co-operate for the sake of the whole group, whilst at the same time providing adequately for every child's interests and ability through games, hobbies, competition, etc.

(f) Beach missions

Advantages/Aims. Relaxed, attractive setting for presenting the gospel to holidaymakers as much as to local children.

Avoid. Boring programmes.

Advice. Have youthful, enthusiastic helpers under strong leadership. Provide lively music for singing. Organise beach games, etc. Alternative in wet weather!

(g) Junior school assembly visits

Advantages. All children go to school!

Aim. To present one Bible principle well.

Avoid. Unwise evangelistic fervour which could close the door not only to yourself, but others.

Advice. Be professional. Script as carefully as you would for a television appearance. Choose a lively song complementary to your theme.

(h) Various other methods

Include weekends away, park missions, children's film festivals, and many more.

2. The message

Unless children go home knowking more Bible truth than when they came, we have failed. Children learn through what they see, hear and do.

(i) *Seeing.* In a visual age we must use visual aids, which highlight the message and imprint it on the child's memory, such as flannelgraph, magnetic boards, words and objects, puppets, films, filmstrips, videos, blackboards, overhead projectors, human beings in drama, etc.

(ii) *Hearing.* A clearly spoken, understandable, interesting, entertaining, purposeful presentation.

(iii) *Doing.* Through quizzes, Bible searching, activity leaflets, conversation, competitions, handicrafts, etc.

3. The child's response

This should be as a result of conviction by the Holy Spirit, not just the persuasion of the evangelist. Invite the child for counselling discreetly.

Aims in counselling. (a) To assess the child's real need (b) To give simple steps, preferably building upon teaching already received (c) To help the child place his faith in God, through his word.

Avoid. Counselling behind closed doors (we have nothing to hide) and dealing with more than one child at a time.

Advice. Link the new convert to a 'nurse' who will care for them and gradually introduce them into the life of the church.

Useful addresses

Scripture Press Foundation (UK) Ltd
Chiltern Avenue
Amersham on the Hill
Bucks HP6 5AX

Scripture Union
Clothier Road
Bristol BS4 5RL

Gospel Light Publications
Shirley House
27 Camden Road
London NW1 9NL

Child Evangelism Fellowship
Barkers Chambers
Barker Street
Shrewsbury SY1 1SB

Christian Literature Crusade
51 The Dean
Alresford, Hants SO24 9BJ

Pickering and Inglis Ltd
3 Beggarwood Lane
Basingstoke, Hants RG23 7LP

4A.2

Youth

Youth culture

For the purposes of this chapter, 'youth' is defined as anyone who is a teenager. A strongly defined youth culture is a fairly recent happening. Originally it was linked with the formation of a totally different musical style in the early 1950s (i.e. rock 'n' roll) together with the corresponding fashions, attitudes and standards which went with it.

At present it would be difficult to identify a 'youth culture'. There are many sub-cultures all with different 'uniforms', musical styles and ways of being. Basically, the desire to be in one or other of these sub-cultures *is not to rebel, but to conform.* Being part of a group is very important for a teenager.

It is very easy to be intimidated by groups of teenagers all with green hair or with pins through the nose. Relatively few of them, however, are really nasty. Most teenagers are looking for an identity and are 'trying things out'. It is at this stage that we need to present the gospel in meaningful terms.

Evangelistic ideas

(a) *Youth club work*

Many churches already run youth clubs with table tennis, darts, etc. Usually it will attract non-Christians. But why have the epilogue every week? Often when this happens it is done with little preparation and the young people 'switch off'. Much better to do something once a month and make it really special and good. If you are in a position to have an epilogue on a weekly basis, change the time round from week to week to make it, say, an inter-logue, prologue etc.

(b) *Films*

There are good Christian films and very bad ones. It is important that if you decide to use a film you make sure that it is suitable in terms of style, length, relevance to audience, etc.

(c) *School work*

This can be very productive in all sorts of ways if it is done properly. (See 5A.7 on schools.)

(d) *Concerts*

There are Christian music groups around of most persuasions. The advice here is to go and see a band before booking them. It may be that they are too loud, or the wrong style, or purely entertainment. It's also worth talking about cost before they arrive.

Some bands will need a speaker after they have finished to give the challenge effectively. Check this out with them.

(e) *Barbecues*

A good event to try – but only in the summer! Food is always an attraction to teenagers, especially if it's free!

Think carefully about when and where the speaker should do the 'gospel slot'. Even on a summer's night it can get too cold to sit around on the grass. It's also disconcerting for audience and speaker if the light fades as he's talking.

(f) *Evangelistic party*

Throw a party with food, drink and some stupid party games. The 'epilogue' probably needs to be fairly light-hearted – just enough to get people thinking and talking to their Christian friends. Perhaps some comedy drama with a message in it would fit in well.

(g) Coffee bar

Believe it or not these still work in some areas! They are best held in a place where a lot of teenagers hang around with nothing to do, e.g. some large council estates. It's very unlikely that people will wander in of their own accord so the Christians will have to go and 'fish' folk in off the street. A card with details on is useful for this. (See 5A.2 Coffee Bars.)

(h) Video night

Some of the best gospel films are now available on video. Filmstrips are also obtainable in this medium. Don't be afraid of using non-religious films as a discussion starter. The best place to hold one of these evenings is in a house. Personal invitation is necessary beforehand. Once again, think carefully how you will follow up the film/filmstrip.

(i) Youth services

These can be very useful ways of reaching church-fringe young people. However, they are of a limited value in reaching the unchurched. It is still a very difficult job to persuade someone with no previous church connection to come to such an event.

When they are used, they need to be lively, modern and to the point. Use music, drama, testimony, etc, but don't overload the programme with gimmicks. Make sure the speaker is on the teenage wavelength and will communicate the gospel.

(j) Large missions

In this sort of event, a number of churches join forces under a central organising body to stage a town or city-wide outreach to young people. When it is done properly and efficiently the results can be astounding. Recently an old garage in Dudley was renovated and used as a venue for evening meetings. Schools work and other forms of outreach were happening during the day. Each evening saw around 1,000 young people at the meeting. Most were non-Christians!

Conclusion

(i) It must at all times be remembered that the best people to reach teenagers are teenagers. Therefore *train your young people to evangelise!*

(ii) Today's youth are todays church as well as the church of tomorrow. This means that there must be a major investment of our time, money and resources into this area of outreach.

(iii) Make sure that you know how you will follow-up your converts before you do your evangelism.

Resources

Films
Christian World, PO Box 30, 123 Deansgate, Manchester, M60 3BX
International Films, 235 Shaftesury Avenue, London WC2
National Film Crusade, PO Box 4, Bristol, BS99 75A
(Address for *Cross and the Switchblade* – film or video)

Videos
Trinity Video, 23 Grafton Road, Worthing, West Sussex
Bagster Video, 3 Beggarwood Lane, Basingstoke, Hants
Visual Communication Services, 143 Tower Lane, Bradford, W. Yorks BD8 9HL

Large missions
British Youth for Christ, 80 Darlington Street, Wolverhampton, WV1 4JD
Saltmine Trust, PO Box 15, Dudley, West Midlands, DY3 2AN
Scripture Union, 130 City Road, London EC1V 2NJ

Follow up material
'Life!' Bible studies by CPO, Ivy Arch Road, Worthing, Sussex
The Way Ahead and *Signposts* (Falcon-CPAS)
Breakthrough, Jim Smith (CPAS)

Training material
Breakthrough, training kit. Details from Mission at Home Youth Department, Falcon Court, Fleet Street, London

Books

Crowdbreakers, Bob Moffett (Pickering & Inglis) – how to be an effective youth leader as well as youth club epilogues, ideas for parties, etc.

Preparing for Adolescence, James Dobson (Kingsway) to help you understand teenagers a bit better.

Power Pack, Bob Moffett (Scripture Union) useful resource for youth evenings.

Buzz Magazine

4A.3

Young couples

'We had expected them to ram religion or the Bible down our throats, but they didn't.' 'It was very helpful.' 'We were amazed that young couples with families were willing to give up a whole weekend just to help us.' 'The meal on Friday was great.' 'We want to continue coming to your church even though we are moving a few miles away.' 'There was something different about you folk at that weekend.' 'We have decided not to go ahead and get married.'

Those are some of the comments we have received following our first three non-residential weekends that we have been holding for engaged couples twice a year.

(a) *Reasons for such weekends*

(i) We were increasingly concerned about the *breakdown of family life* within society. Even in our settled middle-class situation, the evidence within the junior schools showed that we were not sheltered from the disasters of divorce, and the subsequent hurt of children. Where could we begin to make any impact? One place was the marriage preparation of engaged couples and the follow-up of newly weds.

(ii) We were unhappy about the inadequacy of *just meeting a couple who were going to be married* and going through the wedding service, talking about hymns, flowers, confetti – i.e. getting them through the wedding, but saying nothing much about the marriage.

(iii) We decided upon *a non-residential weekend* as it solved problems of night-school, overtime, one partner living somewhere else in the country, etc. It didn't solve, however, the attitude of the couple who felt 'they knew it all', that 'they didn't need to come'. We can't make them obligatory, but we try to encourage as firmly as we can!

(iv) We realised that engaged couples and newly weds were at that point in life where *they wanted the best for themselves*. They were open to helpful and relevant ministry. Their minds were focused on marriage, but that didn't mean they were closed to Jesus.

Such weekends were planned with the full support of the church, to the extent that the costs were underwritten. Couples coming were welcome to make any contribution they wanted to, but were not asked to pay. (Costs included meals, literature, administration, use of premises.) Some of the groups in the church – such as a ladies' group, or a prayer group – shouldered the prayer support for the couples, provided a catering team and three Christian married couples shared in the leadership of each weekend. It is a lovely example of the body of Christ working properly.

(b) *Who is involved?*

(i) *Engaged couples themselves.* We would plan to have a maximum of fifteen couples at any one weekend. Too small a number may make couples self-conscious. Too large a number swamps everyone. Most of the couples – by the nature of society, and the fact that many people still want a church wedding – would find this was their first real contact with a Christian church.

(ii) *The church couples helping.* Previously we had invited a number of couples to meet with an experienced Christian counsellor to be briefed in preparing others for marriage. The couples, whose ages varied between twenty-five and forty-five, would be such that the engaged couples could identify with them. Obviously they had to have a stable home and a stable faith, and share the vision of the weekends. Where young children were concerned, baby sitters had to be found. We asked each couple to commit themselves to just one weekend a year, to be willing and able to lead the group sessions, and to keep personal contact with the couples in their group – usually no more than three or four couples each.

(iii) *Who leads the weekend?* The minister and/or lay church leader, who feel that this is something God has equipped them to do.

(c) What happens at a weekend?

(i) *Friday evening.* Welcome session at 8.00 p.m. Church couples have arrived early. They have met previously for briefing and prayer. They need to be good hosts because the couples will be nervous – they don't know what to expect! Serve the food and drink that is socially right for the area. A good meal helps everyone to relax, talk, and begin to share. A short time of welcome afterwards allows the leader to thank the catering team, welcome the couples, make introductions, explain again the purpose and plan of the weekend, indicate where the cloakrooms are, suggest informal dress, allocate to pre-planned groups, and then to introduce, with the help of the overhead projector, one question – 'What is marriage?' Various suggestions are made for the groups to discuss together. They report back, and the leader can end the evening by talking a little about God's plan of marriage revealed in Genesis 1:26–31.

(ii) *Saturday morning.* Coffee available as people arrive. All feeling more relaxed, and often arriving in good time – a welcome sign! This is the session when we want to get at the real stuff of which marriage relationships are made. We need to deal with hopes and fears, expectations, what they find in each other, what is love and how does it grow, what helps and hinders communications, accepting one another, saying sorry and forgiving. Much of this will be in groups – couples reveal themselves in a relaxed atmosphere, and the Christian leaders can often minister helpfully to them. Then the groups report back and the leader can sum up and teach that you can't go for long without bringing in 1 Corinthians 13 about 'love', and the whole fact that the New Testament parallels the husband-wife relationship with the Christ-believer relationships.

(iii) *Saturday evening* is a very practical and realistic session. Some of the break-up points in marriage are in-laws, money, sex and the children. We have asked a couple, who happen to be a doctor and an accountant, to deal with those topics. Very practical things about family planning or organising a budget are dealt with, and we have relevant questions for the group to discuss.

(iv) *Sunday afternoon*. Session starts about 3.00 p.m. when the leader can go through the marriage service itself, and deal with all the legal, practical and church details. We end with a good tea together about 4.30 p.m. and people leave when they need to, but that tea gives lots of time for relaxed chatting.

(d) *Some final comments and observations*

(i) While the weekend is the major contact time with the engaged couples, it is not the only time. First links were made probably when the couples came to arrange their weddings. Future contacts will be vital. That's where ongoing follow-up by the Christian couples is vital. Couples have been invited to meals, the Christian couple make a point of attending their wedding, and we plan a follow-up weekend – 'Marriage – a year later'.

(ii) The evangelism is low-key. The couples' minds are upon marriage – that is their point of conscious need, but you can't deal with marriage without sharing the gospel: the nature of man as a sinner, the facts of forgiveness, acceptance just as we are, the love of God in Christ, faith and trust, commitment. The very heart of the gospel keeps popping up, and you just bring it in at the most natural points.

Useful books

Starting out Together, Gavin Reid (Kingsway)
Getting Married in Church, Mary Batchelor (Lion)

4A.4

Parents of small children

In any area of evangelism, we need to be aware that if we are to win people for the Lord it will mean 'getting involved'; and if we are to reach families, we must do it by friendship evangelism. It will mean discouragement, hurt, even being misunderstood, but this is true of many areas of evangelism. As we go beneath the surface of people's lives, we will find hurts, problems, guilt and many other needs that only Jesus can meet. So, first of all let us look at some of the typical problems facing young families today.

The problems

Many young mothers feel totally isolated, whether they live in a high rise flat in a city, on an estate in a new town development, or in an ordinary suburban street. They have probably just left work, may not even know the people next door and feel lonely, inadequate and in the need of friendship and support. The young father feels the tensions of broken nights, the new strain on the family budget and the change in the girl who used to spend so much time on her appearance and now always looks slightly bedraggled and smells constantly of dried milk and Napisan. Of course this situation will improve and the new family will begin to settle into a routine, but it may be that due to personalities, circumstances or housing conditions, some of those first tensions will create cracks in the marriage relationship that will never quite heal. The pressure on the family today is greater than it has ever been, and many marriages break down because they have no real foundations built during those first years of having a family. Mum feels 'taken for granted' and Dad feels 'left out' and their relationship begins to show signs of strain. Due to the rosy pictures painted by advertisements of the ideal family, many mothers feel that they have failed because they can't cope, they feel guilty and alarmed because they suffer from post-natal depression not realising that for many women it is a natural part of the birth process.

How the church can help

Obviously not everything I suggest will be suitable for your situation, as it will depend on space, location, size of building etc, but I think most people will find something they can do to contact the families around.

(a) Babysitting

Get the young people in your fellowship to offer free babysitting as part of their service. If the people want to pay, put it to a charity. If you are working in a poor area you will find many who will really appreciate such a service, and it will give rise to some good contacts while giving the young people an opportunity to play their part in the life of the fellowship.

(b) Créche

Run a créche where mothers can leave their children while they go shopping. You will need a few cuddly toys, some pull-along toys, trains, toy cars, books, perhaps a garage, dolls, wooden tray puzzles, crayons, lego, other simple construction toys, balls (soft), musical and activity toys (such as Fisher-Price), simple games, children's Lotto, picture dominoes and bricks. You will also need a supply of squash, biscuits, plastic cups and disposable nappies, cream etc. Obviously your equipment will depend on your premises, budget and the age of the children you are catering for (don't put out small toys if there are toddlers who will put them in their mouths). If your budget is low, ask for toy donations from families in the fellowship, and scour second-hand shops and jumble sales – you can very often pick up some bargains!

(c) *Mother and toddler groups*

These can be run regularly – each week, fortnight, month, using your church, or some other local hall. You do not need permission from the local authority, as it would only be for a few hours per week and the mothers would still be responsible for their own children. The equipment needed would be the same as for a créche, with perhaps some larger toys, e.g. bikes, cars, prams, if the premises are large enough. Organise somewhere for the children to play, and have a rota of people to look after them. You will probably find it best to spend most of the time just chatting, particularly if the people who come don't know each other, or if you have to have the children playing in the same room (its almost impossible to expect a speaker to speak over the noise of several small children, and unfair to the children to expect them to keep quiet for too long). When you do have a speaker, there are many people from the local community who will be willing to come and talk – the Fire Prevention Officer, the Police, Road Safety Officer, Librarian, Doctor, Health Visitor; also you could organise cookery demonstrations (particularly if you live in a multi-racial area where different races could learn about each other's cooking).

The idea of a Mother and Toddler group is primarily not for direct evangelism but rather to provide a setting where those with small children, particularly those under playgroup age, can meet with others and make friends. Obviously there will be real opportunities for talking about the Lord, but it shouldn't be a formal meeting, which could put some folk off, but a relaxed time over a cup of tea to make friends. (If you have difficulty finding premises or equipment, ask a local morning playgroup if you could use theirs during the afternoon.)

(d) *Coffee mornings*

These can be direct evangelism, fellowship times, more practical sessions or a mixture of all three. You may wish to alternate evangelism and fellowship and find that those who are invited to the open times then come to the fellowship times as well. In the fellowship times you could have Bible studies, prayer groups, times of sharing when you pray for and minister to each other. In the open times there is an opportunity for personal testimonies, talks on a variety of relevant subjects, panels answering questions, and occasionally a visiting speaker. What may begin as a ladies' coffee morning, may become mixed due to the unemployment situation. Twice a year – June and December – you could have a special meal to which you invite husbands and friends. Serve a really good meal – a summer barbecue or a three course Christmas Dinner – with a programme of drama, song and a speaker. Sell tickets to cover your costs – people really respond and prefer to pay for their meal. It also commits them to coming. During school holidays organise light lunches in a garden or picnic in the local park (you may also do this as a whole church, each month during the summer after the Family Service).

As this is very informal it encourages people to bring their non-Christian neighbours and husbands along without feeling threatened.

(e) Men's evenings

Encourages men to meet one evening per week with talks about things that interest them, e.g. fishing, car maintenance, do-it-yourself. This can be a valuable way of introducing the young father to the church.

(f) The Playgroup

This can be a vital service in the community and there are many areas which still need more Playgroups. A Christian Playgroup can be an ideal way of reaching people, because it can involve the whole family – get Dads to make equipment for you, ask Mums to make dressing up clothes, put on a programme for parents to come and see. One sure way of getting parents into church is to get their children to take part in the Family Service, and even the tinies can dress up and sing.

Setting up a playgroup is a little more complicated than a crèche. You will need much more equipment, qualified staff and as it will run every morning, Monday to Friday, you will need to get permission from your local authority, who will then come and check your premises, staff etc, before registering you. Most authorities will accept one or two qualified staff present each morning (or afternoon); these can be teachers, nurses or nursery nurses, and many local authorities run courses for playgroup leadership – this will usually involve attending college one day per week during term time. You would then be allowed to run a playgroup, without any other qualifications, although this will vary according to where you live. Your premises will need to have adequate fire precautions, floor space, toilet and washing facilities and heating.

The equipment you need will be similar to the things mentioned for mother and toddler groups, plus more large construction toys, wooden or plastic bricks, paints, sand/water play, scissors, glue, a Wendy House, climbing frame, slide, fabric tunnel, small tables and chairs, pastry, fuzzy felt, more wooden jigsaws and tray puzzles, large wooden beads to thread onto laces, strong cardboard boxes which can be turned into a play cooker etc, activity stuff, collage material – this need not be expensive, in fact 'junk' can provide some of the best 'learning by play' – children will spend hours making pictures out of milk bottle tops, material scraps and other bits and pieces, or constructing 'models' out of cornflakes packets and loo roll middles.

If you decide to open a playgroup, the Playgroup Association will be only too pleased to help.

(g) *The Family Service*

Most churches have some kind of family service. Allow a special time for young children in the service, with their own action songs and story have a supply of small birthday presents for those with birthdays that week, and sing happy birthday to them. If they go out during the 'sermon' make sure they are kept happily occupied, so that they learn to enjoy church and encourage their parents to come.

Parents with small children need to know their problems are not unique. What they want are understanding friends. This is an area where Christians can relatively easily show Christ's love to those around and make an impact on their community.

Useful books

Friendship Evangelism, Arthur McPhee (Kingsway)
Out of the Salt Shaker, Rebecca Manley Pippert (IVP)

4A:5

Childless couples

What is it like?

After a couple of years of trying, visits to the GP, referral to specialists, months of tests, hopes and disappointments, the final interview with that final verdict still comes as a sickening shock. No children – ever.

Please, before you consider evangelism to a childless couple, stop and imagine what it's like.

Most couples look forward to raising a family. They will talk about it, plan and imagine the future and this anticipation adds a dimension to their marriage.

Obviously a number of people marry with no desire nor intention of having a baby. Others wish to wait some years before they start a family. If so they will get tired of other's suggestions that their marriage is incomplete or that they are being selfish. In this whole area, which is so highly personal, we must be very aware of the couple's privacy and never embarrass them with unwanted curiosity.

Every case is different, but apart from those who choose to have no family, here are three typical responses to being dubbed infertile.

Mr and Mrs A.

This couple receive the news calmly, come to terms with it quickly and reshape their plans and lives accordingly. They are not passionately fond of children and have suspected something was amiss for some time. The wife is happy in her job and the love relationship is a strong one. However, beneath all this, there *may* be a stronger repressed feeling that over the years could gnaw away at the marriage foundations.

Mr and Mrs B.

Greatly disappointed and very sad: this man and woman take a while to adjust. They talk about it openly to each other and look into the possibilities of fostering (with today's widespread abortion, adoption is almost impossible). They find the best way ahead and come to terms with the situation well. They will suffer periods throughout their lives when they mourn or even feel bitter about the family that might have been, but on the whole all will be well.

Mr and Mrs C.

The wife in particular is stricken by the news. She mourns and becomes obsessed with babies. The sight of a pregnant woman, a programme about birth, an encounter with a pram will all upset her and she may either actually seek these things out or go to any length to avoid them. The husband is not as upset, but he is badly affected by what his wife is going through, especially as he feels there ought to be something he can do. This marriage is in danger.

Unless a couple decide to ignore it and carry on just as before, the knowledge that they are going to remain childless will mean certain adjustments and decisions must be made.

Do we give up or keep on hoping?

Should we look into adoption or fostering?

What about test-tube babies or A.I.D.?

What do we say to people who ask?

What shall we tell our parents?

There will be repercussions on the marriage relationship. If the infertility problem is with the husband, he may fear, perhaps with good reason, that his wife will reject him in some way. The man may blame his wife for failing to bear him children. There may be bitter conversations, sexual problems and a distancing from one another.

The experience will also deeply affect each individual. There may be a feeling that God is punishing them for something in the past. An infertile wife may feel she is not 'a proper woman'. Her femininity is attacked, her maternal instincts and desires frustrated. What is she going to do now her cherished hopes and dreams of raising a family are dashed? A new career or carry on as before?

For a man, emotive words like 'impotent' come to mock him and that all-important drive of his masculinity is threatened. Aspirations of being a father have to be pushed aside and may be repressed harmfully.

Offering friendship and help

There is often great need for understanding help, but any approach must be very sensitive and prayerful. Here are a few practical ideas that could be used.

(i) Offer a free counselling service (provided there are suitable people to man it) to which infertility clinics GPs etc can refer patients. The NHS can rarely provide this itself.

(ii) When you arrange special outreach events make sure there is a good mixture of people rather than just couples with families.

(iii) Childless women from 25–35 will have particular needs and interests, and would feel left out in the family-oriented women's groups. They will probably enjoy sports and creative activities. A wife with a full time job will be under particular pressure as she tries to fit in housework etc. Single girls of her age may well be in a position to make a relationship with her.

(iv) House groups are a natural way of reaching childless couples. The relaxing friendship of a meal, a talk and discussion afterwards may well lead to their opening up and sharing more of themselves and receiving something of Christ's love.

(v) This may be a time of much heart-searching and wondering about the future. Above all, childless couples are just ordinary people and having suffered the indignity and pain of being 'investigated' will now appreciate just being accepted as they are – but with that loving concern for the particular difficulties they face.

Tell them you pray for them, but beware of ferreting out lovely promises from the Scriptures. Many childless couples do become parents by God's grace, but there are more important issues to be faced first. Pray for that understanding of God's love for each individual, his plan for every life and the wonderful truth that in the Lord Jesus is a rock to lean on that will withstand every problem life can throw at us. Teaching on the way that the Holy Spirit can help will be a lot more help than pointed Bible studies about Sarah, Rebekah and Hannah!

4A.6

The retired

One person in six is retired in Great Britain today, that is 9 million people. The retired are people who happen to be old and, like any other age band, comprise a cross-section of individuals. The temptation to categorise people, and to treat them differently, simply because they are old must be resisted, recognising and responding instead to the needs and capabilities of individuals.

The retired cover a span of thirty or more years. Some may have been forced to retire before the statutory age through redundancy. Most newly retired people are active, independent and free of ties (though for some life is dominated by the care of elderly relatives). Many, though not all, of the over eighties, are, to some extent, physically or emotionally dependent on others, and some are housebound. One in three elderly people live alone, and many of the others live with a relative who is also elderly.

Reaching the retired demands an understanding of some of the experiences common in later years of life and a sensitive approach to the emotional and spiritual consequences. Growing older almost always brings with it loss and bereavement, not only of loved ones by death, but of recognised status through work, of physical amd mental capacities, perhaps of home and possessions and an adequate income. It is not surprising then, that many older people are subject to fear – fear of change, of becoming dependent, of loneliness, of being unwanted, of death.

The gospel, while not ignoring the frailties of old age, holds out the promise not only of hope after death, but also of the continuing presence of the Lord and of fulfilment and fruitfulness into old age, through the renewal of the 'inward man' day by day.

> Even to your old age I am he, and to grey hairs I will carry you. I have made, and I will bear; I will carry and will save (Isa. 46:4).

> They shall still bring forth fruit in old age (Ps. 92:14).

How vital, therefore, that the church, in its attitude to older people should not reinforce their feelings of being unwanted and left out, but rather, in proclaiming the gospel, demonstrate the love, understanding and acceptance which will help them both to face the difficult experiences of old age, and to use to the full its opportunities and possibilities.

Activities within the church

Try to encourage elderly people to be involved in as many *ordinary* church activities as possible so that they do not feel excluded. Make sure that family services refer at least sometimes to the needs and concerns of older people without children at home, or living alone. Remember that while older people may seem resistant to change, they *can* adapt to it, to new translations of the Bible, to modern hymns and songs, to unfamiliar orders of service, but they need to have changes explained to them, and to feel that others are ready to listen to their point of view.

Practical problems

Loss of hearing is one of the most common handicaps in old age, so check that the amplicfiation system is adequate, and consider installing an induction loop system, which enables people to hear what is spoken into the pulpit microphone through their hearing aid. Information about this system is available from the Royal National Institute for the Deaf.

For those with poor sight, large print hymn books, Bibles and prayer books are essential.

Ease of access to the building, and to lavatories, may be crucial in encouraging or discouraging church attendance, so think about ramps, handrails or alternative seating where necessary. Of course, the elderly person must be able to get to the church to start with, so helping with transport may be a first consideration.

Special activities for retired people

There is a place for these within the church. The location and type of area, the facilities within the building, and helpers available will all help to determine which are most appropriate for your fellowship. Providing lunch or tea between Sunday services can be a boon to elderly people who may be very lonely at weekends (and also be a means of integrating young and old). Other suitable activities taking place when only retired people are free include ladies' or men's meetings with talks, activities and outings, luncheon clubs, senior citizens' teas, or, more ambitiously, a day care centre for the more handicapped. Such activities can meet very real social needs in the area and at the same time provide many opportunities for sharing the gospel.

Visiting

One of the most fruitful means of contact is through visiting older people in their own homes. Visiting does not come easily and naturally to all; it needs thought and prayer, as well as tact and patience. The old person may welcome being given tapes (of church sermons or hymn singing for example) or suitable literature (the Bible Society has a range of attractively produced devotional leaflets). If you plan to encourage visiting by church members, be prepared to give guidance and support to those who visit. The Church of Scotland has produced an excellent Visitor's Action File with much helpful information and guidance. Do not forget that older people in residential homes or long stay hospitals may feel isolated and welcome contact with the outside world. These people, and old people living alone, may also greatly appreciate being invited for an occasional meal in someone's home.

Services in hospitals and residential homes

Many churches are able to hold short devotional services for residents in homes and hospitals. This can be a very valuable means of reaching older people, provided they are approached with sensitivity. Their concentration span may be short and the audience will include many frail and handicapped people, so a short, relevant talk, spoken clearly, a service in which the old people are encouraged to participate by choosing hymns, and much love and understanding are needed – and a capacity not to be disconcerted by interruptions or by people falling asleep!

Retired people have much experience of life, and much to offer. The later years bring with them, inevitably, a more acute awareness of the end of life. Above all, the retired have time – time to reflect, perhaps for the first time for many years, on spiritual realities. There are many opportunities for the church to reach out to this often neglected and undervalued section of society.

Useful addresses

The Christian Council on Ageing
C/o Green Norton Court
Green Norton
Nr Towcester
Northants NW12 8BS

Bible Society
146 Queen Victoria Street
London EC4V 4BX

Royal National Institute for the Deaf
105 Gower Street
London WC1E 6AH

Age Concern England
Bernard Sunley House
60 Pitcairn Road
Mitcham
Surrey CR4 3LL

Church of Scotland Board
of Social Responsibility
121 George Street
Edinburgh EH2 4YN

4A.7

Single people

Over the past few years there has been an upsurge of interest in the status, role and potential of single people in our nation. Prompted by the statistical evidence that suggests that 35 per cent of our population could be single at the turn of the century, single people have begun to attract attention, not least the interest of those who have been quick to seize the opportunity of making commercial gain through exploitation of the singles' lifestyle, with singles clubs, discos, single accommodation and singles bars where, if you arrive with a partner, you could be refused admission!

Tragically, the Church has been slow to respond with positive input and ministry opportunity; Sunday schools cater for children, there are meetings for young marrieds, senior citizens and young people, but very little for singles. Maybe leadership still clings to the idea that single people are second-class citizens or people who have 'lost their way', and this apathy and misunderstanding has masked the real potential of reaching a great proportion of our population.

Single people include those who have never married, either by choice or lack of opportunity, separated and divorced people, and those who have been rendered single through the death of a partner. This is a much broader basis than some would anticipate, but when you consider how many people within your own church fellowship fall into these categories it is possible to appreciate the terrific potential.

How to begin

(a) Look before you leap

Talk to the single people in your church and the places where you work. How do they spend their free time? What kind of relationships do they encourage? What fears and apprehensions do they have? Keep your ears and eyes open and begin to learn what makes single people tick. It is so easy to work in a vacuum and not really understand real needs, so make sure you get under the skin of singles to avoid trying to answer the questions that no one is asking.

(b) Choose your leader

Leadership is critical and is perhaps the area where much ministry potential has been lost. The singles' leader should be a positive person, with flair and imagination. He (or she) must be responsible, stable and well adjusted, and leadership qualities should be endorsed by their church leaders. It may be that a married couple could spearhead an outreach ministry; this is often useful when the counselling gets deep, but at all costs avoid those in the congregation who think it would be 'nice' to see the singles pairing off! Matchmakers make horrendous leaders!

(c) Birds of a feather

1 John 1:7 reminds us that because of what God has done, 'we have fellowship one with another'. We are linked because of a common bond in Christ, and if effective evangelistic outreach is going to be launched then

the most valuable asset is the *group* of singles already in the church. They need to be ministering to each other so that evangelism is a spontaneous overflow of body ministry. This is easier to write than to arrange because most single people tend to be very independent and can cope on their own, whereas a team ministry relies heavily upon dependence on each other.

Before being more specific, there are two factors that need to be understood. The teaching in the church should be ministering to the needs of singles and adding to their spiritual growth. This *does not mean* special messages for members who are single, but it underlines the responsibility of providing a balanced diet that caters for all sections of the congregation. This demands an awareness that single people are real people with vital needs. Secondly, the church must support any outreach programme, as spiritual babies who have no cradle, whether married or single, can fall very heavily.

Ideas for action

(i) In launching a ministry to the single population, call all the single people together who attend the church and organise a brain-storming session. Invite ideas for reaching non-churched singles and then debate all the suggestions. Some won't be as wild as they sound. Then decide on a specific event to make contact with other singles. For example, organise a buffet supper, or take over the local Chinese restaurant for a 'meal and message' style evening. Most commercial restaurants will welcome your business, particularly on Monday evenings! Personally invite single people and in the course of your evening share your plans and aims, and ask a well-trusted speaker to share why there is a concern to help single people. This should not be a heavy preaching presentation, but a bridge-building exercise which could lead to more effective personal evangelism. Invitations could also be backed up by volunteers from the church to run a baby-sitting service so that single parents are able to attend.

(ii) Single people can become problem-orientated, and loneliness, depression and isolation are all too familiar, but the listening ear or the offer of help and advice can be warmly received. A church singles' fellowship could form a team of people to operate a telephone help line, the number of which has been published, rather like the Samaritan's service. Contacts with the community on this basis can be wide and varied and you also need to be totally committed to the project because once the novelty has worn off it starts to get tough.

(iii) The building of many new leisure centres has given wider scope for groups wanting to use the squash, badminton, swimming and other sports facilities. Single people use this as a basis for meeting others, and it really can be quite exciting to see how a group of people, who are obviously fulfilled in their lifestyle, attract other people.

Any ministry and outreach venture must be shared fully with pastor and church leadership. Evangelism needs to be soaked in prayerful support, for so much has been attempted with human strength in the past and achieved very little. I have sought to emphasise this perspective, as well as majoring on team work. Singles working with singles on an individual basis are open to all kinds of accusations and pressures, and to be forewarned is to be forearmed.

As the divorce rate rockets, as statisticians point out that one in three marriages are doomed to fail, and as the current trend to remain single longer continues, the number of single people in our community is growing very rapidly.

Reaching people
bearing in mind where they live

4B.1

Inner city

1. Background

(a) A definition of the inner city

The inner city can be defined as an area characterised by poor housing, high unemployment, low academic attainment, a high crime rate, desperation, poverty and intense social deprivation.

(b) The mythology of the inner city

The inner city has, until recently, been the 'no-go area' of Christian mission. An entire mythology has arisen around the problems of evangelism in such places. Difficulties have been exaggerated and the inner city person has been caricatured as an unthinking moron who is unresponsive to the good news. This evaluation could not be further from the truth. The message of Jesus is supremely the good news for the poor (Luke 4:18–19).

(c) Cultural relevance

To tell the good news effectively, the inner city church must be culturally relevant. This requires two things:

a congregation that is local to the neighbourhood rather than 'commuter saints'

the good news proclaimed in such a way that it becomes meaningful to the inner city person

2. Good news to the inner city

(a) A visible gospel

The 'visible gospel' is the gospel encapsulated in the lives of Christians. The church in the inner city should express the life of Christ by practical involvement with people (Matt. 5:16); it should be demonstrating God's compassion and bias to the poor in social action. The inner city Christian should not merely offer the gospel in word but express it in action.

(b) A practical gospel

The packaging of the gospel often makes it irrelevant to inner city people. A middle class church packages the gospel conceptually but the inner city person may think pragmatically. The genius of the Hebrew/Christian revelation is its use of picture language when describing abstract concepts e.g. the nature and action of God (Isa. 63:1–6; Zeph. 3:17). This reduction of God to human thought forms finds its perfect expression in Jesus, God clothed in our humanity, invading earth to make himself known. Consequently, the inner city Christian should train himself/herself to use picture language when telling the good news. Emphasise the power of the good news to change lives and illustrate from personal experience the difference it can make to behaviour, attitudes and relationships. Good news for the inner city is a good news rooted in real life.

(c) *A straightforward gospel*

Tell the good news straightforwardly rather than euphemistically. The inner city person rarely dilutes the truth to make it palatable but prefers abrasive honesty. Tactful and polite language may be considered deceitful and cowardly in an inner city context.

(d) *A corporate gospel*

The inner city person is probably less individualistic than his upmarket counterpart. He or she finds identity within the group rather than in personal achievement. The gospel is remarkably adapted to this kind of person. Salvation is never referred to in individualistic terms. Those who respond to the Lordship of Jesus are not only integrated into him but placed in his body (1 Cor. 12:13).

(e) *A visual gospel*

Never take reading for granted. There are always people in the inner city who read with difficulty if at all. Never assess the intelligence of any individual by his or her ability to read. Often this deficiency is compensated for by unusual powers of memory. Use visual aids and dramatic, easily remembered stories to communicate the goods news.

(f) *A personalised gospel*

The way we tell the good news is often determined by our personality and talents. These insights are not meant as a definitive guide to communicating the good news to the inner city, but have been given to act as signposts pointing the Christian in the right direction. Telling the good news is not learnt in the cloister but in the market square.

3. Some ideas for inner city evangelism

(a) *Multi-racial evangelism*

British inner city areas are becoming multi-racial. White and black churches should attempt to meet together regularly for praise and evangelism. This can be achieved if the pastors of the respective churches have fellowship together and share mutual respect for each other. If churches of different ethnic origin meet, however, cultural and religious tolerance are required. It may be helpful to imbibe the following principles:

study the alien culture

accept the culture with its religious attitudes and expressions as equally valid as your own

experience the culture by involvement with its people until it becomes as natural as your own culture.

In areas of racial tension, a united church can be a mighty instrument of reconciliation and evangelism.

(b) *Open air meetings*

High-rise flat precincts are the ideal location for open air meetings. An imaginatively organised event supported by local churches, can be used to bring a number of people to Christ. Many Black churches have gifted choirs and soloists who can provide excellent music. Testimonies, interviews, street drama and succinct messages can turn high-rise flats into crusade balconies with people hanging from windows to listen.

(c) *Doorstep visitation*

A programme of doorstep visitation is the bloodstream of the inner city church. A booklet or leaflet introducing the church, with photographs of the interior, descriptions of the services, and a list of local amenities, e.g. hospitals, railway stations, can be the first step in infiltration. This can be followed by specific evangelistic visits and home Bible studies.

(d) *Family service*

A family service is an event that is convened to reach the entire family. The programme should include the following:

easily remembered songs for children and non-readers that can be learnt quickly

dramatic sketches (if personnel are available)

a visually illustrated message of no more than twenty minutes.

The family service can be viewed as part of God's counter attack on the disintegration of family life in the inner city.

(e) A pensioners' tea

Pensioners are often trapped, afraid, victimised, robbed and ignored in the inner city. A monthly pensioners' tea can provide an opportunity to tell the gospel. For the pensioner, the most simple journey can be frightening and dangerous. In many inner city areas pensioners have been violently mugged and robbed at least once. They live in constant fear and apprehension. The church must not only be willing to provide tea but also to fetch the elderly.

(f) Social opportunities

Church premises can be used for a nursery, marriage counselling, a citizens advice bureau and legal aid. These social opportunities can provide the bridge into the community.

4B.2

Flat dwellers

You have a concern for a block of flats near your church. How do you reach those living there?

1. Aim

Your aim, as in any evangelism, is to 'make disciples'. This involves making contact with people, helping them to understand the gospel so that they can respond and become integrated members of a local church.

2. Background

You must *understand* and *think through* your particular situation:

what type of flats are you dealing with – privately owned or local authority; housing divided up or high-rise?

what are the sort of *people* you are talking about? This will follow on from the previous question. How would the flat dwellers relate to your church and its members?

where are the flats *situated*? Are there natural geographical or social links with your church?

what already existing *links* does your church have with the flats? Are there church members or families of children in your youth groups living there? Do members have relatives, friends, or work mates living in the block?

Think about the flats themselves:

a block of flats is very different from a street. It has a different sense of community. The occupants tend to lead separate lives, even though they are under one roof.

people often feel *isolated* and *vulnerable*, particularly in high-rise blocks, where there can be a lot of vandalism, mugging, etc. To the casual visitor they can seem defensive and uninterested.

the visitor to flats can find a problem of *accessibility* with answer phones, broken lifts, etc. The arrangement of flats itself can make speaking to people at the door difficult.

As you think these things through, you build up a picture of your own situation, and can begin to develop a strategy.

3. Strategy

(a) *Contacts*

Establishing *contacts* is of primary importance, as these are the people you can work with in direct evangelism. We need to recognise that in urban communities 'where you live' matters much less than 'who you know' in your social network i.e. relatives, friends or neighbours. This certainly applies to flat dwellers. So, be aware of and use the existing 'networks' which exist in the flats concerned.

(b) *Visiting*

General visiting is not always successful, although literature distribution on special occasions – Christmas, parish missions – will give people an awareness of the church. In any visiting the aim is to find 'responsive' people – those who have some interest in Christian things and would like to learn more. Such people can be followed up in more directly 'evangelistic' visiting by people with gifts of evangelism. A problem for many churches is lack of manpower to undertake extensive visiting. In such cases, there may be a place for bringing in a team from outside, e.g. students. Also, there may be existing contacts to be followed up, either through church members, children in the youth groups, or through baptisms, marriages and funerals.

(c) *Home meetings*

In many cities around the world 'home' meetings in flats have been very successful. This is a possibility if you have someone who can host a gathering and invite in their friends and neighbours. People may like to talk about a subject of common interest (e.g. family, work) or hear somebody talk about their faith with an opportunity for questions. (See section 4B.4e).

(d) *Needs*

You should be considering the needs of your flat dwellers, and thinking imaginatively how to meet them. Often it is the elderly and mothers with young children who feel most isolated and in need of friendship. Therefore, mother and toddler groups and clubs for the elderly can be effective ways of creating natural contacts. Groups for men, on 'neutral ground' in pubs or clubs, should be based on the interests of the men concerned. Christians can be involved in groups in which flat dwellers meet and share their concerns, e.g. residents' and community groups. Meeting people in such natural and non-threatening situations makes for good links and helps build up trust.

(e) *Prayer*

We need to recognise the priority of prayer if we are to move forward. Very practically our concern for a block of flats must be expressed in a desire to pray for the people living there, perhaps praying for real contacts to be made there. It is as we pray that we will see God give us real opportunities.

4B.3

Corporation estates

1. The environment

In Great Britain 34 per cent of all households live in local authority housing. The majority of these homes are on corporation estates varying from 500 to 70,000 people. Such housing provision has greatly improved the living standards of many who could not afford to buy their own home. There is, however, an easily recognised uniformity of layout and architecture. The reaction against this loss of personal identity is evident when a householder buys his own council house. The first signs are the changes in external decoration in order to look different. This may take the form of an additional porch or new front door or just a change of outside colour. The tower blocks have highlighted the feelings of isolation. There is no garden fence over which to talk. Unless one happens to come up in the lift at the same time as a neighbour, one may rarely see them. The gospel of Jesus Christ can bring purpose and worth to lives and is able to counter the impersonal factors of environment. Jesus said, 'Even the very hairs of your head are all numbered so don't be afraid, you are worth more than many sparrows' (Matt. 10:30–31 NIV). The local church must be identified with its surrounding community and yet be salt within it.

2. The people

Some estates were part of rehousing schemes or overspill areas or linked with a particular industry (61 per cent of the unskilled labour force of the country live in local authority housing.) The points system for obtaining a house and the order of preference for the housing area you would like has often meant the emergence of an unwritten league table of better and worse housing areas. The families with the greatest social need have taken the first house that is available whatever the area offered. Families with less pressing needs have waited and even turned down houses until their first choice is available. There is a lack of extended family life. The system of housing allocation makes it difficult for the son or daughter to get a house around the corner. It is vital for the local church to meet this need of fellowship life. There needs to be a family atmosphere as in the early Church where 'they broke bread in their homes and ate together with glad and sincere hearts' (Acts 2:46).

3. Reaching out with the gospel

Church attendance is much lower in council housing areas than private housing areas.

For the working class man there is a great cultural barrier to entering a church. This means that the church must go out to visit people where they are. The church is seen as irrelevant, and there is a great superstitious feeling about God. As the body of Christ, our evangelism needs to give a face to this unknown God in Jesus Christ (Acts 17:23; 2 Cor. 4:6).

We must view visiting in three different stages and note particular insights in reaching people on corporation estates.

(a) Pioneer visiting

Initial door-to-door visiting with an introductory slip posted in beforehand explaining the purpose of the visit (e.g. community survey, special events or regular neighbourhood concern of the local church). There is a great deal of good will and open-hearted welcome which should be encouraged when pioneer visiting on an estate. Enthusiasm and humour help people to be relaxed. The joy of the Lord is our strength.

(b) *Contact visiting*

Building a relationship in which we share the love of Christ through regular contact and care with interested homes. This may result from pioneer visiting, or other activities, or links such as relatives, friends or neighbours (Acts 18:7–8). After the intial welcome it is more difficult to see a sustained response on the estate. Some will show initial interest not wanting to refuse, but will find it difficult to follow through to be 'fruit that will last'. This makes contact visiting all the more important but often discouraging. It may mean remembering a birthday, making a hospital visit, or sending a card from holiday. It demands a great deal of time, patience and care and needs to involve as many members of the local church as possible as well as supportive projects (e.g. Family Day Care Centre, schemes among unemployed, schools work and elderly people support). An open-home programme inviting neighbours to see a suitable video has been another means of making contact. The provision of facilities must never replace the nurture of personal, caring relationships.

(c) *In-depth visiting*

Prayerfully recognising people from the circle of contacts with whom we can share an in-depth arranged visit or series of visits to introduce the gospel of Christ. A variety of aids are available e.g. Evangelism Explosion visiting, *Good News Down Your Street* – introductory course to the Christian faith, Nurture/Basics/Discovery groups. Often the local church can develop a turnover of interested contacts but not bring the challenge of commitment. In-depth visiting must include a strong element of 'apprenticeship', (2 Tim. 2:2).

Communication of the gospel must be in simple and clear language which is well illustrated. Faith must be 'caught' as well as taught. Keeping to arranged visits is not so easy where diaries and appointments are less familiar. Include as many of the adults in the household as possible. Discover where each person is in their spiritual understanding and seek to lead them step-by-step to Christ. It is vital to cover such outreach with specific prayer partnership.

4. Leadership and fellowship life

The nurture of new Christians is especially important in an area where there is more instant response but less stickability. The discipling must be ongoing to produce leaders from the grass roots who are able to relate the Scriptures to the real needs of the community. It is important to recognise spiritual gifts more than searching for professional qualifications. So many of the keener young people go off to college and qualify and never return to live on the estate. The Lord Jesus chose a nucleus of ordinary men 'that they might be with him' (Mark 3:14). They were to become the leaders of the early Church. On the estates where there can be so many instant demands upon time it is essential to make time to train leadership.

Fellowship life must be a visible expression of love, joy and peace in the fullness of the Spirit. Jesus said, 'Let your light shine before men, that they may see your good deeds and praise your Father in heaven' (Matt. 5:16 NIV). In a community where actions speak louder than words, worship and witness should involve lively participation and should be less cerebral. Many have family breakdowns, deep hurts and resentments and feelings of rejection, and some find it difficult to cope with life. The local church is more than a first aid post or emergency ward with a turnover of patients. It is the extended family of God in which long-term wholeness is realised.

Further reading

Building with Bananas, D& N Copley (Paternoster)

Built as a City, David Sheppard (Hodder & Stoughton)

New Wineskins, Howard Snyder (Hodder & Stoughton)

Urban Harvest, Roy Joslin (Evangelical Press)

Making Known the Good News to Residents of Council Housing Estates, compiled by Lewis Misselbrook (Published by N.I.E.)

4B.4

Owner occupiers

1. Who are owner occupiers?

(i) They are 'ordinary people', making up the majority of the adult population. They are not necessarily more wealthy than those in rented accommodation. Most have mortgage commitments; these, added to the pressure to keep up with neighbours, often lead to financial struggles. They have a certain indefinable confidence which comes from owning their own house. Unwittingly perhaps, they have a feeling of achievement and status.

(ii) The church has had more success in attracting this section of the community than most others. Many churches in Great Britain have a solid core of owner occupiers, even if they commute into an inner city church in the area where they came from originally.

(iii) Despite this, most are typical, secularised and respectably pagan with little knowledge of the Bible or the Christian faith. The wide easy road is much favoured and concentration on material prosperity effectively blinds many to its destination: destruction (Matt. 7:13). Just because churches contain a large proportion of owner occupiers, it does not mean that there are not thousands more in urgent need of the gospel.

2. Two basic requirements

These requirements apply to all evangelism, but they need constant spelling out.

(a) Friendship

The major reason for failure in reaching people for Christ is failure in building, retaining and enjoying meaningful relationships with those outside the church. As members are sucked into time-consuming church life, they often find a depth and joy of friendship in the family of God which cannot be found outside it. This results in:

- losing contact with former friends
- mistaking surface friendship and nodding acquaintance for the genuine thing
- bewilderment because such 'friends' often do not turn up to events to which they are invited
- a new Christian being most effective in evangelism during his/her first year in faith.

(b) Prayer

This is needed for those 'in the front line' who do the outreach and from the whole church in support. Nearly everyone engaged in evangelism knows this, but evidence points to it not being much practised.

3. Some possible methods

A consistent feature of outreach on private estates in the second half of the twentieth century has been the effectiveness of using *the home*. People naturally enter one another's homes and tend to feel more receptive in the relaxed atmosphere of a home than the more formal setting of a church or hall. So, the emphasis is on homes both of church members and of those we are trying to reach.

(a) Informal use of homes

Christian people should be encouraged to use their homes and practise hospitality. It is also good to get to know neighbours in *their* homes, if the invitation occurs. It is all part of taking people seriously and establishing real friendship. There is no short-cut; evangelism flounders without it.

(b) *Home meetings*

These are usually at the invitation of church members in their own home, although they can occasionally be more effective when the host and the hostess are uncommitted but interested (*see* 3B.4e Home meetings).

(c) *Door-to-door visiting*

This is necessary where there are not many contacts. It is second best because it is less natural than when outreach springs from an existing friendship. However, it is well worth doing, not as an alternative but in addition. There can be two different aims:

(i) *Contacts*. This could more appropriately be described as pre-evangelism than evangelism. The aims are to seek out those who have a basic interest which can be nurtured and to announce the presence of a living church in the locality.

It is necessary to devise a good excuse for calling (*see* 5A.10 and 5A.11). A period of visiting an estate or part of an estate, usually in twos, will nearly always produce a number of good contacts, i.e. friendships to be developed and people to be prayed for. The next stage will usually be an invitation to a home meeting, guest service or an explanation of the Christian faith in their own home (*see* section 6).

(ii) *Direct evangelism*. This requires training and is best when a specific method is used. (*see* 5A.17 Co-operative ventures). It is likely that such methods produce their best results among owner occupiers. They have the major advantage of mobilising church members and teaching them to articulate their faith. They are best used in an area where there are few church members living; otherwise there is a danger that slow witness relying heavily on friendship can be harmed and good work can be undone.

(d) *Good news down the street*

This is a variation on Evangelism Explosion, taking place over about six weeks. People who have expressed interest in the Christian faith agree to welcome into their home, on six consecutive weeks, three church members who explain, in an informal way, about Jesus and how to know him.

It usually needs to be a minister who sets this up and he needs to be persuasive! However, it is a method which has worked and is an ideal means of taking further any interest which may have been aroused by home meetings or contact visiting. In addition, it is an exceptionally effective method of training church members in talking naturally and informally about their faith.

(e) *Guest service or other evangelistic events*

For some reason, owner occupiers are marginally less uncomfortable inside the walls of a church than those who live on corporation estates (which tend to be further estranged from the church). People will come and some will respond. However, they won't usually come unless invited by a *friend*. They won't usually respond unless they have been faithfully *prayed* for.

(f) *Through children*

Many residents on private estates still encourage their offspring to attend church. This leads to potential contact with the parents. It is a strategy used in theory for many years and it has not got a good track record. It is far easier to reach children in the long term through parents than it is to reach parents through their children.

If it is to work, the teachers must see their role in wide terms. They need to be friends to the whole family and this involves regular visits. Parents evenings, similar to those held at schools, can be another bridge, but they must be well done, taking the children and what they do seriously – not just an excuse to preach.

Useful books

Good News Down the Street, Michael Wooderson (Grove booklets)

4B.5

Bedsits and sheltered housing

1. Bedsits

For many city centre churches, reaching people who live in bedsits will be an important part of their evangelistic outreach. With this type of accommodation, we are usually dealing with *single* people, probably students or young 'professionals' working nearby. Often there is a high turnover of people living in them, as people move on to the next step in their lives when getting married or going to a new job. With such a highly mobile population, it is clear that we have to be flexible and organised in our outreach.

A major difficulty is often found in actually making *contact* with people in bedsits. Probably they will be out quite a lot of the time, and often away or busy at weekends. Access to individual bedsits is made harder by answer phones, which also prevent an initial personal contact. People in bedsits may well feel independent, isolated and lonely, all of which is encouraged by the type of accommodation in which they live. We also need to recognise in this group that people's social relationships are fairly unrelated to where they live, since they will be acquired through work or leisure. They will probably feel little attachment to the area in which they live, including the local church.

(a) *How are we to reach such people?*

(i) *Imagination* must play an important part in our thinking. We must find out about the people's needs, how they spend their time, and think how we can go about attracting them. This may include the use of meals, coffee bars, or clubs offering a range of music or sport. Events on 'neutral' ground, e.g. in a local hotel, with a good evangelistic film or speaker, might be valuable. Make use of people and contacts that your church already has in the bedsits.

(ii) Systematic *visiting* and distribution of literature at Christmas, Easter, etc. has a place. Young people are often interested to talk about the Christian faith, and alongside such visiting we could offer coffee evenings or enquirers' groups.

(iii) Finally, it must be added that we need to examine our own pattern of ministry as a church to see if we are catering for these sort of people. Our churches need to be ready to offer effective ministry to *students* and *singles*. Students are away from their roots and need to feel that they can drop in on people for food and friendship at any time. They need the freedom to explore ideas without condemnation, and Christian input at the intellectual level at which they function. With so many churches concentrating on families, single people ministries are a neglected area. A church needs to create a social structure within itself where singles can come for friendship, sharing and ministry. We should ask God to show us how to be more effective in reaching out to those who live in bedsits near us.

2. Sheltered housing

With the elderly population on the increase there is a growing need for sheltered accommodation. Usually such housing consists of separate units (flats or bedsits) on a warden controlled site. There may well also be a common room or recreation room. This type of housing is usually designed for old folk, but can also be used for the physically or mentally handicapped.

With people in sheltered accommodation, as opposed to those in bedsits, the places where they live *is* significant, and gives a strong sense of community and identity. This can obviously be used to advantage in our outreach.

An important first step in making contact with sheltered housing in your area is to get to know the warden and staff. Building up trust and confidence will help you gain access to the residents. Having said this, they will usually be more than happy to see somebody taking an interest in the people.

(i) Find an opportuntiy to visit people in their flats or bedsits. It will probably be best to do so during the day, and could involve a range of church people e.g. older or retired folk, or members of the youth group. Such visiting should be seen as a regular commitment. Make use of existing contacts e.g. church members.

(ii) Arrange outings and/or transport to special events in the locality.

(iii) When thinking of older people, it is possible to hold a short *service* with hymns, readings and a short talk on a regular basis or linked with occasions such as Christmas or Easter. Church people could be involved who would not normally be able to do visiting.

(iv) Get involved in events which encourage a sense of community e.g. outings, parties. This shows that Christians are concerned for the whole person and will help build 'bridges' between the church and the people concerned.

In all of this, the church should *pray* for opportunities in which Christ can be made real through people to this section of the community.

4B.6

Halls of residence, nurses' homes etc.

1. First principles

(i) Christian witness in residences can only be carried out effectively by those actually living-in. A group of Christians, however small, is usually essential, since it is often impossible for visitors to work in a residence without an invitation.

(ii) By their very nature residences represent a unique opportunity for witness. The sense of community, the regular contact with friends day in and day out, the sharing of kitchens and common rooms, and an interest in discussion at almost any hour of the day or night, provide an ideal environment for evangelism. The most sound basis for Christian witness – *genuine friendship and living contact* – is immediately possible.

(iii) This opportunity brings with it a heavy responsibility. It places a premium on *consistent Christian living*, and lifestyle and behaviour which demonstrate the living reality of the gospel. 'Witness' implies not only the need to proclaim but also to live the gospel, to 'shine as lights in the world, holding forth the word of life' (Phil. 2:15–16). We are being closely scrutinised.

(iv) Fellowship groups in the residences are invariably the best *support base for witness*. Where possible it is helpful to establish a weekly meeting of Christians for Bible study, prayer and fellowship. Such groups always face the temptation to become introverted, but should work hard to ensure that their regular meetings are open and intelligible to non-Christians, and that they have regular (monthly?) opportunities for corporate evangelism.

(v) With most nurses/students living in for only one year (and occasionally two), it is essential to work towards the fulfilment of a *strategy*, appropriate to your residence, that has been prayerfully conceived and carefully planned. It is easy for time to slip by without grasping the particular opportunities available (the first weeks of term; Christmas events; Easter; help at exam time; leaving parties etc).

2. Provoking interest

(a) *Door knocking*

There is no need to be afraid of straightforward contact visits, but you will need to have in mind the following:

> it is important to have a strategy – what are you hoping to achieve? What sort of follow-up for interested people?

> don't be too pushy – aim to be sensitive (is it the right time to talk?); have ideas for opening conversations

> it is usually helpful to have publicity or an invitation for a meeting in the Hall; or a literature distribution programme.

(b) *A questionnaire/survey*

Half a dozen well chosen questions on attitudes to religion, Jesus Christ, the Bible etc, appropriate to your residence. As a serious attempt to discover people's views, it is vital that you collate the information and aim to publish it (student magazine or your own sheet). Again, plan how to follow up the interest.

(c) *Bookstall*

A weekly book table in the Hall (get permission), strategically located (e.g. common room, refectory) and at the right time of day. Have a good mix of relevant books, magazines and free literature.

(d) *Social events*

Important in establishing friendships and developing opportunities for informal chats. Try events like a barbecue, Barn dance, Tearcraft evening, etc. Plan how to follow up.

(e) *Those from overseas*

Usually there are quite a few in most residences. They are often lonely and contact must be first and foremost at the level of friendship, helping them to adjust to the unexpected way of life, climate, food etc.

(f) *Bar evangelism*

This is a difficult area, but a gifted evangelist or musician can often get away with a ten-minute presentation, and personal conversations can do the rest.

3. Stimulating thoughtful discussion

(a) *Open meetings*

A whole variety of events can be arranged, many best linked with imaginative hospitality – e.g. pizza, smartie, hot potato, pancake, popcorn, Pooh, poetry/ literature parties, formal dinner.

(i) *Before*. Each Christian invites one or two non-Christian friends (aim for 6–12 in total). Use a small invitation card with details of time, place, discussion topic. Pray hard!

(ii) *During*. Make sure it's relaxed. After the food have someone give a short talk, or show a filmstrip, aimed at provoking discussion. Don't go on too long; have a summary and then allow individual discussion.

(iii) *After*. According to interest, see ideas below.

There is a great variety of possible topics for discussion, from the usual questions ('A God of love and a suffering world'; 'Is Christianity sexually repressive?'), to topics of current interest (nuclear debate, political issues) and matters of academic or professional concern (nurses might consider professional lectures, discussions on ethical and moral issues). Alternatively, try a 'revue' (if you've got the talent) – songs, poetry, drama and a ten-minute talk; or a filmstrip (some good discussion starters from Scripture Union, Falcon, or UCCF); or discussion linked with good evangelistic books.

4. Helping towards commitment

(a) *Bible discussion groups*

Studying the Bible with non-Christians is by far the best way to carry out evangelism in Hall.

(i) Ensure that non-Christians outnumber Christians. Keep the total number small.

(ii) Have a series of 3 or 4 studies, so that people know what they are committing themselves to.

(iii) Have Bibles (modern translation) or Gospels available. Choose the passage carefully and prepare thoroughly. Keep to time and to the text. Conversations can follow afterwards.

(Outlines for such evangelistic studies are available from Navigators, Campus Crusade and UCCF.)

(b) *Personal conversation*

As in all evangelism, this is the best way to help someone come to faith (*see* section 6).

5. Christian fellowship

(a) *Beginners group*

Regular Bible studies in Christian basics for a small group of new Christians in your Hall.

(b) *One-to-one*

Regular (possibly daily) meetings with a young Christian to establish him in prayer and Bible reading. This possibility is another advantage of a residential setting where early morning or late evening meetings are possible. Keep to the same sex.

(c) *Integration into Hall fellowship*

Encourage the new Christian to link up with others in your residence. He or she will have questions concerning the Christian life and his/her studies or profession, amongst other things.

(d) *Local church*

Most important of all. Take the young Christian with you (*see* section 6.3).

Useful addresses

Universities and Colleges Christian Fellowship, 38 De Montfort Street, Leicester LE1 7GP Tel: 0533 551700

Campus Crusade for Christ, 103 Friar Street, Reading RG1 1EP

The Navigators, 86b Coombe Road, New Malden, Surrey KT3 4RB

Nurses Christian Fellowship, 277a Ewell Road, Surbiton, Surrey KT6 7AX

Christian Medical Fellowship, 157 Waterloo Road, London SE1 8XN

4B.7

Satellite communities

There has been a rapid growth, in recent years, of dormitory towns built within commuting distance of our large cities. These towns have their own distinctive moods and peculiarities and present the Church with special responsibilities and opportunities in church planting. For maximum effectiveness the Church should be involved as early as possible within the creation of the new community. This demands a visionary spirit among the Christians within the city to release, support and encourage these with a pioneering attitude to settle and work in the emerging community.

1. Assessing the situation

There is almost certainly a community population with men travelling up to four hours every day to and from the city. A large percentage of the women may well be at work during the day. The general unemployment problem will, of course, affect this from area to area. Surveys indicate that materialism and marital breakdown are the chief social factors. Up to 50 per cent of children of secondary school age will not be living with their original two parents and it is quite common for a child to have had two or even three different surnames by the age of eleven. Estimates of single parent families range from 20 per cent to 50 per cent and the sense of being abandoned, lost and lonely can be strong. These factors will mean that the community is riddled with insecurity and emotional problems that will have a real bearing upon the kind of church that emerges and the type of spiritual help and counselling required.

Among the people there is likely to be a belief in religion and in God but little understanding of true Christianity, and the church is deemed irrelevant.

Special needs within the community will be discovered by close contact and discussion with the people. It has been suggested that the school gate has replaced the village well as the centre of neighbourhood gossip. It may be profitable, if there is sufficient manpower available, to take a doorstep survey to highlight the areas of need. The assessment of these findings will, of course, affect your strategy of witness and evangelism.

2. Advancing the kingdom

(i) In Luke 10:8–9, Jesus indicated a three-pronged approach to the community. We need to be *sociable, sympathetic and spiritual*. Such an approach will demonstrate that the kingdom of God has come to the people. There is no problem establishing first contacts for anyone seriously interested in the life of the community. The following have been tested as meeting points: the schools, the senior citizens' club, the clinic, the doctor's surgery, the corner shop, the shopping centre, the mobile library, the youth centre, the park, the community centre, the library, the pub.

(ii) In some towns *parish steward schemes* have been effective especially when a key family can be located in each street.

Areas of help are made known to the street:

Help available in emergencies: sudden illness, prescriptions at the weekend.

Illness at home or hospital: meals cooked, shopping done, pensions fetched, children looked after, prayed for by name in church.

Elderly or handicapped: visits for company, transport to hospital, training centre or church.

Parents: baby sitting arranged, children cared for while mother is in hospital.

Newcomers: welcomed with offers of friendship, information leaflet giving details of local amenities, shops, services, churches.

One church had 100 requests for help during its first twelve months. The volunteers ranged in age from sixteen to eighty.

One survey asked: 'What is the most important thing in your life?' 62 per cent gave 'My family' as the answer. A Family Counsellor Service could be set up with Christians trained to give help in specific areas. Bristol's Family Life Association has much experience and encouragement in this field. Leaflets, cards and advertisements make the free service known in the city.

(iii) *A free church/community newspaper* delivered periodically to each home is also an excellent service and superb vehicle for the gospel but is expensive, time consuming and demands an expertise that is not always available. Shared by several churches it becomes a distinct and worthwhile possibility.

(iv) Having established our contacts, the presentation of the gospel must be done with care and forethought. Attending a church is frightening for many and the use of homes has many advantages. Video cassettes in the home for gospel films make good discussion starters and first contact social evenings are an opportunity with tremendous potential. Coffee mornings are by no means new but are still proving to be effective in presenting the gospel in an atmospere of friendship. If an epilogue is included it is essential that someone is delegated to care for the children in another room for those few minutes. There is no need to restrict the use of homes to those of church members. A good spirited person in the community will often oblige and will thereby enlarge the circle of unconverted friends present. Programmes of interest are well known amongst ladies' groups (cookery, flower arranging, etc), but what about car maintenance, photography, decorating, jogging, etc for the men?

Some in the community will respond to a direct approach: a series on clear spiritual issues, allowing for open discussion, can prove a draw. The writer presented a lecture contrasting Christianity and humanism in a satellite town and a meal was provided. 150 attended including some of the town council and the Provost. Considerable discussion followed as Christians shared their faith on a personal level.

(v) *Door to door visitations* can be useful in the community if it is well planned. Perhaps its strategic benefit is in discovering the lapsed Christian who has not sought fellowship since leaving the city church or Sunday school. There is a definite ministry amongst backsliders that can prove to be very fruitful.

In adopting any of these methods of evangelism the need will be highlighted for Christian workers to be trained in personal evangelism so that opportunities are not fumbled or lost when the key moment arises to share their beliefs.

3. Anticipating the church

Pioneers of a new church may need to be prepared for a long haul. They should set long-term objectives and follow the projects through. The autonomous and independent church has advantages regarding spontaneity but also has an in-built weakness inasmuch as movement of leaders away from situations can lead to decline or closure of the work. Evolving from the home based group into a rented hall or erecting a new church building continues to be a hotly debated issue. The immense expense involved in building is offputting. However, it does open the door to a complex of facilities tailored for all its needs, not the least being an attractive main hall conducive to worship and congregational activity. Rented accommodation has its limitations, especially as many newcomers prefer to attend a 'proper church', but there are advantages to consider and the income of the church can be channelled into ministry, evangelism and compassionate outlets. In either case, there is a strong plea to maintain the smaller house group cells and make these the base for pastoral care and evangelistic care, evangelism and worship as the vital ingredients for balanced church growth.

Established churches will need to release men and resources to ensure the spawning of these new churches in our satellite communities.

Reaching People
bearing in mind what they do

4C.1

Landworkers

Farmers who work their land and run their businesses are divided about six to four between owner occupiers and tenants. There are great differences in wealth and lifestyle between farmers. Their backgrounds and education are very varied as are their levels of income. Outward appearances may not reflect either their wealth or their intelligence. Some are on the way to becoming employers, others will remain employees.

1. The person

There are also similarities between farmers. Most working farmers are commercially-minded businessmen. Most drive hard bargains. As the capital needs of today's farms are very great there is usually a sense of economy. Long hours are often worked and 'time wasting' is very selective. Most better-off farmers have a hobby or interest on which time is spent, such as the country sports of shooting, hunting, or fishing, or motor sports, collecting items from the past or going to local social events. But outside these work is hard, consistent and usually covers at least part of seven days a week.

Most farmers are independently minded. They are therefore anti-authority and anti-being told what to do. Traditions run strongly, partly due to a strong sense of family and continuity. The past generation is never far away and has to be considered. Often, father keeps control even when a son is well into his forties or even fifties and older. Materialism, while being in a sense as strong as with any other social group, is often coloured by family considerations. Status symbols for farmers are as likely to be animals or pieces of farm equipment as pieces of home furnishing or a car.

Farmers' wives are as varied as their husbands. They are usually intelligent and very hard working and often every bit as conversant with the business as their husbands, though they are almost always supportive rather than dominant.

2. Points of contact

(a) Nature

As land workers are dependant on living things for their income there is great respect for 'nature'. This can also be the church's opportunity. A country minister can appropriately use Rogation Tide in May each year to pray for the area's crops and in times of stressful weather should pray for two things:

that the lesson God is trying to teach through the weather should be learnt that the change needed in the weather should happen.

Jesus stilled a storm. Elijah prayed for rain. James referred to Elijah's praying. Deuteronomy 28 is about farming prosperity as well as other things, and mentions drought, disease and low yields as signs of absence of blessing. For all man's technology, we farmers still grapple with these problems and need God's favour as well as man's enterprise.

(b) Church services

Most farming people would accept that going to church is a 'right' thing to do, though lack of time is a majority excuse. The excuse is a thin one since traditional Sunday service times of 11.00 a.m. and 6.30 p.m. were planned so that those working on farms could be present after finishing their essential Sunday work. The excuse seems more likely to be a reflection of people's feelings about the church service and its irrelevance to his thinking; often understandably so.

Farmers and farm workers are pragmatic people. They can understand real and important issues. Church must be real and important. Worship must seem relevant. Some country folk object to change. Farm folk do too. But if worship has become boring, people will silently object to that by not coming. So objections to change may need to be overruled in favour of relevance, interest and helpfulness.

(c) Births, marriages and deaths

These are as significant in the countryside as anywhere. Local people move house much less frequently than in towns, so more people are interested in each family event. In casual conversation as well as in formal speeches and church services we can give God credit for creation, remind people of his authority over life and death, and introduce Christian counsel on relationships and marriage. The challenge is how to make enough effort for the gospel without being too pushy or boring in our conversation. There is no substitute for a Christ-filled life. Genuine caring about each person is detectable and compellingly attractive. We can rejoice with the celebrators and weep with the disconsolate.

(d) Morality

Farmers are traditional in their morality. Many are very worried about the environment their children are growing up in. Here too is a teaching and evangelistic opportunity. The land worker and his family are subject to the same moral pressures, even though the temptations may not be as frequent as for the town dweller. Man's extremity can certainly be God's opportunity as the interest and prayers of Christians is shown. The gospel's teaching on marriage or on sexual behaviour may become the point at which repentance comes. Traditional strictures exerted by country parents on their children may be rejected. Here again is a chance for Christian, biblical morality to be compared with tradition. The older generation may have to change if rigidity is being applied to unnecessary rules. Conscious that his prosperity is largely not in his own control a farmer often respects those who appear to know about God or have a closeness to him. The country parson therefore has respect and opportunities. However, this respect is mixed with an aversion to authority.

(e) *Relationships*

A Christian has an important role as a peacemaker and that can be helpful to land workers as to anyone else. To offer hope and counsel to breaking marriages may not only restore the couple's happiness, but also avoid the need for disposing through divorce of the farming business and the children's future livelihood. Sometimes disputes arise between neighbours that can be eased by a caring third party. Sometimes, too, prodigal children can become reconciled with their parents when Christian insights on resentment and bitterness are shared with the parents.

(f) *Reality*

Like most people, farmers respond to and respect real faith. A Christian minister who is close to God in his own daily experience will impress anyone. Giving thanks before meals in a genuine way, can therefore be helpful as well as right whenever groups meet to share food. This can be done at NFU meetings, too. Speeches can contain Christian material or themes can be suggested to Young Farmers Clubs

3. Involvement

Farming facilities can often be used by churches or Christian groups, either for fellowship activities or for evangelistic times or just for fun. For example barbecues, camps, rambles, church picnics, nature or farm walks, harvest suppers, barn dances and bonfire parties.

Farmers or farm workers may well be suitable people to help in church as lay preachers, or counsellors, as entertainers for meals or providers of visual aids, or by providing an alternative meeting place.

Remember, farm families are often isolated and if they are not well off may find it difficult to get to meetings. Some country people are shy of large groups and may need encouragement. Reluctance to come to church may just be social shyness. Make personal contacts, respond to individual needs and so build the kingdom of God.

4C.2

Industry

1. Size and distribution of workplaces

British industry consists of more than 30,000 firms[1] employing 8,420,000 of the country's 22,511,000 employed people.[2] Although many firms have fewer than 30 workers, the Kompass Directory lists 6,400 companies with 200 or more workers, 1,470 of them with more than 600.

The table below shows the number of firms in the 16 most heavily-populated cities in England and Wales employing 200 or more workers.[1]

City	Population[3]	No. of workplaces with 200+ workers
London (postal districts)	N/A	740
Rest of Greater London	6,696,008	355
Birmingham	920,389	147
Manchester	449,168	80
Leicester	279,791	79
Sheffield	477,172	78
Stoke-on-Trent	252,351	62
Nottingham	271,080	60
Leeds	448,528	45
Bristol	387,977	45
Liverpool	510,306	42
Wolverhampton	252,447	40
Coventry	314,124	33
Derby	215,736	31
Bradford	280,691	30
Hull	268,302	30

2. Distribution of Christians

Nearly 100,000 Christians[4] are scattered throughout this working world, making everything from tacks to telescopes, biscuits to bulldozers. In insurance and local government Christians form between two and three per cent of the total workforce.[4] In the 'heat' of industry – steelworks, coal mines and car factories – the proportion reduces to about half of one per cent.[4] Even this tiny percentage represents a considerable force. Twenty-five Christians in a factory of 5,000 can make an impact far beyond their numerical strength.

3. Significance of workplaces in evangelism

Fairly even distribution of the larger workplaces throughout the country means that most urban, and some rural, churches are probably situated near at least one factory, and are likely to have members in several. The following are some of the reasons why industry deserves our serious attention.

(a) Time

For many Christians, secular work is their greatest commitment, in time and energy, outside the home. It occupies a huge proportion of life, reckoned in hours of the week, weeks of the year, or years of a lifetime.

(b) Access

A workplace is a wholly familiar area of involvement, into which both Christian and non-Christian employees have unhindered access.

(c) Contacts and relationships

Christians meet more non-Christians through their work than anywhere else. In a week some Christians encounter more non-Christians than a missionary might meet in an equatorial jungle.

At work relationships are formed, some close, others more distant. Christian witness in this context is not the work of five minutes, but recurs through continuing and developing rapport. There is nothing impersonal or hit-and-run about it.

(d) Indispensibility

Industry comprises hundreds of people herded together on one site in our locality, culture, language, and reach. If churches and church members show no interest in their own, or nearby, workplaces, no-one else can do it for them.

For these reasons, churches need a close, prayerful, interest in the working life of their members, and to see this as part of the church's missionary endeavour.

4. Methods of witness

Three main instruments for evangelism exist within a workplace; a Christian fellowship; individual Christians; and evangelism from outside.

Christian fellowships provide a single focus for gospel testimony within a workplace, representing a variety of types and grades of worker, acting corporately in activities beyond an individual's scope, and helping to dispel the 'crank' label so frequently applied to isolated Christians.

Evangelism from outside includes 'platform' evangelism by visiting evangelists, the work of chaplains, and avenues open to local churches.

(a) Evangelism by Christian fellowships

(i) *Meetings.* Regular meetings of Christian fellowships usually take place
weekly during lunch-breaks in a conference room within the factory or
office, or in a nearby church hall. They are publicised by word of mouth,
notice boards, a printed programme, or all three.

Subjects for meetings need to be relevant to everyone, not merely to
Christians. Meetings need titles to arouse interest. Examples of thought-
provoking titles: 'Space and Beyond'; 'How not to be a Christian'; 'God or
Mammon'; 'Eat, drink and be merry, for tomorrow we die'. Ten minutes
at the end for questions and comments to the speaker will clarify misunderstandings, stimulate thinking, and identify genuine inquirers.

A carol service at Christmas is an occasion for preaching the gospel. The
hardest hearts melt slightly at Christmas. Some workplace carol services are
attended by hundreds.

Christian films can be shown. Many scientific, biographical, and historical
films are technically excellent, and, though not overtly evangelistic, convey
clearly the Christian message.

(ii) *Bookstalls.* These may be permitted in reception foyers or canteen
entrances. Christians manning them may sell, give or lend books, and talk
informally about the gospel.

(iii) *'Open' days.* Company 'Open' days attract several thousand people to
tour the works who are confronted by a vast range of things to do and view.
Display stands by Christian fellowships can lead to unhurried, profitable
conversation with visitors.

(iv) *Bibles and literature.* Firms sometimes allow Bibles to be placed in
reception areas or medical rooms, or presented to apprentices, retiring
workers, or VIP visitors, at the fellowship's expense.

Literature racks with give-away gospel portions and tracts are another
possibility, while distribution of thoughtfully-prepared literature systemat-
ically inside the works, or randomly at the factory gates, could also be
considered.

(v) *Open air witness.* For decades a regular feature of shipyard life on
Clydeside and Wearside, open air preaching has taken place elsewhere in
works car parks, or on industrial estates.

(vi) *Buffet suppers.* Invite colleagues personally with a free ticket. The
programme could include supper, musical items, and an apt testimony or
talk.

(vii) *Works newspapers.* Space is often available in works newspapers or staff magazines for reports of Christian fellowship activities, or a relevant testimony or news item.

(viii) *Prayer*. Prayer must surround everything. Have a separate weekly prayer meeting at work, or pray with another Christian in spare lunch or break times.

(b) *Witness by individual Christians*

A Christian, while he may attempt some of the special forms of evangelism included under the previous heading, is always a witness in his every attitude, word and action. He should not underestimate the relationships he builds with colleagues, whether he sees them every day, or fleetingly once a month. If the Christian understands the personality of his colleagues, respects their abilities, welcomes their company, and inquires after their families, he will win their friendship and will have many natural openings to talk of his Saviour.

Some additional means:

(i) *Christian calendars*. On a wall, desk, or machine, a Christian calendar immediately marks out a man or woman as a Christian. It contrasts with most calendars on view, and its message will be a constant, silent witness.

(ii) *Hospital visiting*. Colleagues in hospital or sick for long periods will always appreciate a visit. Serious illness is often a thoughtful time in people's experience, and leaves them open to the caring interest of a Christian willing to spend time, and pray with them. Similarly, the Christian has a vital ministry to the bereaved family and to colleagues when a fellow-employee dies suddenly.

(iii) *Local church interest*. Bring the needs of your colleagues and workplace to your church prayer meeting. This will kindle concern, encourage your own witness at work, and widen the church's local missionary vision.

(c) *Evangelism from outside the workplace*

(i) *Indirect influences*. Is your neighbour a company director? Your witness to him, and your prayers, could have a powerful effect upon the tens, hundreds, or thousands he employs. Your prayers for Christians in work-places which hit the headlines, in whatever connection, could encourage a faint believer, or prosper a witness.

(ii) *Platform evangelism*. By direct appeal to top management, evangelists have entered workplaces to address entire workforces, or preach in canteens at lunch-times. Gospel literature has been distributed, and follow-up arranged. This work has not been confined to places where the top management were Christians. The number of Christian-owned companies, into which evangelists have an open door, are few, though some still exist.

(iii) *Chaplains and town or city missionaries*. Many industries will welcome a chaplain, whether full-time, dividing his hours among many factories in one area, or a minister, clergyman or pastor giving half a day a week to the factory opposite his church. Being a chaplain involves pastoral and welfare counselling, but any chaplain worthy of the ministry must be a concerned evangelist. Town and city missionaries, with their unswervingly evangelical basis, effectively combine this twin function.

(iv) *Nearby churches*. Is your church opposite, or next to a factory. If so, you may find the following questions helpful.

● do any of your church members work there?
● do any other Christians known to you work there?
● how are you encouraging these Christians?
● have you any meaningful relationship with the factory?
● have you offered the factory the weekday use of your church car park?
● have you offered to visit any of the workers in hospital?
● do you know the managing director's name?
● have you, or has your minister, met him yet?
● have you invited the management to your church's annual carol service, or other suitable occasion?

Only good will come of an enterprising, friendly relationship with your local industry.

Notes

1. Kompass Directory 1982 Vol II Companies Information
2. Social Trends 1983 P. 54 – Central Statistical Office
3. 1981 Census
4. Informal surveys by the Workers' Christian Fellowship

4C.3

Itinerants

Nearly 2,000 years ago Jesus said: 'I was an hungered, and ye gave me no meat: I was thirsty, and ye gave me no drink: I was a stranger, and ye took me not in: naked, and ye clothed me not: sick and in prison, and ye visited me not ... Inasmuch as ye did it not to one of the least of these, ye did it not to me' (Matt. 25:34–45, AV).

During his early ministry Jesus had and still has a special love and interest in those who for many reasons have lost that which is most precious to all mankind – dignity and self-respect. Indeed, his final word of command to his followers, and so to us too, was and is: 'Thou shalt love . . . thy neighbour as thyself' (Luke 10:27) – this command has never been revoked.

Down the centuries the Christian Church has largely neglected this particular area of ministry to homeless itinerants (wanderers with no fixed abode). The structural pattern and practice of the established Church (i.e. the denominations) is such, that by and large this area of human need is sadly overlooked by the majority. General Booth, the founder of the Salvation Army, caught this vision of human need: 'while women weep as they do now; I'll fight; while little children go hungry as they do now, I'll fight; while men go to prison in and out, in and out, as they do now, I'll fight – I'll fight to the very end!' Today, the social services of the Salvation Army world-wide embrace all kinds of itinerants and vagrants – young and old. Others, such as the Church Army and independent Christian organisations are also meeting this area of need: soup kitchens abound in most major cities, and most cities have their statutory authority run hostels for homeless men and women.

From personal experience, both in night shelters, local authority administration, and, more recently working in Christian hostel administration, there appear to be three types of itinerant or homeless wanderer, lost in a sea of homelessness and despair:

(a) *The chronically sick (not necessary physically sick)*

They are mainly addicted to alcohol abuse; the Skid Row inhabitant unable to help himself (or herself) – an area of loneliness and degradation – whose only bed for the night is a derelict house or park bench or just the streets (skippering – the common term used among the itinerant fraternity for sleeping rough).

(b) *The passenger*

The itinerant just passing through, finding themselves in a down-and-out situation because of many circumstances, i.e. domestic upheaval, marriage breakdown, inability to cope with life – opting out of a difficult situation, yet not beyond reasonable help. Such people find themselves able to stay in hostels for a period of 6–8 months 'licking their wounds', and then move on, some to return again into society, others to continue in this way for the rest of their lives.

(c) *The institutionalised*

Men and women who have been so long living in hostels that this is their established life-style. Many have lived in this environment for 40–50 years and will only move out for their funeral.

How can we reach itinerants for Christ?

It is my belief that this area of ministry is a specialised ministry, yet it is the bounden duty of every Christian to be a soulwinner – and this includes the itinerants.

(i) There must be a deep love and concern for their material needs . . . (don't talk to a hungry man about the goodness of the Lord until you have fed him); an ability to share their personal problems with patience and understanding, especially with the alcoholic (a study of alcoholism would be of value to any who would serve the Lord in this ministry).

(ii) There must be an awareness of the need to identify with the individual, especially in the area of personal involvement. The Holy Spirit has given us spiritual gifts of discernment, and as we engage in in-depth counselling, the personal worker must surround himself with prayer support, for underneath the outward appearance lie stories of tragedy, heartbreak, and in some cases demon possession (it is advisable to deal with such cases with a prayerful associate, and if necessary be prepared to recommend others who may have specific gifts of deliverance in the name of the Lord Jesus).

(iii) The main problem is how to integrate such itinerants into the fellowship of the Church. This needs careful handling, with love, pastoral care, and deep expressions of love from the whole of the church. Praise God it can be done to his glory as we educate the child of God in this particular area of social concern. Believe me there is nothing more thrilling than to witness a former lonely, broken vagrant born into the family of God and cherished, nourished, loved and made to feel a member of the Church family.

In follow-up, remember that most of these men and women have for years lived independent, lonely lives, and to integrate them back into society will, in most cases mean careful rehabilitation when they move into their own house or flat after sheltered accommodation. This might mean teaching the basics, i.e. how to balance weekly budgets – food, electricity, gas, rent, etc; teaching how to shop again. Be patient, kind yet understanding and firm and you will have great joy as you see the Holy Spirit bringing men and women into a living experience of Christ.

Finally, you may find that this ministry is not spectacular, but with the help of the Lord it will prove to be a blessing.

Further reading

The General Next to God Richard Collier
God in the Shadows Hugh Redwood
Touched by a Loving Hand W. H. Dempster
Supplementary Benefits Handbook, DHSS

4C.4

Professionals and self-employed

Basic principles

Either to protect themselves or their profession, professionals and self-employed people have placed themselves behind very high defensive walls. They often have their own customs and jargon and even sometimes have a particular way of dressing. Perhaps this is more noticeable in the older professions such as law and medicine, but it is just as true, if more subtle, with men in executive positions in banking, insurance, accountancy, shipping, or who are on the management team of a large factory or concern. As a missionary tries to blend into the culture of his adopted country by learning the language to communicate more effectively and assuming national dress so as not to appear too foreign, so anyone working among professional people will find it easier to penetrate the defensive walls if the basic rules of mission are observed. Don't turn up to speak to a group of bankers wearing jeans and a tee-shirt. Always meet people where they are, make sure they feel comfortable and not threatened. Note sometimes in the New Testament the number of times that Jesus did just that.

Places of contact

(a) At work

There are two clear choices, both have their obvious advantages. Many business and financial areas contain old churches and ancient guild or trade halls. Old buildings are not normally off-putting to professional people. They are either familiar from school days, or reminiscent of a college chapel, or simply look like the administrative buildings of the profession. But make sure that the inside of the building feels right too. A building containing rotting church furniture won't do. And the refreshments must be appropriate. A sticky bun on a collapsing paper plate together with coffee-coloured liquid in a polystyrene cup won't be well received by a man who normally has a directors' lunch, or who eats in the managers' dining room. Food can be attractive and imaginative without being expensive. If the choice of building is a hotel, then the food is likely to be appropriate and so will be the ambience of the building. What better place to confer about the Christian faith than the conference room of a hotel already geared to meet the needs of professional business people.

(b) Outside work

Supper parties are ideal for small groups and even better for one-to-one contacts. The setting and the relaxing nature of the meal can provide a marvellous opportunity to present biblical truth and even to lead someone to Christ. If it is a supper party where a speaker has been asked to present a brief message, it is only good manners to tell the guests what to expect, so that they don't feel trapped.

Over the last century Christians who have large country houses have invited friends and contacts to a weekend houseparty. Here again the surroundings and the opportunity to walk and talk at leisure, to converse over a meal or after a game of tennis have made houseparties ideal for evangelism. So much so that large groups of like-minded friends regularly hire boarding schools in the summer months for week-long houseparties. A speaker will be invited to talk after breakfast or after supper. Again, the surroundings have meant that the right bridges have been built and many have come into the kingdom while enjoying a week's holiday among friends.

The approach

(a) Content of the message

There is a place for testimony: notable Christians who have seen success in their professional lives; a moving story of someone converted in prison or who found the reality of God while bankrupt, or the simple testimony of 'what God has done in my life'. Professional people are normally used to spotting fiction in the national press, business reports or in the balance sheets; so be very careful about facts and detail.

However, the more regular diet at meetings must be a careful exposition of biblical truth. Again, professional people are well used to considering a presentation of facts on various aspects of their business, so they will certainly listen to a well presented Christian message. Judicially aimed publicity for a series of talks by someone who is used to speaking to professional people will help.

Make sure that anyone booked to give their testimony has some plan of what they are going to say and understand the importance of keeping to time. Any meeting organised for professional people must keep to time. The most able evangelist, or most compelling speaker, can't get through to a group of men whose minds are beginning to wonder how they are going to get to their next appointment on time.

(b) Women's lib and all that

Whatever we feel about the equality of women it is still clearly true in England that the business professions and financial world are dominated by men. We may want to change this but this is the present position. This male domination is further complicated by an apparent shyness that could be the result of upbringing and schooling. It means, however, that the teaching and appeal of meetings must be directed towards men. Those women who want to attend the meetings will. There can be counselling and nurture classes for them, but the main thrust should be to attract men. If the thrust is the other way round, at the moment it would appear that men won't be attracted. This is a sociological fact that could be changing as women's lib seeks to redress the imbalance, but at the moment it needs to be recognised.

(c) *Big bonuses*

There are several bonuses that are to be enjoyed in seeking to evangelise the professions and the self-employed.

(i) Leading people to make decisions for Christ. Of course, you will find people in the professions who are hesitant and indecisive, but generally speaking this must be the most decisive group in the country. Decision making is their job; they are used to making decisions in the boardroom and in the market place. Therefore, present the facts clearly, show the steps to be taken and invite a response.

(ii) Another bonus is in the area of aftercare once a decision has been made. In response to the new technologies, professional people are used to bringing their knowledge up to date or studying new techniques and methods. Therefore, once a decision is made men and women will want to learn the basics of the new life; its nature, its behaviour and its practice.

(iii) Perhaps the biggest bonus to be reaped is not the area of response but of the future. Jesus clearly had a special place in his ministry for the professions and the self-employed. It was after all from this group that he chose twelve to be with him for training and who were eventually commissioned for rather special tasks. Jesus chose the twelve because he recognised their potential. We have no reason to say that Jesus ceased to have a special regard for this group. Therefore, there is much evangelising to be done, much training and perhaps in the future we will see a vast army of ministers, evangelists, preachers, pastors and missionaries, as Jesus *TRUSTS* his future work to the natural heirs of the original twelve.

4C.5

Unemployed

Someone has commented that unemployment is the fastest growing industry in Great Britain today! At the time of writing (mid 1983) approximately one in seven of the workforce is without a job. If we include as unemployed those who are not registered as such and those on temporary Government schemes, there are well over 4 million people unemployed.

Biblically it is clear that God's intention is that man should work (e.g.

Gen. 1:27–28 and 2:15). Doing and being belong together. Without delving too deep, it is obvious that unemployment is not part of God's desire for people. However, this tragic situation does give Christians an opportunity to demonstrate the love of Christ in very practical ways.

1. Difficulties

There are a number of problems related to reaching the unemployed:

(a) *Apathy*

Understandably, apathy can become a big problem if you are out of a job. It shows itself in lots of ways: staying in bed all morning, state of dress may deteriorate; many stop going down the job centre. This disinterest in life may well show itself if a person is presented with the gospel – 'What's God done for me?'

Apathy amongst unemployed Christians can be another difficulty. As we shall see later, the best people to reach the unemployed are the unemployed. However, Christians on the dole may have real problems getting motivated to do evangelism.

(b) *Where do you find the unemployed?*

One obvious place is on the dole queue, but it is not an easy place to have an extended conversation – people normally want to 'sign on' and get away as quickly as possible. The places to go will vary from area to area. A pub at lunchtime might be a good place, a park or shopping precinct. Many stay indoors for much of the day. The venue will also vary greatly with age and sex.

(c) *Unemployed women*

As far as I am aware, no one has worked out a means of effectively reaching unemployed women. The reason for this is mainly two-fold. Firstly, there are far less women who are unemployed than men. Secondly, a woman who leaves work is likely to simply revert into being a housewife.

(d) *Commitment*

Evangelism amongst the unemployed is usually a long-term commitment. This will cause problems since there is a tremendous turnover in people moving off the register and on to it. (On average 300,000 register and slightly less sign off per month.) There are certain types of people, however, who tend to get stuck in unemployment. These are:

the unskilled young

people over 55

those known as the 'long term unemployed'.

Recent figures showed that 36 per cent of those without work were under 25, another 15 per cent were over 55.

(e) *Effective manpower*

The most effective evangelism amongst those out of work will be done by those in the same boat. But there are proportionately far less Christians without a job than their non-Christian contemporaries. Whereas the national figure for unemployment hovers around the 13 per cent mark, it is unusual to find anything near that figure in an average congregation.

2. What has been tried?

Here are the four main ways that I know of which have had some evangelistic content in them. Obviously there will be variations on these themes.

(a) *Support group – Christian*

The idea here is that of a small group of unemployed Christians meeting together on a regular basis (i.e. once a week) for fellowship, but also to pray for and reach out to non-Christians.

One such project is called 'Genesis' and operates in Leeds. Here a group of twelve Christians meet in a cell group and also go out into secular drop-in centres and the local job centre to witness.

On a larger scale, British Youth for Christ is at present endeavouring to link up some of the 600 people on its unemployment register into similar groups for outreach purposes.

The specific advantages of this form of evangelism are:

Christians who are out of work have the day-time free, as do unemployed non-Christians

the former can relate to the latter in terms of problems and difficulties since they are going through the same thing.

(b) *Support group – non-Christian*

On a big council housing estate in Barking, near London, a self-help group has been established which consists mainly of a dozen non-Christians. A full-time volunteer team of Christians are working on the estate specifically amongst the unemployed. They got started by using a questionnaire in order to survey the area and make contacts. Of the people they interviewed, around 75 per cent said they would be 'very interested' in joining a self-help group.

The evangelism conducted in this way is obviously low-key. The idea here is to show Christian concern in action. Evangelism and conversion is then a by-product of this concern.

(c) Dole queue evangelism

It is impossible to know how much of this happens in an informal way – my guess is very little. Observation has shown that most people want to get in and out of the signing-on booth as quickly as possible.

Organised evangelism of this kind has often failed because:

it has been done by the employed

Christians have been too pushy – it's a long term thing in most cases

as mentioned before, people want to get 'signing-on' over and done with.

It is possible, however, to hand out well-produced leaflets at the gate advertising a special event or drop-in centre. It's probably not wise to hand out gospel tracts!

(d) Drop-in centres

This is potentially the most expensive method of evangelism amongst those without paid employment both in terms of finance and in terms of effort. It is, however, at its best the most well-rounded form of outreach into this particular group of people since it attempts to cater for the 'whole man' i.e. his physical, social and spiritual needs. One organisation which was set up in 1982 to give help and advice in this area is 'Church Action with the Unemployed'. It is supported by the major denominations and can provide both literature and personnel to assist in the setting up of a drop-in centre. British Youth for Christ is also very much involved in the establishing of this sort of work and employs a national officer to advise on schemes.

An example of a Christian-run drop-in centre is 'Crossbar' in Derby. It is sponsored by the local Youth for Christ committee and has been open since November 1982. At the time of writing (mid 1983), the centre is used by approximately fifteen different people per day. This may sound small, but the work tends to be slow, progressive building.

The main lessons learnt and problems faced by those who have opened drop-in centres are listed below:

(i) Don't think you can just open up a church hall with a table tennis table, dartboard and kettle. This is likely to attract no one. 'Crossbar' is housed in an old Anglican mission hall. £16,000 was spent on materials to renovate and re-structure the building. The labour came free of charge from the Community Task Force using YOP personnel. The main hall is carpeted throughout. There is a bar serving a range of soft drinks as well as hot meals at very cheap prices. The recreational equipment includes: two brand new table tennis tables, two snooker tables, darts, a weight training machine, bar football and two space invaders.

One of the problems in attracting people is that they receive free passes to many recreational activities run by the council. There are also secular drop-in centres with good facilities. So there is competition.

(ii) Think carefully about your aims and objectives. What are you trying to achieve? If you do this it will help you to plan before you open and it will keep you on course once you have opened. Which age group are you trying to attract? It's unlikely that young and old will come to the same venue. What are you trying to provide? Is it merely recreational? How will you conduct your evangelism without getting a reputation amongst the local unemployed as a 'Bible bashing' drop-in centre?

In Derby the emphasis has been upon attracting people through the recreational facilities, the cheap food and the pleasant atmosphere. The onus has been upon the staff to build relationships of trust with the clientele over time so that witness has been a natural progression.

(iii) Getting the necessary finance for a project such as this can be a problem. There are several sources of funds.

local churches and Christians are usually willing to give to a combined project

charitable trusts may be willing to help. You will need to put a very strong case, however, as there is a tremendous call upon most trusts. A directory of trusts can be obtained from reference libraries. Local firms may be willing to give financially to a worthwhile project, or they may help with materials

statutory help through urban aid grants and various other grants are often changing and being added to, so it is difficult to give much more information. The local council and MSC office should have details.

(iv) The geographical location of the building is important. Some research needs to happen as to where the highest concentration of unemployed in your chosen age bracket live.

(v) Staffing the centre adequately is critical. If you are rich you could employ someone. It may be possible to work out a volunteer rota. 'Crossbar' has five staff – one full-time and the others part-time. All of them are paid by MSC under the Community Enterprise Programme (CEP). The work they do is under the control of the Derby Youth for Christ committee. It was the final decision of Youth for Christ who was appointed to the staff. It may be worth looking into this possibility.

(vi) Publicise your centre well. There are various ways of doing this. Have a card printed with the details of what's on offer on one side and a map of how to get there on the other. You can distribute these at the local dole office. Posters in local shops is another way. Make use of local press and radio – they are usually interested in these sorts of projects.

(vii) One of the spin-offs that has been discovered from this sort of work is that when it is done properly, a tremendous amount of credibility can be gained with secular bodies (e.g. social services) and with so-called 'liberal' churches.

3. Conclusion

(i) Working in evangelism with the unemployed is a long, hard process. You are working, generally speaking, amongst some of the most unmotivated people in our society. (NB This is not *always* true.)

(ii) The unemployed are reachable with good news. The best equipped people to reach them are those from the same class and in the same predicament i.e. unemployed Christians reaching unemployed non-Christians.

(iii) Long-term evangelistic strategies in which relationships can be formed will eventually produce the most fruit.

Useful addresses

Church Action with the Unemployed, PO Box 576, Aston, Birmingham, B65 QL

BYFC, Unemployment Projects, 80 Darlington Street, Wolverhampton, West Midlands, WV1 1DG

4C.6

Service personnel

Evangelism amongst service men is as old as the gospel itself. Our biblical basis for such work goes back to our Lord himself and the birth of the Church in the gentile world at Caesarea.

Matthew 8:5–13	Christ's commendation of a soldier's faith.
Matthew 27:54 Mark 15:39 Luke 23:47	In the shadow of the cross a soldier confesses his faith in Christ.
Acts 10	The Church in the gentile world is born in a soldier's home.

1. A background to the serviceman

The services are a microcosm of society in general. Men and women come together from various walks of life and are bound together in a comradeship and friendship which is very real. In the regiments and units of the services there is an *esprit de corps* such as is not common in other walks of life. These personnel train and work hard together. They give of their best for Queen, country and regiment, whether it be on the battleground, in the communications centre, the military hospital, or in the realm of athletics and sport. They have a very real sense of belonging to each other and their comradeship is such that they would on many occasions give their lives for each other.

This background must be born in mind by any who seek to work amongst them for the gospel. There is a sense in which because of their discipline und environment, they fall into a specialised category as far as evangelism is concerned.

2. The Church in the services today

The British forces are fortunate to have a full-time chaplaincy in all three services. The chaplains operation is directed by a chaplain general or chaplain in chief, while unit chaplains are appointed to most arms and units of the services.

All chaplains are ordained ministers of the various denominations both Anglican and Free Church. Any work of evangelism to be carried out amongst the men and women of the forces must be done in co-operation with the chaplains. That is why various Christian bodies in this country are found working alongside these men.

Here is a list of some of those involved:

Para-church organisations

   (i) The Soldiers' and Airmen's Scripture Readers Association (SASRA)
  (ii) Miss Daniells Soldiers' Home
 (iii) The Royal Sailors' Rests (Dame Agnes Weston's Rests)
 (iv) Mission to Military Garrisons (MMG)
  (v) Miss Sandes Soldiers' and Airmen's Homes
 (vi) The Salvation Army Red Shield Clubs
 (vii) Toc 'H' Clubs
(viii) YMCA
 (ix) YWCA
  (x) Church of England Service Institutes
 (xi) Church Army
 (xii) Methodist Church Service Centres

Serials (iii) – (xii) form what is known as the CVWW (The Council of Voluntary Welfare Workers) who in the main are engaged in running canteens and bookshops for the forces, while at the same time carrying on a spiritual ministry on their premises.

Serial (i), The Soldiers' and Airmen's Scripture Readers' Association has for 146 years been engaged in personal evangelism and in the provision of Christian fellowship for servicemen and women.

Because of the security at military bases, those who desire a ministry amongst service personnel need to be accredited agents of one of these para-church organisations recognised by the Ministry of Defence. Many opportunities do exist for men and women to work in this area. Small units nation-wide need part-time Scripture Readers, while other organisations are on the lookout for suitable personnel to work in their establishments. Miss Daniells, for example, have a strategic centre in Aldershot in the home of the British Army.

3. The Christian in the services today

With the growth in our day of the peace movement, there are many who feel that the services is not the place for Christians. I feel, however, that while respecting the views of such people, those who find themselves in the forces today as a witness for Jesus Christ have a tremendous opportunity for Christian service. Here is a mission field of Britain's youth who need Christ. The history of forces evangelism tells the story of many who thank God for the day they found Christ on board HM ships, on RAF stations, or in an army barrack room.

Because of the rank structure of the services, the Christian officer has many opportunities with his own status, while the Christian solder, airman or seaman has a similar opportunity to live and speak for Christ amongst his service comrades. While all rank fellowships are encouraged in many areas, evangelism is most effectively carried on amongst those of equal status.

4. The Christian worker in the services today

Mention has already been made of the para-church organisations recognised by the Ministry of Defence. To work as a full-time or part-time worker in the forces, one must belong to one of these. What qualifications are therefore necessary? These will vary depending on the area of work being sought, but broadly speaking, they need to be:

ex-service personnel

balanced committed believers

men and women with a deep sense of call and commitment to the services

inter-denominational in their views

willing to work alongside service chaplains who may not hold the same doctrinal positions these workers will have a gift of personal evangelism with the ability to engage individuals in a spiritual conversation which may begin on purely secular lines

like Cornelius in Acts 10:2, they will be devoted, God-fearing and prayerful.

5. In summary

(i) Service personnel are reached best by those called to witness within the profession and through the church in the services.

(ii) By full and part-time evangelists working with the para-church organisations mentioned.

(iii) Civilian Christians in garrison towns or areas of high service population can encourage service Christians by providing hospitality and fellowship. Some can gain access to camps by becoming part-time evangelists.

(iv) Evangelical churches in areas of military population should seek to build bridges between themselves and the service churches and Christian fellowship groups. Service Christians should always be encouraged to witness corporately on camp as well as part of a local church fellowship.

(v) Some methods used in forces evangelism:

man to man witness

character training sessions (official chaplaincy periods which are part of the serviceman's training)

films and video

rest and recreation rooms at special events such as military tattoos

distribution of Scriptures and gospel literature

fellowship groups on stations for corporate witness

ladies' coffee mornings and Bible study groups

good news clubs and Sunday schools for children

agents of the Soldiers' and Airmen's Scripture Readers Association are allowed the privilege of access to camps in order to proclaim the gospel to men and women where they live and work

many men from other nations work alongside our servicemen. They also are reached through the distribution of Scriptures in their own tongue.

Having read this section of the manual prayerfully, seek the Lord regarding your involvement in this strategic sphere of service for the Lord.

4C.7

Office and shop workers

Background

Office and shop workers are likely to be more literate and numerate than the average and so evangelism here tends to present fewer practical difficulties as the majority of British Christians today are found among those of above average educational achievement. This means that opportunities for co-operative evangelistic action among Christians will probably be greater among office and shop workers than among industrial workers. Moreover, office and shop workers probably find it easier to grasp the fundamentals of the gospel, at least as presented by the average Christian, and are more likely to have basic information from Sunday school and RE lessons which can be built upon in personal Christian witness. They may also have more knowledge of what is going on in the world, thus giving opportunities which in discussion can be turned towards a consideration of Christian truth. (Whether this higher standard of education and religious knowledge necessarily makes Christian conversion more likely, as distinct from Christian witness easier, is a moot point.)

On the other hand office and shop work is often demanding of the worker's whole attention, thus preventing conversation unrelated to the particular job in hand. Moreover, depending on circumstances, separate offices may give less opportunity to get to know people, particularly those of senior grades. Furthermore, in big cities, there tends to be a rigid compartmentalisation of the commuter's working and private life which can dehumanise the office *persona* to such an extent that conversation about the fundamentals of life is inhibited.

Opportunities

(i) Strong influence from the peer-group, which is part of the camaraderie of the shopfloor and which can make Christian witness and conversion so costly there, is normally much weaker in the office or store: greater individuality is permitted and therefore greater freedom for eccentric religious choices.

(ii) Separate offices give the opportunity for private conversation about religion which may simply be impossible in the industrial plant.

(iii) Lunch hours, and other less busy moments, give more opportunity for Christian witness than we are often prepared to admit.

Individual witness

(a) *Conduct*

Three basic principles of individual Christian witness need to be considered as each applies specifically in the office or shop environment. It remains essential that the Christian's life be thoroughly consistent with the Christian testimony to which he aspires – in working closely with colleagues in a department over a period of time, under pressure or not, it is impossible for the real 'you' not to become obvious, especially through conduct in unguarded moments. Without this true Christian life, witness is bound to be undermined. This implies that we must live up at least to our colleagues' expectations of how a Christian ought to live, even if they would not consider those standards as applying to themselves. Today, matters of personal ethics are bound to be very important in establishing the witness of Christian life, but there are other areas which are important and which Christians often seem to overlook:

(i) Obligations to employers in keeping the terms of our contracts of employment, e.g. observance of working hours; satisfactory standards of work; no pilfering, including misuse of photocopying machines, the telephone and stationery (even for church purposes).

(ii) Obligations to colleagues, e.g. in seeking to defend them against managers when the latter are being unfair; participation in staff welfare committees, charities and the trade union branch may be a further way of expressing this concern.

(iii) Care about professional ethics in our field of work – however badly instructed colleagues may be in ethics generally, they will probably have a pretty good idea of proper professional beheaviour in their chosen field of employment (e.g. contract, confidentiality, inducements, etc) and the Christian must ensure that he goes the second mile in such matters.

(iv) Most office and shop workers will soon become responsible for at least some staff. They will be particularly observant of the Christian's conduct as a manager, especially in matters which specifically affect their interests, e.g.

courtesy and consideration in exercising management responsibility; this need by no means conflict with firm and positive leadership

sympathetic consideration and care for staff in personal matters (requests for leave, over family events, etc) and with personal problems like bereavement and marital difficulty. This implies that the Christian must know his staff

scrupulous fairness (i.e. justice) in handling career matters such as staff reports, promotions, and disciplinary proceedings a healthy and open recognition of our own professional and personal weaknesses which make life difficult for others in the department!

(b) *Friendship*

It is of prime importance for the Christian to get to know as individuals those to whom he is seeking to witness, preferably before the process of intensive oral witness is begun. This requires systematic effort to develop *genuine* friendships, to find out what makes people tick, and to seek to assist them with any personal problems which they may have, *before* serious emphasis is placed on the gospel. Put the other way round, the maxim is 'Start by evangelising those who are already your close friends.' It is helpful to develop these friendships outside the office, e.g. by inviting the individual to your home or for a game of squash; later it may be possible to invite the person to church or to your home to a supper party to hear an evangelist or other senior Christian speak.

(c) *Proclamation*

It is not sufficient to rely on life and friendship alone as the vehicles of Christian witness. These may be necessary conditions of Christian witness but they are normally not sufficient in themselves: many Christians live admirable Christian lives in the office but have little evangelistic impact because they make no Christian *proclamation*, no concrete effort to talk to colleagues about their personal need or about Christ. The most important requirement here is the determination to find ways and means of speaking to colleagues about spiritual matters and to invite them to events which may stimulate them to start thinking about them. In the right circumstances, most people – even prim, middle-class, Home Counties' people – are quite willing to talk about these matters. Opportunities must be actively sought, however, chiefly by keeping on the lookout for references in conversation to matters of faith, conduct and life which give the chance to explain the distinctive Christian approach to such matters. To this end, it is also worth identifying oneself as a Christian in a specific external way, e.g. by wearing a Christian symbol as a badge or brooch – they provide a useful talking point. And there is no need to worry endlessly about whether the first two points above have been satisfied before faith is spoken of.

Provided that individual Christians in the office or shop recognise the priority of the Great Commission, they can do a great deal as individuals through personal witness and the use of their homes and local churches to bring the gospel to colleagues.

Corporate witness

Provided that individual Christians in the office or shop recognise the priority of the Great Commission, they can do a great deal as individuals through personal witness and the use of their homes and local churches to bring the gospel to colleagues.

Where the homes of colleagues are dispersed from the workplace and there is a compartmentalisation of work and social life, Christians in the workplace should seek to co-operate in evangelism. Here again, the problem often appears to be priority and motivation: most evangelical Christians have the aim of using Christian Unions and other groups for evangelism, but all too often these groups appear to be designed to meet the spiritual needs of Christians, to provide the spiritual food and fellowship which in principle every Christian should be receiving from the local church of which the New Testament requires him to be a member. Arguably, the primary purpose of Christian groups in the workplace should be evangelism and the immediate nurture of those converted as a result, with the object of linking converts up with a local church in their neighbourhood as soon as possible.

If the members of Christian groups in the office or shop are active in personal witness (as previously outlined) the arrangement of evangelistic meetings by the Christian group should provide a useful focus to the evangelistic work of individual members. It would be good to see more Christian groups organising such evangelistic efforts.

It may, however, prove difficult to attract colleagues to meetings in the office or shop which obviously have an overt religious purpose especially as attendance may be the subject of adverse comment by other colleagues. Examples of other mechanisms which can be used in the office or shop are:

(i) Co-operation between Christians and other social interest groups where such exist e.g.

with music societies to arrange carol and Easter concerts, and recitals of religious music at other times (at the least, the programme notes can be used for Christian proclamation); there may also be clubs for middle-brow and pop music which can be used in the same way

with drama groups to mount plays with a Christian message (e.g. those by T. S. Eliot) or readings of Christian literature; or to extend invitations to Christian drama groups to perform

with film societies, for showing of films such as *Chariots of Fire*.

with sports societies, to invite Christian sportsmen to speak (e.g. Christian members of the Tennis Club could persuade the committee to invite Gerald Williams to speak at the Annual Dinner).

(ii) Arrangement of discussion of professional matters, especially professional ethics, which have an obvious spiritual angle – colleagues will often be very ready to participate in such discussions if their views are invited.

(iii) Arrangement of meetings at which senior and respected people in the business or profession who are Christians can speak – if, for example, the company chairman or managing director is a Christian, some staff will probably turn up to hear the boss speak! Such meetings may be more effective if associated with lunch or dinner to which colleagues can be specifically invited to meet the speaker.

(iv) Co-operation with a local evangelical church to arrange lunchtime services, talks and debates by prominent Christians, the programme being well-advertised in the workplace.

(v) Persuasion of the office or shop management to appoint a local evangelical minister as chaplain to work in co-operation with the personnel and welfare services; he in turn could use Christians in the workplace as a resource to help him with his work.

These suggestions are clearly more applicable in the larger organisation. In the smaller concern, the onus will be on the individual to apply the general principles suggested earlier. The Christian with an effective testimony may in such circumstances, however, be better able to persuade the management when vacancies occur, to appoint other Christians to assist in the task.

A note on witness by sales staff to contacts in other organisations: the general points made above in respect of personal integrity obviously apply to itinerant sales staff. The special problem faced by such staff is that their contacts within the firm may be comparatively slight, while contacts with people in other organisations are much greater but usually of a fleeting kind. Here, the special character of witness bears comparison with that in colportage and doorstep evangelism. There is less opportunity to develop close personal friendships over a period of years, so a Christian needs to identify himself from the start and take the first opportunity for witness presented – despite what has been suggested above, people are sometimes more ready to open up on religious matters to a comparative stranger than to a close colleague. The wearing of a specific Christian symbol is of particular value in this profession; among other advantages it enables fellow Christians to identify each other quickly and so to encourage each other in co-operative witness all the earlier.

4C.8

The hospitalised

This term usually covers two broad categories of patient. Their spiritual needs may be the same but their situations will require different forms of 'reaching' whether by church initiatives and groups or by individiual workers.

Short-stay patients

There are the hundreds who nowadays spend only three to twelve days in a hospital bed plus a few days convalescing in day rooms or annexes. Close and repeated contact is hardly possible. Indeed, one doubts whether people never before visited or spoken to about spiritual needs should be exposed to any kind of church outreach whilst lying prone in pain, discomfort and anxiety, in drugged confusion, or great discomfort after an operation. The Hospital Chaplain is best to counsel and pray with such people. However, it is possible that a student helper or a regular church visitor, if he has won the trust of the nursing staff, could be encouraged to have a word with a suicidal patient full of guilt and hopeless misery, or some young woman upset in conscience by an intended abortion of her baby.

Once in a while the church visitor may be able to reach out caringly to someone who is longing to express sorrow and shame over 'causing so much trouble to everyone'. Anxious parents and relatives waiting outside accident and coronary wards may respond to your simple words of sympathy and hope and may even welcome a little prayer card. But beware of the children's wards where young parents may ask the same kind of difficult questions about God as you are just then asking yourself. This work needs a very special kind of church visitor who can relate the ways of God to such people's needs.

Short-term wards for eyes, skin-diseases, angina cases etc., are not suitable places for organised services or group visits. Yet it would be a godsend if someone could reach them with large-print scripture booklets, text cards of 'comfortable words', and good clear get-well cards – also the only Christian hospital magazine now available. It is a comfort to realise that even in short-stay wards a sincere open conversation and prayer time between a Christian visitor and a believer lying in one of the beds can make quite an impression on nearby patients who hear far more than they seem to.

Long-stay patients

There are many kinds of long-stay patients with an amazing variety of needs. There is no single formula for effective outreach.

(a) The mentally ill

The largest permanent population is to be found in the severely subnormal and the mentally ill sectors. Some Christians will feel led to visit them and witness to them in word and prayer, in songs and pictures. It is a heart-breaking task since so few of us know how to accept their strange approaches and peculiar forms of loving welcome or warm interest. Few of us know how to pick up faint signals from them; few of us truly believe that the Lord can carry the precious seed of the gospel along channels which the Spirit secretly prepares. Surely he who opens the eyes of the blind and unstops the ears of the deaf is also able to unlock the doors of the heart and set the prisoners free.

(b) The geriatric

Almost as large a group – indeed it is getting larger – is the geriatric, most of whom are classified medically as terminal. We prefer to look upon them as just waiting to turn the last corner on the great road to eternity. These 70–95 classes increase year by year and they are still living souls. They have fewer and fewer visitors as sons and other relatives grow old and infirm, whilst their former club, team, union branch or church and chapel forget them. How can church based evangelism or pastoral outreach meet their needs?

(i) Remember they will be in the same bedspace or chair month by month so that you can develop contact and then gospel witness slowly, caringly, wisely.

(ii) Old folk respond at length to the caring voice and the warm young hand holding theirs. Sooner or later they will tell you about their losses, their doubts, their sadder memories and adventures, then at last the very private need comes out: 'How can I stop being so bad tempered when I'm ninety-seven. Isn't it too late to change?' or 'I'd like to have the same faith as Mrs Bloggs had before she passed on.'

(iii) Please let them travel back along timeways to their own youth and their own home environment. You will then find out their spiritual roots – if they have any.

(iv) In the dayroom anything you say to a hard-of-hearing aged Christian is overheard by all the others despite competition from the TV.

(v) Be ready for rebuffs. Some old dear will say 'Go home and have your tea now' or 'Why are you speaking so long with that old Annie' or 'Leave me alone; I can't go creeping back to God now. I've always done what I pleased.'

(vi) Be ready for sudden song or chorus from an aged Christian or a flood of Psalms and verses from those who were well instructed in their youth. Join in with them.

(c) General wards

Your first problem is finding an access. It is easier in geriatric wards than in the other long-care wards such as the post stroke recovery wards, or nervous disorder cases (or special gynaecological wards). All of us will learn soon enough that we have to conform not only with a crowded timetable in each ward but with a definite hospital ethos and attitude.

(i) Become an occasional helper to the chaplains and to accept that you will be restricted by the same code as he has to observe as an employee of the Health Authority. Chaplains are rarely evangelists, not because of liberal theology but because each training manual and hospital guideline has sentences like these: 'Chaplains do not push religion at people. They are concerned with meeting the religious needs of patients and staff *who express such* needs ... Chaplains are there to listen rather than to talk ... Real listening is a healing process and a channel of God's Spirit ...' If you decide to become a chaplain's helper you must accept the same principles.

(ii) A number of Christians could be encouraged by their churches to take up auxiliary forms of hospital service such as night-orderlies, therapist helpers enabling patients to recover speech or movement; receptionist-telephonists who so often break the dreaded news and can offer the first comfort. Even the hospital hairdresser could do faithful service. All these can reach patients and relatives in their hour of need.

(iii) Join the Hospital League of Friends. Evangelicals often frown upon this because of their social and fund-raising activities, but why not take up the non-social tasks such as arranging flowers, bringing in library books and healthy magazines (some Christian ones). You can sit and knit in a ladies' day room as one keen chapel lady I know does while she gossips the gospel. You could help them write their letters or just offer to be their telephone contact. Who knows how the Lord will lead you in time to some present-day Lydia?

Whoever feels led to reach out to the hospitalised as an individual will need the three golden rules of humility:

pray before you greet them

listen carefully before you speak with them

feel your way into their lives before you address them.

(iv) Outreach by group or team work has been tried in many forms – the most common being the Christmas carol-singing, with or without the choirboys. Surprisingly little is heard as yet of churches taking the trouble to prepare taped greetings and video-recorded services from the patients' own churches. Yet this would be a wonderful opening as the patient concerned will want to share his joys with the other long-stay patients. As an alternative, one can lay on a special programme for the Hospital Radio, but this can be a patchy business in some busy wards. Citizens Band could have been used but as it has been so sadly abused that the authorities will not usually agree. Group visits could be quite a blessing and a challenge to categories such as stroke, nervous and geriatric cases – but will all intending communicators please remember that sick or weakened or aged patients cannot cope with fast tempo lyrics, rapid testimonies, and hurried talks and dialogues. Be gracious; give them time to absorb what they hear; and give it in clear simple ways. In the near future, singing groups may be removed from all wards and told to use the day rooms only. There again the choir or band must see that they have the well-loved hymns, not the latest gospel-hit or modern Scripture chorus or some raw song of appeal. Can church groups remember to convey the message not through a separate address but through well thought out comments between each hymn, whether chosen by some patients or in some cases chosen for patients.

(v) It may seem strange that one of the most effective ways to reach long-stay patients is for the pastor or church visitor to encourage Christian patients to start witnessing and to show a caring attitude. My allies now include a 92 year-old ex primary leader who shares her 'Words of Comfort' or her 'Confidence' booklets with new patients; a 64 year-old man who offers to pray alongside any man going for operation; a dear spinster who when wakeful with pain would speak of God's mercies to other patients and to her night nurse. The Lord can use his children and servants in fruitful ways, but our task is to encourage them, provide them with booklets etc., and, above all, pray with them – for those prayers will be heard. The church leader's visit could be creative as well as comforting.

The message

One question remains – what gospel are we meant to reach the hospitalised with? Is it the gospel of sin, guilt, death and judgement, or do we show forth the God who is willing and able through Jesus Christ our only Saviour, to enter their lives at any moment – soon or late? Tell them that the Lord will enter in to guide the puzzled, lift up the downcast, heal the bruised, steady the confused, fill the long nights with his presence. Above all, he comes in mercy to answer prayers, to open a way back from the darkest paths, to deliver and restore, to forgive, to grant a last 'sure and certain hope' to those who humbly trust. These words lack theological exactitude but at least the hospitalized can understand them and then respond to the Spirit of Christ channelled through your church and you. As you reach out to them for him will you first lift them up before the Lord in prayer? And will the church which urged you *to reach the hospitalised* be faithful in praying for them – and for you?

Useful books

Readings in Sickness (SPCK) *Visiting the Sick* (Mowbray) *Making Use of Illness* (Mowbray booklet) *Watch With The Sick* (SPCK) all by Norman Auttons

How Not To Visit The Sick, Maxwell (MMS booklets)

Role of Faith in the Process of Healing, Jackson (SCM)

Understanding Loneliness, Jackson (SCM)

Healing Gifts of the Spirit, The Healing Light Sanford Agnes (Arthur James Press)

Halfway to Heaven, Sinclair (Hodder & Stoughton)

For use in wards

Prayers of Help and Healing, Barclay (Fontana)

Prayers for the Sick, Hollings & Gullick (McGrimmon)

Words of Comfort, Scripture Gift Mission (Radcliffe House)

Confidence, Light of the World (Trinitarian Bible Society)

Bible Society Leaflets for use in hospitals

Evangelism Through Specific Projects

5A.1

Evangelistic services

The potential of evangelistic services within the local church is greater than many Christians think! We seem to have lost the habit of bringing others to church. Some churches have fallen into the deadly trap of having their meetings for 'the Saints in the morning and the Sinners in the evening' but, unfortunately, nobody has told the sinners about the arrangement so they do not turn up! But across the country, in recent years, churches of all denominations have been re-discovering the value of evangelistic services, which present in a clear, biblical and a challenging way the truth about Jesus Christ.

Often, a minister or church leader when faced with the challenge of planning evangelistic services responds with the heartfelt cry 'But I am not an evangelist'. Paul's words to the young church leader, Timothy, still hold true today, 'Do the work of an evangelist' (2 Tim. 4:5). It is the responsibility laid upon all called to teach, lead and feed the Church of God to remember the primary task of the Church is that of *mission*. The purpose of this section is to give practical ways in which evangelistic services can be planned and used to reach non-Christians.

Basic steps

(a) *Examine*

Take a long hard look at your congregation. It is worth noting approximately how many non-Christians you can regularly expect in morning and evening services. Some church leaders having undertaken such an examination have been forced to admit that they get more unbelievers in the morning than in the evening service. Accordingly, they have planned their evangelistic services for the morning congregation. An examination of the congregation needs to take into account not only how many non-Christians regularly attend but how often do casual visitors attend? What age group are they? What background do they come from?

Moving out from the church, the examination needs to take into account the local community. Does the church have an established link with members of the community? Do people come for special occasions such as Easter, Harvest, Christmas?

If the result of this examination shows that the community has no real contact with the church, then this is where bridge-building work must begin. Door-to-door visitation, a regular community letter to all the houses in your district, and stimulating Christians to get involved with their neighbours are some of the steps that perhaps need to be taken.

(b) *Evaluate*

So often in our sermons we tend to answer the questions that nobody is really asking. A good exercise for anyone seeking to communicate the gospel is to evaluate the people that we are preaching to. What is their social background? What is their intellectual ability? What are the sort of needs and problems that they are facing in their lives day by day? The gospel is, of course, a timeless, changeless message. However, if we look at the apostle Paul as a model of a communicator of the gospel, then it is obvious that he tailored his approach to the audience to which he was speaking (see Acts 17).

(c) *Educate*

If God has given to the leaders of a local church a burden for specific evangelistic services to reach those outside the kingdom of God, then that burden must be shared with people we lead. They are the bridges to the non-Christians. We need to educate Christian people to *pray* for non-Christian friends and relations.

Christians within a local church need to be educated into the habit of inviting such friends to attend services that are designed to reach them with the gospel. We would do well to undertake a serious programme of teaching and encouraging believers to get into the habit of regularly inviting their friends to services that are geared to people who are searching and are open to hearing some answers.

The opportunity for evangelistic services within the local church fall into two distinct categories:

Special occasions

As well as the major festivals of the Christian year (Christmas, Easter, Harvest etc.), churches often have a regular family service or parade service for a uniformed organisation. In addition, there are added evangelistic opportunities such as Christenings, Baptisms, Confirmations etc. Often these are occasions when non-Christians attend in large numbers. It is worth bearing this in mind when structuring not only the sermon but also the whole form of the service. In addition, remember that the offer of some free take-away literature at the end of such a service has often sown a seed in a person's life that has ultimately borne fruit in their coming to a full commitment to Christ. Take a look at your church calendar for the coming year and circle in red ink such special occasions and make them a target for the prayers of the church fellowship as well as your own preparation. Pray and plan for God to use these occasions to bring people to a realisation of all that the Lord Jesus Christ can do in their lives.

Specific series

Having undertaken an evaluation of the congregation and community, it may well be that you discover a need to plan within the church year a specific series of evangelistic services. The period of time involved can vary from a few weeks to, in some cases, a whole year of structured services with the object of clearly presenting the Christian faith.

The following guidelines are given as positive suggestions to help you in your planning.

(a) Plan carefully

If you have taken an honest look at the needs of the people that you are wanting to reach, then you should have filled up a piece of paper already with thoughts and suggestions. For example, you may wish to take, as a series of services, questions that non-Christians often ask. You could use a title such as 'Now that's a good question!' Then week by week deal with some of the basic questions that non-Christians ask about the Christian faith. For example:

If God is a God of love why is there so much suffering?

How can I know that God exists?

Why do Christians say Jesus is the only way to God?

Is there life after death?

Is there life after birth?

Another idea for a possible series maybe to take the title 'What Jesus said about . . .' and then you could link in to various passages from the gospels that deal with issues that are very relevant for today such as Marriage, Work, Leisure, Money, Sex, Caring for Others etc. Whatever you decide after prayer and reflection, the series needs to be presented in a clear and relevant way. Avoid the 'Language of Zion'. Ask the most recent converts in the church to evaluate the outline of the series and ask if it would have helped them find Christ!

(b) Tell your people

Make your evangelistic series a target for prayer for the whole church. Encourage the members of your church to look in faith to God for great things to happen. Encourage them to pray in small groups (i.e. prayer triplets), encourage them to pray corporately – and encourage them to pray specifically for people by name. We so often underestimate the power of prayer. The best organised and professionally advertised evangelistic service is useless unless God breaks through into peoples lives.

(c) *Advertise*

There is simply no substitute for good advertising. Often Christian meetings have failed because organisers have skimped on advertising. There are many ways of approaching this. Some churches have found it valuable to take space in a local paper to advertise a coming series of meetings. Another suggestion is to use an attractively produced programme card, setting out the subjects to be covered and giving a warm invitation for people to attend the series. But the best advertising in the world will not get bottoms on pews! *Any* publicity must be backed by personal contact and real interest from members of the fellowship.

(d) *Follow-up groups*

A special series of evangelistic services often produces a group of people who, although they have not yet made a definite Christian commitment, are interested enough to attend a follow-up group. It is worth thinking about the possibility of creating a weekly group linked to the special series of services. This could provide an opportunity for people to ask questions informally. One church has come up with a unique title for their follow-up group 'Agnostics Anonymous'! Such a group needs to have at the leadership level people competent not only to answer searching questions but also able to give care and friendship to people seeking to know more. It would be valuable if the minister, or person responsible for speaking during the special series of meetings, was put on the spot in this group to answer questions arising from his messages. It is not as comfortable as being within the security of the pulpit, but it is a lot more biblical! Most of us had queries that needed answers before our conversion, and such a group provides the opportunity for relationships to grow and such questions to be raised.

(e) *Calling for commitment*

The subject of appeals is one with a history of controversy in the Church. Whether you take the view that it is right to call people to some form of public commitment – or if you feel that such a practise is unhelpful – we must all agree that *the* appeal of the gospel is for people to respond to Jesus Christ in repentance and faith. In a special series of evangelistic services it is important to explain to non-Christians attending how they can receive further help or answers to their questions. This may take the form of handing in a card at the end of the service asking for a visit from a member of the church or, alternatively, it may be an invitation to join a follow-up group as described above.

Some churches have successfully used an envelope system. Early in the service an announcement is made that any one wishing to think through further the question of commitment to Christ may ask, at the conclusion of the service, for a special envelope. The envelope contains items such as a

John's Gospel and a *Journey Into Life* plus a letter from the minister explaining the implications of committing one's life to Christ. Someone wishing to think over things at a deeper level can take the envelope home with them and, as the letter suggests, telephone the minister or church contact within that week to arrange an appointment for a visit. At the conclusion of the message, the attention of the congregation is once again drawn to these follow-up envelopes and people are invited to ask for one as they leave. It has been found advisable to make a note of the names of those asking for an envelope, so that some follow-up can be initiated by the church if the contact does not respond within a week.

This may seem extremely clinical, and some may object that if the Holy Spirit is doing his work we need not bother with such 'techniques'. Experience shows that people who are seeking to know God do not always ask the right questions in the way that we expect them to! As well as proclaiming the gospel we need to make sure that we are available to *explain* the gospel, and to sit and talk at depth with people who want to know more.

A healthy growing church is a church engaged in the task of mission. Evangelism is not just something we are meant to 'do' as if it were some extra-special activity, but, rather, the whole church life is to be that of a witnessing community.

10 helpful hints for evangelistic services

1. Plan the whole service carefully. Include testimonies that are clear and relevant. Use hymns and songs that communicate the joy that can be found in Jesus Christ.

2. Arrange some light refreshment at the conclusion of the service as this encourages visitors to stay and mix.

3. Use the opportunity to have a bookstall with copies of the Bible and a wide selection of evangelistic books. Give a few minutes in your service to a 'Book-spot' and introduce briefly some of the titles available.

4. At some point in the service, explain in basic terms what you believe as a church. Don't give them your statement of faith. Remember, with the abundance of cults today it is a wise thing to identify yourselves and the message with historic Christianity.

5. Encourage others to share in the leading of the service.

6. Have some experienced Christians with name-badges (first names only preferably) circulating at the end of the service among visitors. Explain that such people will be happy to help with any questions that may have arisen.

7. Have warm and sensitive stewards on duty! The type of welcome a person receives can make a real difference to the way they listen to the message.

8. Beware of overkill. Keep the service to a reasonable length, and make the earlier part flow rather than stagger!

9. Provide Bibles in the pew and encourage the congregation to follow both the Scripture reading and the sermon for themselves.

10. Plan your follow-up carefully. *Before* you begin, make sure you have people willing to telephone and visit new contacts, and set up a good workable system to assist this.

Further reading

I believe in Evangelism David Watson (Hodder & Stoughton) – particularly ch. 8 'Evangelism and the Local Church'

A Guide to Effective Evangelism Through the Local Church, David Greenaway (One Step Forward Publications, High House, Walcote, Lutterworth, Leicester LE17 4JW)

5A.2

Coffee bars

In the early 1960s young people met to drink coffee, chat amongst themselves and listen to music. The lighting was subdued, the atmosphere relaxed and the dress informal. The youths loved it, the church used it, and 'coffee bar' evangelism was born.

Why?

(a) *Is it a valid method?*

Flexibility is the key to the early church's methods. They engaged in mass evangelism Acts 2:14, personal witness Acts 8:30, home meetings Acts 5:42, literature work John 20:31.

(b) *Why run a coffee bar?*

(i) All Christians can be involved. They can be waiters, waitresses, washers-up, sweepers, prayer partners, makers of coffee, decorators, car park attendants, electricians, personal workers.

(ii) Every person deserves to hear the gospel in an atmosphere in which he feels relaxed.

(iii) Effective evangelism ultimately comes down to person-to-person contact.

(iv) All that happens in a coffee bar should be geared to implementing these important principles:

to involve everyone

to make the guests feel at home

to make personal conversations possible and effective.

(a) *Where to hold it*

(i) Church or neutral hall? The latter is preferable because for most young people the church is only good at running jumble sales and whist drives.

(ii) Church halls have regulations concerning smoking, and sensitivity is needed about the volume and kind of music used. All these create unwanted tensions.

(iii) Churches are strategically located on housing estates where the people are but the social life, invariably is not. Young people migrate to those areas where there is action.

(iv) Use neutral premises. The local council will provide you with a list of independent halls for hire. Look out for empty shops, garages or supermarkets, buildings due for demolition but not about to fall down. You may be able to persuade a local cafe owner to open up in the evening and hand the running of the place over to you. You will need to negotiate terms.

(v) Go for smaller rather than larger premises. Big rooms half filled are half empty to the customer. The friendly atmosphere is lost.

(vi) Contact the neighbours. Explain what you plan to do and why. Drop in to your local cop shop and inform them about the event.

(vii) Check parking availability.

(viii) Do you have electricity and running water?

(ix) Are there adequate toilet facilities?

(x) Heating. Too hot is better than too cold. At least you can turn off what you have.

(xi) Is it hard wearing? Some wear and tear will occur. Too many big windows are a nightmare.

(b) *Decorations*

Make them bold and imaginative with the aim of creating a warm, friendly atmosphere. Coloured lights and lowered ceilings help.

(c) *Give it a name*

This fixes attention on something other than a vague coffee bar.

(d) *Background music*

Don't use live groups as background music. Try cassettes or records. Not too loud. The aim is to take the chilly edge off the room not to drown out conversation.

(e) *Refreshments*

Selling them means less waste and mess. Avoid plates of biscuits and bowls of sugar lumps on tables. They could end up as missiles.

(f) *When to run it*

(i) Once a week makes it a youth club and produces staffing problems. Vitality quickly dissipates and workers need continual motivation.

(ii) A concentrated activity lasting five to eight days is best. There is less disruption to the church programme and the discipling of converts and follow up of the 'interested' can take place during the ensuing months.

(g) *Getting people in*

(i) Tickets are best. They make the holder a privileged person and give the event credibility.

(ii) Tickets should be well designed.

(iii) Supply your workers with tickets to hand out to their school friends and work contacts. Carefully distribute some around the area in places where young people congregate. Avoid spreading the tickets around as if they were leaflets. This detracts from their value.

(iv) If you use tickets you must have a ticket collector at the door. As customers leave at the end of the evenings, give each one a ticket so they can come back another evening.

(h) *What time to start-finish*

The earlier you begin the younger your age group will be. If you want young teens fine, if not start around 8.30–9.00 p.m. End around 10.30–11.00 p.m.

(i) *Get Christians into contact with guests*

(i) If Christians are placed at every table, the visitor gets an impression that the place is full and may exit. You always look for an empty table in a restaurant! So why shouldn't he. Keep your workers heaped around a few tables and let them drift across to welcome visitors after an appropriate 'settle-down' time.

(ii) Advise workers how to introduce themselves. Something like 'Hi, my name is . . . Welcome to our coffee bar.'

(j) *Music*

(i) Arrange a platform/stage wherever possible for the group. Remember they need adequate space to play in.

(ii) Make sure the group understand what you expect from them.

(iii) A group requires:

a place in which to change and pray

an earthed power point and where its located

time to set up – 40 to 60 minutes

if they come straight from work or a long distance – something to eat and drink

realistic expenses. Not just petrol money, but something for the upkeep of equipment and support of their ministry. Fix this when booking the group – don't leave it until end of the evening.

(k) *Think about the spot*

(i) Preacher follows the group and can be introduced at start with them.

(ii) Message needs to be relevant, reasonably short, and contain a clear biblical explanation of what it means to be a Christian and how to become one.

(iii) If personal counselling is offered make sure there is a well marked, accessible warm room. Have in it all the literature your counsellors will need.

(iv) Use the message to encourage Christians to re-stimulate their table conversations by asking, 'What do you think about that statement on forgiveness?'

(v) Further response to the talk can be gathered by inviting questions from the floor. Offering pencils and paper for written questions plus the facility of a cassette recorder for spoken questions.

(vi) Films and film strips should be used carefully.

(vii) The same speaker each evening gives continuity.

(viii) Testimonies of local Christian youth will add impact.

(l) *Training*

Untrained helpers are a liability. Run a training course that people have to attend in order to work on the team. Four to six sessions covering personal witness; spiritual fitness; answering questions; starting conversations; leading people to Christ will help.

(m) *Prayer*

(i) When a worker reaches the conclusion of his conversation he can go into the prayer room and wrap it all up in prayer.

(ii) Older Christians and surplus workers can exercise a supportive role in prayer.

(iii) Keep the prayer team well informed of the needs in the coffee bar. Specific prayer brings specific results.

Who?

The quality of your workers will make a bigger impact than the excellence of the venue. Better to have a team of spiritually alive Christians in a poor hall than spiritual pygmies in a magnificently organised place.

5A.3

Supper and luncheon clubs

Scattered liberally through the gospels are accounts of Jesus enjoying the company of friends over a meal. When Matthew wanted to introduce his new friend to his fellow tax gatherers he invited them to a meal, and it is concerning this occasion that Jesus said to the pharisees and teachers of law, 'It is not the healthy who need a doctor but the sick. I have not come to call the righteous but sinners to repentence (Luke 5:31–2).

Our country has many classes, cultures and characteristics, but these are all drawn together in one common physical need: eating and drinking. Jesus recognised these as vital times for evangelism. If we are to reach people where they are we must use these times, when our friends and neighbours are most relaxed and receptive, to introduce Jesus to them. Our methods must be flexible catering for the varying needs of different areas, but with the same Jesus to introduce, people can be reached from the urban poor to the affluent, in twos or threes or in hundreds, in homes, halls, hotels or restaurants.

The following guidelines will help in the setting up of supper and luncheon clubs.

Prayer and preparation

Prayer is a priority in all we do. Thus it is assumed that a small group of concerned individuals will form the primary planning group. These will engage in:

(i) Individual prayer leading to:

(ii) Collective prayer resulting in:

(iii) The small planning group giving guidance to:

(iv) The larger working group of hosts and hostesses.

(v) Plan a suitable programme for your area with sufficient time between events for:

(vi) Two prayer and preparation meetings, when:

previous events are reviewed

tickets discussed

requests shared and prayed for.

(vii) Print clear programmes for invited guests with topical titles and clear details of date, time, venue and speaker.

Hosts and hostesses

Whatever you choose to call them it is essential to have one or two people caring for a set number of guests before, during, and after each event (i.e. husband and wife for a couples' dinner, hostesses for lunches). They should be:

committed Christians with a vision to participate in the events as part of an ongoing relationship, sharing with their guests an active and meaningful faith

willing to be at the prayer and preparation meetings

willing to follow up and develop relationships between events in their homes and churches

willing and able to counsel.

Christians unable to take the responsibility of being hosts or hostesses should be encouraged to support by bringing friends and praying.

Tickets and tables

From Wimbledon to Wembley, on trains or in planes, we are a ticket orientated society. People feel secure and committed with a ticket. Tickets also greatly improve the efficient running of a supper and luncheon club, ensuring careful check on numbers, care of guests, secure finance, and a channel for basic information.

(i) Issue tickets to hosts and hostesses at the first prayer meeting, giving plenty of time for prayerful and careful distribution.

(ii) The price, date, venue, table number, and hostess name should be shown clearly on the ticket.

(iii) Hosts and hostesses commit themselves to distribute a certain number of tickets.

(iv) Money and final numbers brought to second prayer meeting.

(v) The size of tables will vary. The ideal situation is to have one hostess in charge of each table (e.g. table seating eight guests including hostess).

(vi) Tables should be numbered and the hostesses name clearly seen. A flower arrangement and menu are attractive additions.

(vii) For larger occasions a table plan aids smooth direction of guests.

(viii) Place names are an added help.

Home, hall or hotel

The venue is going to vary with each area but here are some factors to take into consideration:

(i) Have you the personnel and facilities to do your own catering (i.e. large home or church premises)?

(ii) Are you in an area where friends and neighbours are used to eating out?

(iii) Are your guests more at home on neutral ground – home, hotel or community centre?

(iv) Has your area suitable hotel or resturant facilities?

(v) Negotiate the best terms with the management regarding the price of the meal.

(vi) Check how long before the meal you may have access to the room and state whether you require the bar to be open.

When venue is established good working relationships with staff are important.

Speaker and subject

These are not essential to a supper or luncheon, but unlike the early Church we do not have Jesus visibly with us sharing a meal, so his presence can be made known through a speaker, singer or special feature, to stimulate discussion and questions during and after the meal.

(i) The planning group should meet regularly to pray for, discuss and book speakers for a programme of events.

(ii) The secretary should invite speakers in good time in a clear letter including:

> date
>
> time
>
> venue
>
> length and suggested title of talk
>
> aims and size of event.

(iii) A reminder letter should be sent two weeks before the event, repeating the details, and giving clear directions of how to reach the venue.

(iv) Overnight accommodation should be offered if the speaker is travelling from a distance.

(v) Gift for travel, time and effort should be realistic and sent before the event.

Feature, finance and follow-up

Feature

Some clubs find it helpful to use a feature – soloist, practical demonstrations, book reviews – before the meal and speaker. This helps relax guests, captures attention, and breaks the ice.

Finance

There are two main views about financing a club.

(i) The price of tickets takes into account the meal, printing, speakers expenses, postage, flowers, hire of venue etc.

(ii) The price of the ticket should only cover the meal and all other expenses are covered by God through Christian giving.

Follow-up

Have available:

(i) Free literature e.g. *Knowing God Personally*, Campus Crusade For Christ or *Journey Into Life*.

(ii) A room for counselling.

(iii) Facilities to record talk if the speaker agrees for this to be done.

(iv) Book stand.

Useful address

The Christian Lunch and Dinner Club. Mrs Helen Cooke, Umberslade, Shoreham Road, Otford, Kent TN14 5RN.

5A.4

International students

1. The situation

The United Kingdom has up to 100,000 international students. They can be found in all types of educational establishments in the public and private sectors.

Many of these students find the culture very different and not at all what they had expected. International students come to the United Kingdom from every continent, every culture and every religious background.

International students are in an alien environment and suffer from the loneliness and isolation that this brings. They need love and care.

Such love and care is not only a good idea – it is also biblical!

When an alien (stranger or international student) lives with you in your land, do not ill-treat him. The alien living with you must be treated as one of your native-born. Love him as yourself, for you were aliens in Egypt. I am the Lord your God (Lev. 19:33–4).

2. The potential

International students are often much more open to consider new ideas than they would be in their own culture. They are away from family and cultural restrains and this provides an opportunity for investigating new concepts.

This can be both positive and negative. We have the exciting role of making it positive by introducing them to Jesus Christ, both by lifestyle and words.

Many students are from countries closed to conventional missionary work – what an amazing opportunity to share the Good News.

Many international leaders once studied in the United Kingdom and many of the present students will become the people who make decisions and effect changes in their cultures.

International students need the opportunity both to give and receive. Christian international students often have much to give our churches and fellowships and it is good to really work at drawing them in. Non-christians can stimulate world knowledge, provide fascinating cultural insights and enrich our lives.

We must start with the *similarities* rather than differences and we must treat people as people. Some similarities are that all are made in the image of God, all are students and all come from families. To learn to love international students as ourselves, we must first of all identify with them.

3. The strategy

(a) Friendship

This comes both first and last. Our desire to share the Good News of Jesus Christ must arise out of this. International students will quickly see through us if our love is not genuine. How can we demonstrate friendship?

(i) By being with them.

(ii) By doing things with them – studying, sports, activities, shopping, trips etc.

(iii) By hospitality – many international students are older and miss the atmosphere of the family or the privilege of being in a home, whether of a single or married person. To see a Christian family at work can be a remarkable testimony to the power of the Good News – particularly as it is not only in the West that family relationships are not what they should be.

Christmas can be a particularly lonely time and a good opportunity for welcoming people into our homes and explaining the Good News of Jesus Christ.

(iv) Be abreast of the real situation and problems of international students with regard to fees, accommodation, language, studies, politics of their country (do not criticise) etc.

(b) *Welcoming*

For one Middle Eastern student there was six months of loneliness before being approached by a Britisher, who happened to be a member of a Christian Union. How much better if he had been met and welcomed when he first arrived in the country.

The time when most relationships are built up is in the first few weeks of a person's stay. We need to be geared up to ensure that this happens. You will need to contact the college(s) for information and to offer your services.

Here are some possible steps:

(i) See if any 'welcome campaign' is conducted in the area – if there is one, fit in with it. They are frequently run by Christian Unions and/or the British Council.

(ii) Discover the best place to meet students – normally the railway station. Permission is usually needed to do this.

(iii) Arrange for people to show the students to their accommodation; perhaps have cars available to help with luggage.

(iv) Organise activities that could help the students settle in e.g. a local tour, shopping, advice on how and where to buy, use of local transport, where to eat etc.

(v) Have an international reception to welcome students. Have a host and hostess (preferably people of some experience) show films on the UK or on the area, give an introduction to living in the town and welcome them. Food is an important part of all events.

(vi) The impetus of these activities can be kept up by occasional special activities during the rest of the year. What about a bonfire on November 5th, a Christmas reception, a Pancake party, an Easter film, a post-graduate dinner, an end-of-year evening, a weekend in the country? Show them *your* culture.

(vii) Remember

● the secret is not to organise many activities, but to organise well. (Activities would also depend on the number of students in the area and contact with them.)

● a personal invitation is worth many circulars

● be sensitive to cultural differences in food, male/female relations, and humour.

(c) *Literature*

Books explaining the Good News, and above all, the Bible itself can play a major part in helping international students come to an understanding of the significance of Jesus. It is sometimes helpful to have literature in other languages, particularly Middle Eastern ones.

4. Conclusion

Friendship with international students can be particularly exciting and rewarding.

Useful address

If you want any practical help, please contact:
UCCF, Overseas Student Centre, c/o 38 de Montfort Street, Leicester LE1 7GP (Tel. Leicester 551700).

5A.5

Men's breakfasts

A room full of fifty or sixty men, not in a bar, club, or watching a sporting event but in Christian fellowship is unusual. Men are notoriously diffident and difficult to reach. The competitive and acquisitive ethic of their working lives brings them into conflict with the teaching of Jesus. Rather than feel themselves hypocrites they leave religion to their wives and children.

We must meet men where they are and a Men's Breakfast (developed by Canon Roy Barber) not only does this but it also provides support and fellowship for Christians. Moreover, for outsiders, it provides a peer group where they will not feel exposed.

Evangelism among men is best achieved in a men's context with a men's speaker. The venue may be a church hall or a secular restaurant. The time must be early enough both to challenge and also to allow members to get away in time for work.

There will be three areas of strategy that will concern us:

1. Choice of speakers

(i) The speakers should be Christians who are able to speak with conviction from their own experience.

(ii) It is good if speakers are well known.

(iii) It is even better if speakers are able.

(a) *Their topics*

(i) It is good to have a clear evangelistic address, perhaps twice a year, designed to carry conviction and so result in commitment. Members should be made aware of these times so that they can bring their uncommitted friends.

(ii) On other occasions it will be useful to have speakers who can relate their faith to their work and life so as to give members of the fellowship a vision of how their own life may be inspired by Christian ideals.

(b) *Their recruitment*

(i) It is very important that speakers are invited in good time. Many of the best speakers have full diaries for months ahead.

(ii) It is important to keep an eye on the news and watch for Christians who sometimes most unexpectedly may appear in the public eye.

2. Organisation

(a) *The kitchen team.*

Sometimes wives come to the rescue, but a men's team at the heart of the breakfast breeds *esprit de corps*. Sixty men can be catered for at 7.00 a.m. if a team of four can be on duty by 6 a.m. A roll and butter could be served followed by bacon and sausage, coffee and marmalade. The leader will need to know numbers a few days early for catering purposes. Remember, 10 per cent will oversleep so do not cater for all the tickets sold!

(b) *Sales team*

Tickets should be sold for the price of the breakfast. Most tickets for the next time will be sold at the breakfast itself. Thus it is important to have one of the team collecting tickets or money on the door while another sells tickets for the next breakfast. A record should be kept of those who buy tickets and members should be encouraged to buy two to bring a friend – the most satisfactory way of promoting growth.

Notice of the breakfast should be given in good time although the push to sell tickets can be left to the last fortnight. Longer than this is counter productive.

(c) *Preparation team*

A small team of people should prepare the venue the night before so that the kitchen team can get down to business early in the morning.

(d) *Post-breakfast team*

This will usually fall to retired men who do not have to get off to work early. Their endeavours will allow the breakfast team to come in and listen to the speaker, knowing that the subsequent washing-up and clearing away of tables is being looked after.

(e) *Prayer*

The pre-breakfast prayer group can meet just as effectively the previous Sunday evening after church as at 5.00 a.m. on the day, or on the evening of the night before.'

3. The meal itself

(a) *Punctuality*

If men are to come regularly they must be able to trust the organisers to let them be away on the dot. Thus it is important that the Chairman (be he lay or clerical) sits down with the speaker promptly. Grace is said and initial notices given out, members and their friends are welcomed, and details of the next breakfast are announced, with a word of thanks to those who have got everything ready.

The speaker will have been given the pattern of the occasion and told that he will have twenty minutes to use as he likes.

By 7.30 a.m. the meal should be almost through and the Chairman can then rise and introduce the speaker. Some, particularly politicians and Trade Union officials, will talk for seven minutes and then ask for questions. Others, particularly clergy, will speak for twenty minutes and then sit down promptly. At five minutes to eight the speaker should be finished and the Chairman is able to thank him (and the kitchen team), close in prayer and wish the men a good day as the rush for the door begins.

(b) *And the follow-up*

A good speaker will have provided enough material for members to find talking points during the day at work. An evangelistic speaker will stand by the door as the members stream out to allow men who want a word to speak briefly with him.

Finally, the Chairman will write to the speaker to thank him, enclosing his expenses.

Thus the breakfast will have done its work, and as a spin-off will have given encouragement to members and congregation alike.

5A.6

Local church mission

When Jesus Christ first mentioned the Church, it was not in connection with baptism, communion or church discipline and organisation; Jesus spoke about *power*. The people of God are to be powerful people! 'On this rock

I will build my church, and the gates of hell will not prove stronger than it' (Matt. 16:18).

The teaching is clear; when the Church of Jesus marches forward in his power, then the evil one has no protection. The word of the Lord to Joshua has a modern day ring. 'I will give you every place where you set your foot' (Joshua. 1:3).

So we need to mobilise the thousands of churches and fellowships that already exist in our land. The local church has enormous advantages over all other para-church organisations when it comes to the task of evangelism. It has a recognised area for its outreach; it may be the whole, or a clearly defined part, of the town, one village or a cluster of villages. It already has some standing in the eyes of the community and has often been involved in outreach before.

The local church should also have the advantage of being an integrated people. The people of God have joined themselves to one another in loving fellowship; known in the area and known to one another. A local church should have an organised team. The grace gifts of God will have been recognised within the body of believers. People will have already begun to minister with the strength that God gives in the area which he has indicated.

Basic Principles

(a) Follow-up

(i) A strong argument must be made for the importance of follow-up in local church mission. In this way you avoid squandering energy on outreach projects that are totally unrelated to your ability or capacity to cope with. A village church with a membership of twenty senior citizens will probably follow-up more effectively on some other senior citizens, and maybe one or two younger couples, rather than on the gang of teenage motorcyclists who invade the village every Saturday evening. Even if a bridgehead is established by having a youth mission with a special youth speaker and his heavy rock band, it is unlikely that Mrs Brown's organ playing on Sunday will hold the lads. That is not to say that the lads shouldn't be reached, but it is the task of the larger town church where the lads live and work. Nor should any church feel that it cannot break out from the past and break new ground. The principle, however, stands firm – *plan the follow-up programme before you plan the outreach mission.*

(ii) If there is to be any genuine discipling of new believers it will involve discovering more teachers and group leaders within the church and training them to train others. In this way you avoid the danger of trying to make every new contact fit into a church's straight jacket. For example:

'If you're really keen, you must come to the prayer meeting,' But if no one has helped that new believer to talk to God, either they will adopt the jargon, which is often meaningless to them, or fail to contribute at all.

'Come to our Bible study,' must offer more than a series on 'The Minor Prophets in the Exile of Israel', particularly if no one has yet helped them to buy a Bible in readable English.

Follow-up of this calibre will involve the ministry team in fulfilling a biblical pattern of leadership; a distinctive leadership style which trains others to be, in turn, effective trainers (see Eph. 4:11–13).

(b) *Gifts*

Looking at Ephesians is a reminder that within the church there are some with the God-given gift of the evangelist. Some of these may be lay members of your local church. Their gift should be recognised and they should have opportunities to develop their skills. Both the early Church and the present day Church have been blessed with the gift of the itinerant evangelist (Acts 8:40 and 2 Tim. 4:5). Don't hesitate to call in the outside helper. Sometimes we are too near the situation ourselves to see the wood from the trees. We miss some of the opportunities and strengths which the sympathetic outsider immediately notices. *Building on your strengths must be considered a basic principle of local church mission.*

Look first at the things you are good at. If you have a number of Christians who enjoy having folk into their homes for coffee or for a meal then use these homes for evangelistic evenings. If you have members who are professionally trained caterers, who turn every church meal, with ease, into a banquet, then consider the use of dinner parties with an after dinner speaker. However, make sure that the entertaining fits into the normal expectations of your guests otherwise it could prove very embarrassing for them.

(c) *Expectation*

Another principle for a single church mission is to always do one unusual thing in every half year; one memorable happening. It could be the use of an unusual venue for a Christian event. Set at least one faith-exercising and faith-stretching target. Allow the Lord to push you out into deep water on at least a couple of occasions every year (Luke 5:4). Expect the Lord of all greatness to do great things.

Planning

The practical planning of a local church mission centres around finding five key people. These people will all be possibility thinkers; Christians with vision, drive and initiative. Under the guidance of the Holy Spirit they make the impossible become possible. Key people do not have to be extroverts but they must have the God-given ability to enthuse others into doing the preparation work to make the Lord's work possible.

(a) *Prayer person*

Someone who emphasises the priority of prayer needs to be discovered and set free from all other responsibilities. Prayer, in local church mission, is the priority and needs to be recognised as such.

Appoint someone to this position who has the 'gift' of prayer. If they, themselves, pray about all aspects of the outreach, they will know how to guide others in prayer. Ask Christians from other churches to pray for you; a church with one hundred members could enrol five hundred prayer partners from the Christian friends of its own members.

Encourage every individual to pray for the mission outreach every day. The prayer person has another vital task; to develop and inspire the corporate aspect of prayer. The New Testament speaks more about praying together than praying as individuals. So appoint someone who can inspire others to pray. Avoid a long-winded person who takes twenty minutes of a thirty minute prayer time just explaining the items for prayer! Appoint, as prayer person, someone who can also communicate through the written page, so that regular items appear in your magazine guiding the Christians in their praying. Give out as many details of answered prayer as possible, always respecting people's right to anonymity and privacy. Telephone round when there are urgent requests for prayer. Some of your widowed ladies may well be your best prayer warriors, giving time to immediate prayer for immediate needs.

Whatever else a church learns through local mission, it should certainly learn to pray. The mission outreach will focus and sharpen the church's prayer life.

(b) *Follow-up person*

Choose an optimist, a visionary, someone who is persuasive, able to convince church committees about the need for responsible change. The greatest threat to any Christian fellowship engaged in effective evangelism comes through the changes needed in long-established programmes in order to accommodate new believers. Church groups often become irrational and totally resistant to change – and their resistance results in the loss of some of the new contacts made. No one advocates change for the sake of change, but to expect a new-born Christian to attend, and immediately fit into, the church's routine programme of activities is tantamount to baby-battering!

The follow-up person must immediately take notice of the God-given gifts which the new believers are seen to possess. Though young in the faith, they are, none the less, functional members of the body of Christ. Talented men and women who are leaders in the secular world will come to know Jesus through your local church mission. Within weeks they will make rapid growth in the faith. You do not have to wait five years before giving such people a job to do.

The place of the minister, pastor or full-time Christian worker is crucial in the follow-up of local church mission. It is good if they can be released from all other routine church duties for the whole month following a time of mission. They are then able to concentrate on helping with (but not conducting as a solo performance) the follow-up programme. The main task of caring for new-born Christians is the responsibility of the many within a fellowship, not the few.

(c) *Publicity person*

However long your local church mission is planned for, the fact remains that your church members and adherents, the parents of children who come to your organisations, and the folk on and beyond the fringe of the church will not attend your meetings unless they hear about them. Key person number three is, therefore, the publicity person.

Your publicity must be good, attractive, simple, readable and it must make people want to come. Your mission must appear newsworthy. Your publicity person will have, or must develop, contacts with the local press, radio and television.

For your publicity person you need someone with boundless optimism, unlimited patience and unquenchable persistence. Appoint someone who dresses well and has a good sense of colour combination. The younger man or woman will usually produce more creative ideas. If you have a real 'expert' in this field within the church, then, obviously, use that person, but make sure they really do have the talent. Do not automatically appoint the person who works at the local printing works. Their real gift might be clerical or in administration – not publicity. Do not be afraid to use the recently converted advertising representative; that's why God sent him to you.

Whatever you considered to be a reasonable amount to spend on publicity should be doubled. This will enable the publicity to be attractive enough for your Christians to want to give it away and for the non-Christians to find it eye-catching enough to read. Remember, effective publicity for five days of special outreach is almost as expensive as that needed for a fifteen day programme. However, you have to take into account the stamina of the believers in fixing the length. The project should be long enough to stretch and exercise your faith and to establish the priority of evangelism in the church's life, without leaving the believers utterly exhausted and unable to care for the new converts.

(d) *Resource person*

This member of the team acts in the happy knowledge that the Lord supplies generously, through his people, when they are motivated to give for the extension of God's kingdom. There are two tasks for the resource person:

raising money for all the expenses of a mission
co-ordinating the wise use of other gifts.

You will need offers of hospitality, homes for evangelistic home meetings, cars for the taxi service, baby/granny-sitters and the stewards who can give a gentle, but warm, welcome to outsiders.

Because this job includes the wise handling of financial resources, the obvious choice is someone who finds finance figures easy to handle; people in accountancy and banking are highly eligible, *but those who are pessimistic or miserly should be disqualified*.

(e) *Co-ordinating person*

He/she covers any task which does not obviously fit into any of the other four departments. Appoint an unflappable personality; someone who can make incisive decisions. Some of the decisions may turn out to have been less than the best possible, but a delayed decision is always a wrong one.

Choose someone who can help everyone else to set realistic faith goals. A 'faith goal' is a target beyond that which you can achieve by ordinary hard work and efficient organisation, but not so unrealistic as to be beyond the faith of most church members. Appoint someone who knows how to nag effectively in order to keep everything on schedule and on target.

What will be the result of all this thought, prayer, and effort? What will there be to show for all the expenditure of time and finance? The usual result can be stated very simply. The Lord seems to entrust to a church the number of new-born spiritual babies which that church can cope with.

So, start like any couple preparing for a new addition to the family. Start with your follow-up programme. Then get involved in the exciting work of local church mission.

5A.7

Schools evangelism

Background
(a) *Schools evangelism*

Schools evangelism can often be viewed romantically but:

(i) *It is not*

a 'limelight' evangelism constantly in the Christian public's eye

an instant work. In an 'instant' society immediate results are often expected but gaining credibility, trust and respect of staff and pupils can take time

for those who can't 'make it' in a job and so 'try' Christian work.

(ii) *It is*

important and strategic. An experienced schools worker/evangelist can talk to more young people in a few days than most churches would reach in a lifetime.

Most young people make their life's decisions regarding job and beliefs whilst at school and so it is vital to use the opportunities available in a responsible way.

(b) *What does the law say?*

The Education Act of 1944 states that assembly/worship is compulsory and religious education is compulsory (It is interesting that religious education is the *only* compulsory subject.)

(c) *Advantages of schools work*

(i) Where else do you get:

a ready made 'captive' audience – the largest 'mission field' in any community

no hire of halls

no providing 'bait' to attract.

(ii) You meet them on their own territory and so fulfil the *go tell* commission of Jesus not the *come listen* commission we have made.

(iii) Experienced outsiders, offering a *free* service to schools, can have a real impact because they are not 'establishment'.

(d) *The schools evangelist*

(i) This is not the work for every evangelist and it needs a certain 'breed' because it is totally demanding.

Physically. Five assemblies, forty periods, five lunchtime activities and evening events can be quite tiring!

Spiritually. This is the real 'frontline' of battle and not the cosy confines of a church.

Mentally. Having to remain fresh, alert and mentally agile is also very draining.

(ii) Not every evangelist can cope with schools:

some can only impose answers rather than debate and listen to the 'real' questions

in school we can 'teach' but not 'preach'.

(iii) The schools evangelist needs to:

understand young people and their culture

use 'language' they can understand

know why you believe what you believe and how to effectively communicate that.

Opportunities

(a) *What can we do in schools?*

One-off visits

A week's involvement/mission in the life of a school

A term at a time with a particular group(s).

(i) *Assembly*, either as a 'one off' or series. Often hard because of limited time and the prejudice of pupils to them, but an opportunity to create maximum impact quickly so:

get one point over well

don't overrun your time

stop when you're winning

do the unexpected – if it helps your point

Be informative
    factual
    interesting
    challenging on their basic ideas of God, Jesus, the Bible, etc, but *not* giving an appeal

use humour – if it's natural to you. Jesus did and it can break down barriers but it shouldn't be taken as a reliable 'thermometer' as to the success of an assembly.

(ii) *The lesson.* This is where more dialogue can happen and more effective communication take place. So, in addition to the above points on assemblies, it is important that:

lessons are well prepared. The more planning there is here the more freedom you have to change direction

expose yourself honestly to their questions and the answers you give. An outsider can often 'personalise' his answers in a way that a teacher can't

be visual – chalk pictures, films, filmstrips, objects, flashcards, questionnaires, sketches, pupil involvement, music, etc, all help. What they 'see' helps in remembering what they 'hear'.

(iii) *The Christian Union.* Alongside the assembly this is a way that a school may often 'test' your worth for involvement in lessons. Obviously there is more freedom in what you say in a CU because the pupils are there voluntarily.

(b) Worker/staff/pupil relationship

A fine art!

(i) *The teacher.* You become the 'authority' figure with the pupils and yet it needs to be relaxed authority where the pupils know their limits. Some teachers stay, others leave. You can encourage either depending on your confidence and relationship with the teacher. But remember he/she legally has the right to stay.

(ii) *The pupil.*

be unshockable! Double meanings will be 'read' into what you say given the chance

be sincere and friendly – sometimes first name terms can help

encourage dialogue and involvement

learn how to ask 'open' questions – not just requiring 'yes' or 'no' answers

what you wear and how you conduct yourself is important, so:

be yourself, but

don't allow pupils to resent you by being too casual and

don't let teachers resent you by undermining their standards in the school.

(c) Creating the contacts

(i) Prayer – the basic requirement. Schools have been opened up through consistent prayer.

(ii) Work through any contacts you have from the headmaster downwards. If no contacts exist then:

write a brief letter of introduction informing him you'll be in touch

telephone later for an appointment

visit the head and/or staff and state clearly what you can offer in a wise, sensitive and honest way. Remember they'll be suspicious

make it clear there's *no charge* to the school

be courteous and write immediately after any contact regardless of the outcome.

(d) Schools missions

(i) This is where a 'self contained' week's involvement in a school(s), under a special theme, can become a mission linked into a local church(es) which can:

pray for the week

be a base for coffee bars, concerts, films

even help in financing the week.

(ii) A mission can have its own lunchtime activities.

Final thought
You may be the only 'face' many young people will be able to give to Christianity!

5A.8

Films

If you are going to use films in evangelism effectively there are some very basic factors to be considered and questions asked.

1. The audience

Exactly who am I wanting to reach when I show a particular film? It is not sufficient to assume that every film available with a Christian message is suitable for anyone we can get into the hall.

So, as a priority, you need to decide who you want to influence most when you show the film. Do you want to challenge people who are totally ignorant of the Christian faith or entertain Christians?

2. The venue

The best place to show a film of course is a cinema. With secular cinema audiences on the decline cinemas can often be rented at realistic prices from the large entertainment companies that own them. However, this may not always be possible as many smaller towns no longer have public cinemas.

To use a public cinema will probably mean that you will need a 35mm print of the film you wish to use. The majority of Christian films available for hire in Britain are issued in 16mm only so your choice of film will be considerably restricted.

In an age of technical excellence people are quick to criticise when they find it difficult to understand the speech from a film, blaming the film itself, the projector, or more frequently the projectionist. All three have been known to be at fault on more than one occasion, but in the majority of cases the problem lies with the acoustics of the building.

Generally speaking, a long rectangular shaped hall with little or no balcony, walls and windows covered with thick curtains, well carpeted and filled with people, provides the best acoustics for showing a film.

If you are genuinely wanting to reach non-church going people, maybe you will have to avoid church premises altogether and go to suitable premises that are non-threatening.

I have seen a whole ministry of evangelism develop in prisons over the last fifteen years as a result of initial visits to show films with a Christian message. Don't forget that films can be shown with great effect and few acoustic problems in the open air. One of the largest film audiences I have ever had was one hot summer's evening for an open air show with the screen erected on a seaside bandstand.

3. The film

Generally speaking films that can be used in evangelism can be placed in one or more of four different categories.

(a) Feature films

This type of film has the widest audience appeal and can be used very effectively with people with no church background. Many of them are of suitable technical quality and have a good enough story to warrant the hire of a cinema or large public auditorium for areawide impact. They can also be used with great effect in a small hall or even a home meeting.

(b) Documentaries

Documentary films have many uses in excess of their primary purpose of providing information. When used thoughtfully they can be valuable tools for evangelism and effective discussion stimulators. The subject matter under documentation in the film can be used as a basis from which to present the gospel either directly or indirectly.

Sermon films, particularly those featuring such a gifted and well-known preacher as Billy Graham, can be used with great effect in locations which may never receive a personal visit from the evangelist himself.

(d) Discussion starters

Films of this type are usually of short duration (thirty minutes running time or less), deal with a specific issue or topic and may even be of a documentary nature. This type of film is excellent for providing a Christian perspective or viewpoint on the everyday issues and problems of life where a sermon or more direct presentation would be inappropriate.

4. The preparation

(a) *Before the day of the film show*

(i) Check that the hall has adequate black-out facilities.

(ii) If the show is to take place after dark and you do not plan to use black-outs check for any inconveniently placed street lighting which may shine into the hall.

(iii) Check that the hall has suitable power points in which to plug your projector.

(iv) Ensure that your power lead is of sufficient length to reach from the power point to the projector.

(v) Know where all light switches are located and which switch is connected with which light.

(vi) Become well acquainted with the geography of the hall and building. Be aware of where fire exits and fire extinguishers are located and be conversant with the safety regulations for the building.

(vii) Check that you have the correct projector lens and a projector lamp of sufficient power to provide an adequate picture for the size of the hall.

(viii) Check that the screen you intend to use is large enough for the size of the hall and that it can be erected high enough to allow the film to be projected above the heads of the audience.

(ix) Check that the hall will be opened up ahead of the advertised time for commencing the show to allow you adequate time to set up the equipment.

(b) *Before the film show*

(i) Set up the screen, speakers and projection equipment well before the advertised time for commencing the film.

(ii) Ensure that the screen is the correct distance from the projector for the picture to just fill the screen, and that it is exactly at right angles to the projection beam.

(iii) Position the extension speakers above the head-level of the audience and angled facing the opposite corners of the hall.

(iv) Where possible run all cables around the wall of the hall.

(v) Always clean the projector gate before threading the film.

(vi) Check the leader on the film for torn sprocket holes before you thread the film on to the projector.

(vii) If the film is on two or more reels check to ensure that the first reel you show is in fact the first reel of the film.

(viii) After threading, run the film through the projector until just before the first picture frames appear. Do not start the performance by running the whole of the film leader through with the projector lamp on and the volume turned up. Rather, start the performance just prior to the first picture frame or the first bars of music from the soundtrack, which ever comes first, and gradually turn the volume up to the required level.

(ix) If you are using one projector and there needs to be a break in the showing while you change reels, warn your audience beforehand.

Resource material – film libraries in Great Britain

International Films
(Incorporating World Wide Pictures)
235 Shaftesbury Avenue
London WC2H 8EL
Tel. 01–836–2254

Fact and Faith films
120 The Rock
Bury
Lancs BL9 0PJ
Tel. 061–764–1538

Christian World Centre
P.O. Box 30
123 Deansgate
Manchester M60 3BX
Tel. 061–834–6060

Light and Life Films
42 Fountainhall Road
Edinburgh EH9 2LW
Tel. 031–667–1607

Evangelical Film Library
67 Linnet Drive
Chelmsford
Essex CM2 8AE
Tel. 0245–59475

Agape Films
4 Avondale Road
Hove BN3 6ER
Tel. 0273–737068

CTVC Film Library
Foundation House
Walton Road
Watford WD2 2JE
Tel. 0923–35444

5A.9

Street happenings

Declaring the good news of Jesus Christ in the marketplace can be the most exhilarating experience of evangelism. On the streets, on the beach, a public house, carparks, city squares, playgrounds and housing estates, people who would normally be too inhibited to enter a building to hear the gospel can be entertained and challenged unexpectedly – not having had time to harden their hearts on the way to a meeting. For them, the whole event has the freedom of spontaneity – something is happening in town! – they are free to stay and free to continue their shopping.

Jesus preached in the temple and in the synagogues, but the greatest part of his public ministry happened unannounced in the open air. People crowded round, off their guard and perhaps surprised by their own interest: a leper was healed, a funeral cortege interrupted by a resurrection, cripples walked, stories were told, something extraordinary occurred by the power of God and the way for the gospel was suddenly open into the hearts of the astonished onlookers. Public signs and wonders and entertaining preaching continued with unashamed energy and joy as the Christian church grew. We should pray for such miraculous crowd-pullers today, but they are difficult to plan! Effective outdoor proclamation can and must be carefully prepared. Presentation is the key and outside you get the attention you deserve.

Presentation

(a) Visual impact

Although different styles of presentation, such as soap-box preaching, open-air services with choirs, brass bands and testimonies, singing-groups and 'religious surveys' are time-honoured methods of street witness, in an age of television nothing beats visual power for holding attention. Even chaining yourself to a lamp-post (to illustrate the bonds of sin) might command greater interest than shouting your message at passers-by through a loud hailer! Something *seen* is often something remembered. While the experienced solo preacher may still have some success, he must entertain as well as harangue his audience; much better for the evangelist to be part of the colour and exuberance of the best street-theatre performances, where he could act as continuity man, linking and commenting briefly on the sketches.

(b) Music

The predominance of musak radio and myriads of buskers today tends to encourage people to drift past music on the streets. However, music accompanying well-rehearsed and vigorously performed song-and-dance routines will grab the attention and create a confident relationship with an audience at the beginning of a presentation. Anything with a dynamic beat is preferable to songs that would be more suitable to the context of worship. Dance sets the mood, makes people happy and makes the music 'watchable'.

(c) Handling crowds

No street-theatre group, even a bad one, will have an apathetic audience. In the latter case, they will have no audience at all. If they are good they can hold a large crowd for up to half an hour, moved, entertained, angered and intrigued, but never indifferent.

(i) *Gather a crowd* by announcing 'town-crier style' your performance; by wearing colourful costumes and setting up brightly painted props (boxes, a ladder, a door, whatever you need) on your chosen site. It helps to have a few normal looking friends standing around, displaying nonchalant interest, to instigate a crowd. (They should not be clutching piles of hand-outs too blatantly.) Noise, energy, a song-and-dance and then begin.

(ii) *PA* is illegal in a public place without permission. It has also the disadvantage of keeping people at a distance; you want them in close for the atmosphere and for the conversations afterwards.

(iii) *A small audience* which is attentive should not be underestimated. I can remember one performance given to three people and a corgi – two of those people were converted.

(iv) *Temperature.* You may become very warm acting, singing and preaching; your audience may become very cold watching you. Beware of winter performances.

(v) *Length.* Aim for about twenty minutes. This allows time to communicate clearly and for conversations to develop before people move off.

(vi) *An uninterrupted flow.* Once the presentation is underway, it should continue without a break. A ten-second gap, a fluffed line, an obscure subject or confused linking can all lose an audience.

Preparation

(a) Choosing a venue

Study your area and find a place where people naturally gather to relax or where there are always plenty of passers-by. Ensure that everyone will hear and see properly (a raised area, free from heavy traffic noise is best) and that your crowd won't anger traders by obscuring shopwindows or anger the police by obstructing traffic or pavements. Sometimes, playing *towards* a building, rather than against it, will help the acoustics. Always obtain permission from the local council when using public property and inform the police of your activities.

(b) Timing the performance

For tourists and holidaymakers this may not matter much, but local residents will be more inclined to stop and listen during a lunch hour or on Saturday afternoons.

(c) Selecting material

Experience will be the best judge of what works and what fails. Avoid material which is too 'wordy' or cerebral. Concentrate on creating enjoyable *characters* and let them convey the message. One point well-made is sufficient for each sketch and five minutes or under is an optimum length.

Although everything needs to be big and bold, with vivid characters and plenty of action, this doesn't preclude subtlety. Skilful mime can be very absorbing on the streets, either alone or accompanying clear narration. Remember, a good sketch is more than a sermon with arm-movements. Rehearse all sketches and links until they are tight and confident.

Performance

(a) Identify yourselves

It is wise to state clearly and regularly throughout the performance who you are and what you are doing. Most people are suspicious of the many groups and cults which button-hole them on the streets and they need reassurance. If you can, identify yourselves with a local church which people may have heard of. All crowds fluctuate, so continue this process for those who have just arrived.

(b) Entertain

The importance of our message as Christans will not necessarily command attention of itself; we must also present it in a way that is genuinely entertaining. Seriousness is not diminished by a humorous context. If people are enjoying *the way* we are saying things, then *what* we are saying will be more carefully listened to. A couple of short, funny sketches, by way of an hors d'oeuvre will pave the way for the main course.

(c) Presence

All the cast must be able to command the stage and project their voices properly.

(d) A clear objective

Street-theatre can simply be a good way of advertising another event (a mission meeting or guest service where there will be a fuller explanation of the gospel). At other times it will be an immediate lead-in to personal conversation with strangers. Think carefully about the end of the show. It is always better to finish with a piece that generates a friendly atmosphere encouraging people to chat, rather than finishing with, 'God will judge your wickedness'. By all means communicate this message earlier, but end with something lighter.

(e) *Heckling*

Hecklers are best ignored if possible, unless you are adept at repartee. Even the most aggressive are usually disarmed by face-to-face conversation afterwards.

(f) *Prayer*

Intelligent prayer before a performance will give it a spiritual cutting-edge. On many occasions, I have seen open Bibles and lively conversations after an inspired street-theatre presentation.

Useful book

Time to Act, Paul Burbridge (Hodder & Stoughton)

5A.10

Visitation

Very early in its existence Christianity was recognised as a 'contagion': the Roman civil servant Pliny wrote to his superiors from Asia Minor about 112 AD complaining of the spread of the faith: 'The contagion of that superstition has penetrated not the cities only, but the villages and the country.' Our aim must be to expose the non-believer to a strong 'strain' long enough for the disease to be caught and for the person himself to become a 'carrier' and go on to infect others.

Visiting has long been used as a means of making contact with others with a view to sharing the Christian faith.

(a) *Evangelism Explosion*

This has been one of the most effective schemes in recent years. It was pioneered in the USA by James Kennedy and is now widely used in Britain. It mobilises the congregation in teams of three to undertake a carefully planned operation of systematic evangelistic visiting. It majors on an impressively thorough preparation of the teams and provides them with a clear model for leading people to faith in Christ. (More fully discussed in 5A:17 Co-operative ventures.)

(b) 'Challenge'

The *Challenge* newspaper round is a scheme that builds in a long-term contact with people. *Challenge* is a monthly tabloid newspaper designed for outreach. Full of human interest stories presented in Daily Mirror style it is eminently suitable for regular distribution in areas where there is little or no contact with the church.

(c) *Bible Society*

The Bible Society encourages all the churches in a locality to engage in a joint enterprise distributing a gospel to every home with a personal recommendation from the visitor. The provision of special covers for each locality ensures that a *Good News for* . . . campaign has local appeal and can be launched with considerable publicity. This blanket coverage of a whole town or suburb will uncover a number of worthwhile contacts.

These are three well-tried ways of making personal contact with non-believers. However, most evangelistic visiting schemes suffer two serious disadvantages:

(i) They fail to provide sufficient 'space' for contacts to be exposed to the Christian faith long enough to influence them decisively.

(ii) They require visitors to work under considerable pressure of time, which either leads to a 'failure syndrome' on their part or the temptation to get a 'result' at any cost.

Much evangelistic visiting never gets beyond enabling the visitor to make the initial contact and to uncover the spiritual need. It does not allow sufficient time to develop a relationship of trust and confidence between the visitor and the contact so that the claims of Jesus may be presented in a meaningful way.

(d) *Good News down the Street*

It was dissatisfaction with this aspect of most evangelistic visiting which led to the devising of the scheme described in *Good News down the Street* (Grove Books, 1982). If Jehovah's Witnesses and Mormons can gain access to people's homes for a course of instruction lasting weeks or even months why shouldn't the Christian church do the same? Why not offer people a series of informal discussions to take place in their own home? A session a week for six weeks would provide adequate time to build relationships between the visitors and the contact, to present the central claims of the Christian faith, to dispel the distortions and misunderstandings, to provide an atmosphere of trust and confidence in which people could be helped to take a step of faith without feeling pressured on the human level.

The question then arises, who in the congregation would be able to take part in such a scheme? People won't be falling over themselves to volunteer

– to place yourself at the mercy of complete strangers for six weeks is, after all, a daunting prospect for most church members. How can this difficulty be overcome?

(i) Provide a simple outline for each session with brief notes so that the church members have something to guide them. Not only does this give them confidence but it also has the advantage of enabling new information from the Scriptures to be fed in each week and ensures that discussion moves on towards a conclusion. The challenge to commitment can be written into the course material, thereby removing a lot of the pressure from inexperienced church members about how to negotiate the most critical aspect of the whole exercise.

(ii) Send people out in teams of three. Not only do they encourage one another but they provide a wide range of Christian experience and cultural background for contacts to relate to. If the contact is interested enough to invite a team at all, three members will be as welcome as two. If each team is involved with only one household (as is advisable) the relationships that are forged over the weeks mean that there is little difficulty linking new Christians into the fellowship of the church.

The informality of the home situation is important to the success of the scheme. People feel at ease in their own home and will readily express their true feelings. They are on their own ground and if we always make it clear that we will withdraw the team at any time, they do not feel threatened. It is important to allow people the freedom to explore those areas of life and faith which are of concern to them, while encouraging them all the time to measure their opinions against the teaching of Jesus. The team's role is not to provide 'pat' answers, but to help them discover answers for themselves by sharing with them ways in which a living faith in Jesus Christ and an understanding of his teaching can make all the difference.

The effectiveness of this approach can be measured by the fact that figures taken over a period of nine years in two very different parishes show that 70 per cent of those who invite a team into their home become Christians and go on to become active members of the church.

Resource material

Challenge Literature Fellowship Ltd, Revenue Buildings, Chapel Road, Worthing, West Sussex BN11 1BQ

Good News down the Street, from Grove Books, Bramcote, Notts NG9 3DS

5A.11

Surveys – questionnaire evangelism

I know a sales representative who makes it his business to observe people. He loves watching them and their reactions. He asks careful questions, and listens to the answers. He seeks to understand people's hopes, joys and sorrows. Not surprisingly, his sales records show that his time and effort have not been wasted.

The Church is not renowned for a similar commitment to observing and understanding her audience.

There is no doubt that we have a daunting task. Ours is a media-dominated and mobile society. Family bread-winners often work a long way from where they live. These factors have all encouraged growing social isolation. It is hard work getting to know the people in our neighbourhood. However, do we want to be effective in our communtiy evangelism? If so, we must get involved in that community and find out what the people think.

An excellent way to begin is by using a community questionnaire (see Community Religious Survey). There are several benefits:

(a) *Systematic survey*

The questionnaire can be the basis of a systematic survey of your community. The results should be tabulated and analysed. You will discover information that will help you make your church services and evangelism more relevant. A community so surveyed will respond warmly to hearing the results. *They* would like to know what their neighbours think! It is also a matter of integrity that the analysis should become public knowledge. Circulate a summary report, or better, publish it in the local paper. Write an evangelistic article to go with it!

(b) *Training*

Ordinary church members must share in the task of visiting. The average Christian runs away at the thought of initiating a spontaneous conversation on the doorstep. An erroneous view is also reinforced in his mind: that for visiting you need to have the 'gift of the gab'. The questionnaire helps the ordinary Christian *get involved*. It gives him the chance to come face to face with the views, prejudices and needs of his local community. Furthermore, through using such a formal 'tool', he will be developing his own conversational and listening skills.

Community Religious Survey

Note for Interviewer: Please circle appropriate number(s) or the number(s) which come nearest to the reply given. You may find that some questions may not have to be asked.

Inner city 1   Suburb 2   Town 3   Village 4   (5)

Male   1   Female 2   (6)

Under 18 1   19-25 2   26-35 3   36-40 4   41-60 5   Over 60 6   (7)

1 Would you say you hold any religious beliefs?

Yes 1   No 2   Unsure 3   (8)

2 Would you say you are

Christian 1   Moslem   3
Jewish   2   No religion 4
Other (please write in) _____ (9)

3 ● (IF CHRISTIAN) What denomination are you?

Church of England/Episcopal 1   Free Church   3
Roman Catholic   2   No denomination 4
                             Sect   5   (10)

4 ● (IF CHRISTIAN) How often do you go to church?

Once a week   1   Several times a year 3
Once or twice a month 2   Once a year or less   4   (11)

5 ALL. Which of the following sentences describes you best? (read them)

I definitely believe in God   1
I think I believe in God but I am not sure   2
I believe in God at times but not at others   3
I definitely do not believe in God   4   (12)

6 ALL. According to your belief, who is Jesus Christ?

Son of God/God in human form 1   A prophet   4
Just a (good) man   2   A legend/myth 5
A good teacher   3   A madman   6
Other (please write in) _____ (13)

7 ALL. What do you believe will happen to you when you die?

Don't know   1   After life (unspecific) 3
Heaven/Eternal Life 2   Cease to exist   4
Other (please write in) _____ (14)

8 ALL. In your opinion, how does a person become a Christian?

Live a good life   1   Believe in God 4
You are brought up a Christian   2   Join a church   5
Believe in Christ as personal saviour 3   Don't know   6
                                            Other   7   (15)

9 ALL. If you could know God personally, would you be interested? Yes 1   No 2   Don't Know 3   (16)

(c) *Discovering interested people*

The questionnaire helps you discover the 'ripe fruit' – people who are ready to move on in their quest for spiritual truth. The questions used in the 'example' survey are very helpful. Answers often show a clear interest which can be followed up immediately or at another visit.

(d) *Advertising a church event*

In one neighbourhood, a church was screening the film *Jesus*. They designed a questionnaire which invited people's response to other productions on the life of Christ (e.g. *Godspell, Jesus Christ Superstar* and Zefferelli's *Jesus of Nazareth*. The church gained useful information and made good evangelistic contacts. They also invited most of the community to the local film showing. Of 800 people who eventually attended the film, over half were non-Christians.

Practical details

It is a simple, but important, matter to prepare for questionnaire visiting in the neighbourhood. All the usual rules for house-to-house visiting should be observed.

a pre-visit letter from the church is essential

streets should be carefully assigned to church members working in pairs

an adequate filing system should be maintained to avoid duplication and other mistakes

visiting church members should be properly briefed. They should be encouraged to live out on the doorstep those hallmarks of Jesus Christ's ministry: grace and truth.

The introduction

Visitors should *know* their introduction.

Example

'Excuse me. My friend and I are from .... church. You should have received a letter from the church about our visit. We are trying to learn what people in the neighbourhood think and feel about God. If this is a convenient moment, would *you* help us by giving *your* answers to nine questions? ... We would be happy afterwards to try and answer any questions you may have for us.

Conducting the interview

Questions on the sample shown should be asked just as they are written. Answers given should be accepted without critical comment. At the end of the questionnaire, visitors should express their appreciation and invite any questions from the householder. This is an act of courtesy before the visitor takes his leave. However, such an invitation allows further discussion to take place at the *householder's discretion*. There may well be an opportunity for the visitor to draw attention to one of the answers given on the questionnaire. There may be the chance to share part of his own story of what Christ means to him. Interest may be such that he can briefly explain the gospel message. There are several outlines available in Christian bookshops which are ideal for this purpose.

Some will be quick to condemn such an open-ended approach. However, it is not really open-ended. The visitor finishes the questionnaire and invites any questions from the householder.

Normally, he would leave after expressing his appreciation for the valuable time given. He wants, however, to be available. If the householder is clearly interested, it would be perfectly appropriate, sensitively, to continue the conversation. Moreover, the visitor is a Christian, not 'like a horse or a mule, without understanding, which must be curbed with bit and bridle' (Ps. 32:9). He is not doing a commercial survey; he is getting involved, being a friend, learning about his neighbourhood, and seeking to be a fitting representative of Christ.

Useful address

Copies of the Community Religion Survey can be obtained from Campus Crusade for Christ, 103 Friar Street, Reading, RG1 1EP. Permission to reproduce the questionnaire should be obtained from Campus Crusade for Christ.

5A.12

Small group pre-evangelism

Carol started her path to Christian discipleship through a pre-evangelistic post-natal support group! Ken, not being noticeably in need of post-natal support, found his way into Christian fellowship by means of a 'Getting to know you' evening. The common factor here is that the local church began their ministry towards them before a detailed presentation of the gospel message was made. Carol and Ken were under no pressure to respond immediately to Christ. Consequently, they were able to feel that the local Christians cared for them as people first, rather than just as souls to be won. This gave them time to consider the situation, one thing led to another, and within a few months both had given their lives to Christ.

Principles behind pre-evangelism

Two main reasons spring to mind suggesting the need for pre-evangelism:
(a) evangelism is more than words (b) people are generally further back in
their understanding of the Christian faith than we give credit for.

(a) *Evangelism is more than words*

This insight stems from taking the incarnation of God in Christ seriously.
When God wanted to reveal himself to mankind, he did not do so through
a philosophical treatise. The Word became flesh, God became man. Before
he opened his mouth to speak, Jesus stood where we stand tempted, human
and vulnerable. The role of pre-evangelistic projects within a church
programme is therefore partly a silent witness to the nature and character
of God.

(b) *Limited understanding of Christianity*

'The Whole Story' is an attractive title for a series of evangelistic presentations, but there are many who are not ready for so much at one sitting.
Actually, it can be a tremendous relief to realise the place of pre-evangelism.
A nervous young Christian standing on the door step during an evangelistic
visiting programme will be relieved to realise that he may be used of God,
probably not in bringing someone to Christ in one fell swoop, but in helping
that individual several stages on towards faith. To be honest, most of us
moved step by step towards our response of commitment. Perhaps from
antagonism to indifference first, then from an indifference about Christian
things to a vague interest. From there on to a specific desire to know more,
finally to an openness and readiness to face the challenge of personal faith.
Of course there are many side tracks and detours, as well as steps in-
between. It helps to know that there is some structure and pattern to it.
Pre-evangelism is all about helping people from one step to another in the
earlier phases.

Specific projects

Recognising the need and place of specific projects for small group pre-
evangelism, there are, broadly speaking, two starting points. One is the
group set up to meet an immediate pastoral need, through which friendships
may be formed, invitations issued to other events and personal witness
carried on. The other is the deliberate setting up of discussion groups for
those who wish to explore major issues, including, but not exclusively those
with Christian insight.

(a) Post-natal groups

On a large estate with many young families in their first homes, the arrival of baby number one, not to mention two and three, can be something of a traumatic event. A group of young Christian mums meet, not for Bible study and prayer, which is catered for elsewhere, but to provide a support group for others in the same predicament. Funnily enough it is a great relief to know that you are not the only parent pacing the floor with a crying child at 3.00 a.m. Through this pastorally oriented post-natal support group, Carol found some helpful friends, plus a Christian perspective on things and invitations to other more overtly evangelistic occasions.

(b) Residents association

Another church using this pastoral model set up a 'residents association' for its neighbourhood. Friendships were formed and the gospel was seen practically at work in the everyday world.

These groups are not about under-cover work, evangelism in disguise or simply a means to an end. They are in themselves a part of the good news, God with us and God for us.

(c) Getting to know you

The 'Getting to know you' idea is really quite simple and very un-threatening to those who take part. It is church rather than community based.

Ken was invited, along with his wife, to meet with four or five other couples who had all recently looked in on the local family service for one reason or another. The group was completed by two Christian couples, regular members of the congregation. The evening was held in the home of one of them and a light buffet supper provided. All very low key, relaxed and easy. Informally, all got to know one another. The evening was concluded by each of the Christians speaking briefly, introducing an aspect of Christian and local church life, practical information and personal testimony. The evening closed with an invitation to pursue the issues raised at a subsequent 'Basic Christianity' course.

Ken, along with other participants, took up the invitation to meet weekly on six occasions to explore the Christian faith. The following Basic Christianity course enabled participants to talk together about their own doubts, questions, hopes and ambitions. Ken, after asking some astute questions, became a Christian early on in the course. Now, almost two years later, every participant in that group fulfils some important ministry within the life of the local church.

(d) Agnostics Anonymous

This is another way into pre-evangelistic work, more suitable perhaps for those who do not yet own up to a very deep personal interest in the claims of Christ. Unlike our alcoholic counterparts, we don't believe that only those who are sufferers can help towards a solution! There is a Christian input on such topics as war and peace, or life after death.

Once the concept of specific projects for small group pre-evangelism is accepted as valid, then the opportunities and possibilities are endless. There are probably as many different approaches as there are varieties in the needs and experiences of our local communities. Certainly there are young mums who need support, and agnostics who ought not to remain anonymous.

5A.13

Holiday clubs

Thinking 'holiday club'

For several years holiday clubs have been a bright spot in the spectrum of children's evangelism. They are no holiday for the leaders of course! Club work is time consuming, physically demanding, and requires much thought and preparation. But they're run when children are on holiday and have time on their hands, so we can share the good news of Jesus in a relaxed atmosphere of fun, friendship and creative activities.

Making the first move

To begin, we must take a look at our resources, and ask these questions:

(a) *How much room do we have?*

Holiday club is much than a meeting, and the children will need room to move. Some of the time will be spent all together, the rest in small groups for team activities. Chairs are not essential (except for tired workers!); children will sit happily on the floor to watch and listen, and stand to do craftwork, but adequate table space *is* important – overcrowding will cause tension and frustration.

(b) *How much equipment do we have?*

Basic equipment such as piano, board and easel, possibly overhead projector and screen etc, are usually stock-in-trade.

Craftwork materials should present no problem. We can make sure of odds and ends of paper, card, material, containers and so on, though we shall probably have to buy glue and paints. It is the 'durables' that are often in short supply. Sufficient numbers of scissors, paintbrushes, pencils, staplers, etc., are vital if the children are not to become bored because they can't get on! Durables are comparatively expensive, but money spent will be a wise investment, and of course, they can be used again next year!

(c) *How many helpers do we have?*

One of the joys of holiday club is the close relationships that develop between team leaders and their children. To foster this the child/leader ratio should be as low as possible – ideally not more than six or eight children in a team. In addition, helpers will be needed for road-crossing patrol, serving drinks, running a bookstall or tuckshop etc.

If the potential number of children far exceeds our resources it will be wise (and necessary) to enrol the children before holiday club starts, and 'close' the membership when the number we can effectively cater for is reached.

What shall we do?

'Do a little and do it well' is the best maxim if we're planning our first holiday club. A one-week club, held each morning from Monday to Friday, with, perhaps, one games afternoon, and a family activity on the Saturday or Sunday, might prove ideal. When this is decided we need to plan the timetable and activities. Here are some suggestions.

(a) *The daily programme*

9.00 a.m.	Helpers meet for devotional time and last-minute preparations
9.45	Children arrive and register at their team tables
10.00	All together for worship and learning session
10.45	Break for drinks, use of toilets, etc.
11.00	Into teams for work-sheets and craft activities
12.00	All together for any notices, awards, and final prayer
12.15	Children go home. Helpers clear up and prepare for tomorrow.

(b) *The worship and learning sessions*

This is the focal point of holiday club, and, attractively led and presented, will prove really worthwhile and enjoyable. The main ingredient will be: songs, prayer time, quiz (e.g. questions on today's theme or yesterday's story), Bible reading and/or memory work, and the talk.

(c) *Work sheets and craft activities*

Worksheets are made up of puzzles, questions, colouring etc., based on the day's theme, and possibly including a 'think spot' summarising the lesson. They should take about fifteen minutes of team-time, and children can either do these individually, working at their own pace, or as a group exercise with the team leader. When completed, the sheets can be added to each child's folder, to be taken home at the end of the week.

Craftwork doesn't have to be complicated to be enjoyed! Ideas can be based on our theme, e.g. depicting Bible stories and situations or they may be quite unrelated, e.g. kite making, but equally effective in cementing friendships between leaders and children.

Topical tips

The best way to learn how to run a holiday club is to run a holiday club!

(a) *Punctuality*

That is, the *leaders'* punctuality is essential for the smooth running of the club. Helpers should be in a position *before* the children arrive so they have their full attention from the word 'go'. Punctuality is particularly important when teams move to and from their tables, and the timetable is easily eroded! Give team leaders five minutes' warning before they have to end a session, and be firm about a prompt move when the time comes.

(b) *Incentives and rewards*

Children love (and deserve) to be rewarded for *trying hard* and doing well. A simple points system with small awards given, perhaps at family service, will add greatly to the children's enthusiasm, and will enhance team games and competitions.

(c) *Leaders' prayer time*

A good relationship between workers, and a clear 'spiritual perspective' are vital if holiday club is going to reach its full potential, and yet they can easily be lost in the pressure of work.

(d) *Follow-up*

An efficient registration system will supply the name, age, address and any church connection of each club member. The final task of team leaders could be to visit the homes of their children – this will strengthen the link between many families and the local church, and for some it might prove to be a stepping-stone into the kingdom of heaven!

Further reading

Know how to run a holiday club, Gordon Pettie (Scripture Union)
Know how to tell a story, Clifford Warne (Scripture Union).
Know how to teach every child in Sunday School, (Scripture Union).

Resource Material

For holiday club publicity

Samples of suitable leaflets and posters can be obtained from:

Christian Publicity Organisation, Ivy Arch Road, Worthing, W Sussex BN14 8BU

Thrift Printing, Chapel Works, Chambercombe Road, Ilfracombe, N Devon EX34 9PQ

For visual aids and teaching materials

Scripture Union, 130 City Road, London EC1V 2NJ

Scripture Press, Chiltern Avenue, Amersham on the Hill, Bucks. HP6 5AX

Child Evangelism Fellowship, Barkers Chambers, Barkers Street, Shrewsbury, Salop SY1 1SB

5A.14

Town and city-wide

Introduction

Throughout the New Testament, the dominant picture of the spreading of the gospel is that of the royal herald. The messenger of Imperial Rome who hit the towns of the ancient world was someone whose actions and communication were so prominent that no one could be ignorant of his presence or of his message. This is the objective of town and city-wide events. Our aim is to raise the profile of the gospel so high that no one in the area will be ignorant of at least part of its content and everyone will become aware that the Church of Jesus Christ is very much alive and kicking. The strategy to obtain this objective can be stated simply: to gather under a single banner for a limited period all those who believe the orthodox Christian faith, and present the Good News to the great mass of ordinary people in the area in a language that they understand and in a cultural setting in which they feel at home. Let us look at what this will mean under four different headings: Preparation, Practicalities, Programme and Preservation.

Preparation

(a) Local planning groups

(i) *Launching the project.* Most special-event evangelism happens because a small group of people having a similar vision, form themselves into what is best described as an 'ad hoc' committee. The responsibility of this ad hoc committee is to seed the idea of the event locally by seeking the opinions and talking with local Christian leaders and ministers; also by seeking, discreetly and tactfully, the prayers of local Christians. No assumption should be made at this stage that (a) the event will definitely happen or (b) that the ad hoc committee will have anything other than a temporary existence. Having established that there is at least some desire amongst local Christian leaders for an evangelistic event that will lift the gospel before the whole town, the ad hoc committee may then contact appropriate preacher/ preachers/singers, etc, with an enquiry as to (a) their interest (b) their availability. They should then invite local clergy and Christian leaders to a convenient meeting, perhaps over breakfast, where they may meet with the principal speaker and receive an outline of the suggested event. In subsequent discussions the ad hoc group should be superseded by or absorbed into the new official committee. This new group will be responsible for the main organisational burden, setting up working groups which will be responsible for various aspects of the planning. To a large extent the character and quality of the main committee will be determined by those of the ad hoc committee preceeding it.

(i) *Relationships with the visiting team.* Just as relationships within the local committee are of paramount importance, so a warm and loving relationship with those visiting to help in the event or events is vital. We dare not ignore the fact that our Lord Jesus said: 'I pray that they may be one, so that the world may know that you have sent me.'

(iii) *Publicity and information.* This is an area in which the Church has frequently failed. Some spectacularly outstanding disasters have been directly attributable either to bad publicity or to lack of information. First, it is absolutely essential that when a large-scale event is being considered *all* local churches are kept thoroughly informed of plans. Information should be sent to them, whether or not they show initial interest.

With regard to publicity, some terrible mistakes can be avoided simply by employing the services of a skilled graphic designer. *It is not worth trying to avoid the relatively small professional fee involved by employing someone in the church who is 'interested in art'.* Ask the designer to provide you with a logo which can be used on every piece of publicity from posters down to small handbills and letterheads. Consider using large hoardings for maximum impact in the shortest possible time; nothing beats the use of enormous posters all over the city. Think carefully about approaching the local press and tell them what is going on. Especially emphasise to them any aspects that are going to be totally different from the normal church approach. Where an event is being planned especially to attract young people, it is better not to state this on the publicity, but rather to allow the flavour of the publicity itself to convey implicitly that this event is for youth.

Finally, remember that a great deal of money can be saved on publicity by putting the printing work out to tender and obtaining a number of quotations from different printers.

(iv) *Finance*. The fact must be faced from the beginning that no event that is going to attract the attention of the whole town or city is going to be easy to arrange or cheap to mount. In larger towns and cities the budget will almost certainly run into tens of thousands rather than hundreds. Wrongly presented, these figures may produce alarm and panic among the Christian population or, alternatively, feelings of outrage. Part of the finance committee's job, therefore, is a public relations exercise aimed at telling people why the money is required, how much venues cost, etc. Most important of all, it is the job of the finance group to impart to all concerned *a spiritual vision for the financial burden*. People need to understand that it is still true that 'God's work done in God's way in God's time will never lack God's supply'. We serve the Lord of all things; he is more than capable of meeting the needs. However, it is true that in Great Britain the whole subject of money in the minds of many Christians is fraught with fear.

(b) *Prayer*

Nothing is more vital than prayer. Historians of revivals and evangelism tell us that no great revival or evangelistic event ever took place without believing prayer as its foundation. My urgent plea is that not one meeting of the central planning group or of any other working group should take place without a major part of its time being spent in prayer. It is simply not good enough for the meeting to open and close with a single prayer; there should be in every gathering together of the people involved in the planning of the event an extended time of prayer. In addition, the people of God themselves must be drawn into the spiritual battle:

- encourage them to pray in twos or threes, meeting at least once a week, praying for at least twenty minutes and each member of the group to bring three names to that prayer session for whom continuing prayer will be given until they become Christians

- set up monthly prayer breakfasts and invite all local Christians to join together in believing prayer

- call the local Christian communtiy to spiritual battle in an appropriate number of half-nights of prayer; use these occasions to pray in depth for the town and for the coming event. Use large-scale maps and calendars, etc, to bring home to people the enormity of the task and the urgency of the time

- just before the event, call a whole night of prayer and use this to emphasise that just as we know the dawn will come, we are confident in our battle against the kingdom of darkness that the light of the gospel will triumph in the end.

Use the half-nights and full night of prayer as occasions of real spiritual warfare.

John Wesley said: 'God does nothing except by prayer.' Billy Graham has said: 'There are three secrets for successful evangelism: prayer, prayer and more prayer.'

(c) Witnessing

Remember that the visiting evangelist is primarily gifted to reap that which others have already sown. It is part of his function to sow good seed, but his prime task is to be a reaper in the harvest-field of God. He cannot reap where there has been no seed sown, therefore as soon as a special evangelistic event is planned, encouragement and training should be given to all local Christians to begin to witness to their friends, neighbours and relations, but the most important kind of training is 'on the job' training, the kind that can only come when an experienced person takes an inexperienced person under his wing and shows him how it is done.

(d) United church rallies

The success of any large-scale evangelism depends partly upon the confidence with which it is regarded by the Christian public. In order to boost that confidence it is a good idea to set up a series of monthly united rallies especially for Christians. They should be aimed at teaching, inspiring and building the faith of Christian people, and this teaching should be set in the context of worship that is contemporary and exciting and incorporating many different styles of music. Events of this kind will help to build a constituency of people who have grown accustomed to worshipping with each other and whose confidence in God is growing as a result of seeing him working in these preparation meetings.

(e) Ministers' retreat

Any large-scale evangelistic event which is successful in its aim to bring many new people into the kingdom of God will inevitably bring upon the ministers of the town new pressures and responsibilities. Wise planning for an evangelistic event will therefore include planning for a ministers' retreat to be held mid-week, staying away for at least one night and preferably for two nights. The schedule should avoid too many meetings and allow plenty of time for fellowship and prayer together. It is important to choose as speaker for such an occasion, a minister whom other ministers can respect because of his proven track record, who creates an atmosphere of warm, loving acceptance because of his own catholic spirit, and whose ministry can refresh the vision and spiritual life of those who hear.

(f) Preparation weekend

Inevitably, in any large-scale evangelism there are those who form an inner circle of enthusiasts. Amongst them will be committee members, stewards, choir and band members, prayer co-ordinators and general enthusiasts. It is good to get these people together over a weekend period for a time of envisioning and encouraging: if at all possible the main speaker at this weekend should be the principal speaker for the coming evangelistic event. Most people have very little confidence in movements or in organisations; the human psychology is constructed in such a way that we all have the capacity to identify with another person as leader and to feel him 'our man'.

Practicalities

(a) Length of the event

Since our already stated objective is to communicate something of the content of the gospel to every person living in the target area, only a few world-famous personalities such as Billy Graham or Cliff Richard could achieve such an effect in just one day. Our aim is to penetrate the pagan structure of our society and this will undoubtedly take time. Evangelistic events of this type are variously described as missions, campaigns, crusades and festivals, but generally their penetration timetable is similar.

During the first week, most of those responding to Christ will be from the churches and church organisations. During the second week those responding will tend to be fringe members of the church and friends of church members. During the third week an increasingly large proportion of those responding will be total outsiders with no connection with church whatever. An explanation of this is possibly the cynical feeling amongst church members that they will not invite a non-Christian friend to anything unless they have first found it to be acceptable themselves.

(b) Venue

The Lord Jesus commanded us to go into all the world and preach the gospel. He did not ask us to erect special buildings and then invite the world to come to us. Evangelism of the completely unchurched is therefore usually more effective on neutral territory: local town halls, secular youth clubs, school assembly halls, dance halls, cinemas, theatres, exhibition centres. Where these are too expensive, not available, or in the wrong location, or felt to be too predictable and therefore boring, radical alternatives can be sought. There are many abandoned warehouses, old factories and other derelict buildings, the temporary use of which can often be arranged at no cost at all. Refurbishing a building of this kind is an enormous project, generating a great deal of interest and publicity and utilising the services of an army of young and old enthusiasts. Often materials can be had free or very cheaply and special employment and training subsidies may be had from central Government. The overall effect is to put before the people of the town a concrete parable of what God can do. He regenerates the derelict and makes useful the useless. Local radio and television stations and local newspapers all love it. Finally, don't forget the novelty value, during summer months, of a large marquee.

Whatever venue you use will undoubtedly need a team of stewards whose principal concern will be the physical care of the venue and of ushers, whose job it will be to make sure that the audience is comfortably seated and strategically situated – this function is particularly important on those nights where audience numbers may be low. A word of warning here – all too often stewarding and ushering is thought of as a menial task suitable for the untalented and uncommitted. Remember that many visitors will make contact with only one Christian during the evening – the person who shows them to their seat. Give the stewards and ushers a high vision of their calling; remind them that the Psalmist said: 'I would rather be a doorkeeper in the House of God than dwell in luxury' and that Jesus said: 'I am the door.' It is a godly and Christ-like calling to be an usher at an event of this kind.

(c) Aid centre

All too often the attitude of Christians to the problems of our urbanised and secularised humanistic society seems to be: 'Serve you right, pull yourself together.' It is vital to counteract this impression, especially in our city centres. A step towards this is the setting up of an Aid Centre to operate before, during and after the evangelistic event. Wherever possible, it should be set up in the actual premises that are being used for the evangelistic event. Only mature counsellors should staff this centre and if possible it should be kept open from the early hours of the morning to late at night with a 24-hour 'phone number for emergency use. The counsellors should have immediate access to a series of telephone numbers linking them with lawyers, doctors, social workers, etc. Additionally, in some areas a centre like this can achieve a worthwhile redistribution of children's clothes, etc. Obviously the purpose is to demonstrate the concern of Jesus Christ for the whole person.

(d) Transport

Where an event is held centrally, it may be difficult for those living in outlying areas, especially on huge council estates, to make the journey. Bus timetables are not always accurate or reliable. Therefore it is worth considering providing transport to and from the venue. Coaches can be hired relatively cheaply; alternatively it may even be better to buy a second-hand vehicle and then re-sell it to a local church after the event.

Programme

(a) Staging

Whatever the style of the event, it is a fact that the audience must be able to see and hear what is going on. For this to be so it is obvious that an adequate stage must be built. It should be high enough to ensure that every member of the audience will clearly see what is taking place on stage. It should also be deep enough and wide enough to ensure that there is room for all the activities that are likely to take place upon it. Drama often requires a lot of empty space, but a band and choir will tend to fill the stage with equipment, microphones, etc. The stage area must be carefully managed in order to avoid chaos in full public view.

Whatever the nature of the event, lights will be needed on the stage if only to help direct the eyes of the audience to that area, and of course a good sound system will be necessary if the audience is to hear clearly what is going on without distortion and feedback. For any large-scale event it is well worth considering hiring professional sound and light equipment and personnel. No matter how knowledgeable, very few hi-fi enthusiasts are really capable of managing a large sound system. There are several Christian companies specialising in this field of work — it is well worth using their services.

(b) *Music*

I said earlier that our strategy was to present the gospel in a cultural context in which the unconverted and unchurched feel at home. The vast majority of ordinary people spend up to 80 per cent of their working and leisure day within the sound of popular music. It is vital therefore that music in an evangelistic event is tailored to make them feel at home. I believe firmly in the value of worship in evangelism, but I think it must be styled so as to make the unchurched feel that this is a place where they belong and this kind of singing is something they are going to enjoy. A music director should be chosen who has a wide musical interest and is prepared to train a band and choir in singing everything from traditional hymns through to modern 'gutsy' choruses. A good line-up for a band would be: piano, electronic keyboards, bass, lead guitar, rhythm guitars, drums, clarinet, saxophone, trumpet, horns, violins, etc. In other words, utilise local musical talent in order to achieve a variety of sound, a rich tapestry in which can be woven many different styles of music. However, a carefully chosen group of enthusiastic singers whose hearts are committed in love to God and to each other, can do more to generate a sense of excitement and of good news than almost anything else. It is worth bearing in mind some practical points:

the singers concerned must be willing to be converted to the kind of music about which we have been speaking

it is often wise to operate a discreet age barrier.

It is better for a choir to generate an impression of exuberant youth than of exhausted age! The whole area of music is one that is of vital importance, since few things have been used so mightily under God in evangelism as the powerful singing of his praise.

(c) Drama

In an age where there has been an unprecedented expansion of interest in church use of drama, it is worth pointing out that there is a great deal of difference between a small sketch put on at the morning service and the same sketch presented to an audience of several hundred unconverted people. A cringe factor which is almost unnoticeable in one situation will become unbearable in the other. It may therefore be worth considering using one of the professional Christian theatre companies rather than trying to upgrade the performance of locally available groups. Whatever decision you reach on this matter, the drama itself should be witty, pithy and pointed and should have real biblical content. Bear in mind that drama is much better at asking questions than answering them. It is therefore a valuable introduction to the preaching, providing it is asking the right questions. Although some have sought to make this an area of controversy, there is no doubt that the use of drama follows on a sound biblical pattern, both in the parables of Jesus and in the actions of the prophets of the Old Testament.

(d) Preaching

The first aim of evangelistic preaching is to proclaim the good news, and the best way to proclaim good news is to present that good news personified in Jesus Christ. As we present Christ to men, we convict them of sin, because the Bible says that sin is coming short of the glory of God and it is Christ himself who is the glory of God. At the same time the preaching must also present the fact that sin is the transgression of the Law. The Law of God represents his minimum demands on us and the Life of Christ represents his maximum demands. In preaching, our aim is to communicate the truth about Christ effectively by the power of the Holy Spirit so that the hearts of men and women are moved to love him, their minds convinced about him and their wills commanded by him. We must therefore present not only the benefits that Jesus offers but the demands he makes. We are asking people to join a kingdom and they cannot join a kingdom unless they kneel in obedience to its king. Jesus Christ is not a constitutional monarch; we must therefore emphasise to people that we asking them to join the Church of Jesus Christ and to be subject to him forever. Finally, remember this: there is nothing more awesome in the hand of God than a holy man. If you are a preacher, be holy, and if you are inviting a preacher to your evangelistic event, pray that he will be holy above all.

(e) The invitation

When mounting an evangelistic event it is important that those responsible for organising it should agree together about the opportunity that they will give to the hearers to respond. There are many methods that may be used:

contact your pastor later

come for discussion and dialogue in another room

pray silently where you are

fill out a card with your name and address

raise your head while other heads are bowed

come and meet me at the front while others leave

stay in your seat while others leave

stand up and stay standing

walk to the front at the end of the sermon.

Whatever the method used, some basic principles remain the same. First, never manipulate the audience – avoid emotionalism. Do not demean the gospel or degrade the King by begging and pleading. Questions such as 'Who will be the first?' 'Is there another?' give an appearance of desperation which is unworthy of messengers of the King. If you have music during the appeal, make sure that this avoids slushy sentimentalism and the 'let's sing the last verse again . . . again . . . again. . .' syndrome. If people are to be called to public commitment, make sure the call is a tough one. We are after total commitment to Christ, not just another generation of pew-warmers. Where you intend to use counsellors, avoid the world's charge that we use them to 'prime the pump' by asking them not to go forward until several enquirers have already made that public step of commitment. The gospel has its own internal power – it will draw men to Christ.

Preservation

(a) Counselling

When the gospel has been preached and an opportunity for response has been given, there is clearly a need to provide for those who have indicated response a listening ear and wise counsel. It is difficult to imagine a more crucial task than the training of those who are to undertake this particular job and unquestionably it is a training which produces great benefit for those trained. In fact it is well known that many people first truly commit themselves to Christ in the course of attending classes for training in counselling others. And yet the training of a counsellor is not just about leading someone to Christ. It is training someone to recognise the needs of the one who has responded. For those who come forward come into several categories, among them are (i) the uncommitted unbelievers; (ii) the uncommitted believers; (iii) the secretly committed believers; and (iv) rebellious believers. A good counsellor must know how to recognise these different categories and also how to recognise when he or she has hit a problem which is beyond his experience or ability to cope with. For instance, some occult problems are best left to experienced counsellors. We are in the happy position that there are some very good materials available for the training of counsellors. However, even the best materials are no substitute for a good teacher and it is important that the one doing the training of the counsellors should be experienced at what he is doing, an enthusiast for the job, one who can envision others. A good teacher using good materials can perform an invaluable task for the church by liberating hundreds of ordinary, silent Christians to become positive, powerful witnesses for Jesus Christ.

(b) Continuing care

(i) *Individual.* Each one of those coming forward should be linked with another individual if they are not already so linked. In general, most of those coming forward will have been brought by a Christian friend. However, towards the end of a mission, many will be coming whose church background is non-existent and whose friends are all non-Christians. In this situation it may well be the counsellor who must first take on the individual care of that Christian. In general this should mean visiting them at least once a week and befriending them - taking them out, inviting them round for meals, taking them ten-pin bowling as well as to the church. The individual care of the individual who responds to the gospel is absolutely vital if the integrity of the message is to be guarded and the honour of the Lord Jesus to be enhanced.

(ii) *Nurture groups.* No factor has had such a decisive influence on the development of large-scale evangelism in the last few years as the development of the concept known as nurture groups. It has been responsible for a radical improvement in the number of those who turn from a moment of decision to become lifetime disciples of Jesus Christ and servants of the local church. Those who are to lead such groups should be trained before the event in groups of no more than ten that meet weekly to study the word of God and pray together. Each member of the group covenants to pray for the other members daily, and this provides the potential nurture group leaders with the experience of what it is like to be a member of such a group. After the evangelistic event is over, each person who has indicated a response to Jesus Christ is assigned to such a group, and there, as they meet weekly, learn to study the Bible, relating it to daily life, praying over it and praying for a group of people with whom they become increasingly bound together in love and in the service of Christ. In many places church life has been greatly enhanced by making such groups a permanent part of the church programme. However, where it is felt necessary to make the nurture groups a temporary feature, they should have a life of at least three months in order to give time for the new Christian to become settled in his faith.

(iii) *Church.* Where some people have responded to Christ from right outside the church family and have no history of involvement with the church, it may well be wise not to involve them initially in much in the way of church life, but rather to allow relationships to grow at nurture group level to the point where church worship and membership becomes a natural outflow of the life of God in the convert. However, the church itself needs to be prepared for the kind of changes that will have to happen if a previously unchurched convert is going to feel at home in the body of the church itself. Take a careful look at your church, and especially its worship services. Do they make sense? Is there a good biblical reason for doing the things that you do or are you simply following custom? Don't forget that for the new convert the most important thing is his new relationship with Jesus Christ and secondly his need for relationships on the human level. Whatever helps those two processes in the local church is a benefit. Whatever does not help those two processes is directly hindering the advance of the kingdom of God. Be prepared to be radical with your church. After all, the Church of Jesus Christ is the only organisation on the face of the earth that exists for the benefit of non-members.

Resource material

In my view *Breakthrough* is the best counsellors' training kit. Available from CPAS, Falcon Court, Fleet Street, London.

5A.15

Ongoing inter-church evangelism

'I didn't know they existed.' 'I thought we were the only church really preaching the gospel.' 'They are real believers down at St John's!' Those are just three of the standard comments which can be heard after a period of inter-church evangelism. Area projects tend to leave you aware of others who do actually believe as you do.

'Lord, we saw a man driving out demons in your name, and we told him to stop, because he was not one of us.' 'Do not stop him,' Jesus said. 'No one who does a miracle in my name can in the next moment say anything bad about me, for whoever is not against us is for us.' (Mark 9:38–40).

Perhaps in that comment from the master himself there lies the principle for inter-church co-operation.

After being involved in some city-wide or national project and having discovered other believers in other churches in your area, what do you do?

It would be foolish to try and pretend that every church is the same or that co-operation in one national programme of evangelism deals with all the tensions that have existed in the past. So:

(i) Be prepared to be honest about your suspicions. They thought that you were unsound as well!

(ii) Seek to be gracious in your acceptance of another believer even if he worships in a different way to yourself.

(iii) Be generous in your commitment. On going, inter-church evangelism is only going to be worthwhile if it is backed by a generous allocation of time and finance.

(iv) Be adventurous in your programme. if your area projects turn out to be no larger than projects you could do yourself, then you clearly chose the wrong projects on which to co-operate.

Ideas

Inter-church evangelism has all the makings of a good story. If your joint venture is exciting it will make the front page. And if it does that, then one of the national daily papers might follow it up. Then you're on local radio, followed by television opportunities, and all for the glory of God.

(i) How about hiring the new concert hall, which is just being built, for a Christian activity? Or better still, make the first event ever to be held in that place a Christian happening.

(ii) Which category would you like your area group of churches to be included in, when it comes to the Guinness Book of Records? The longest hymn singing session? A continuous reading of the Bible – one Christian per chapter or one Christian per verse – in the open air, of course.

(iii) Premiere showings of the newest Christian film can be an obvious joint venture. Hire the cinema and prove to the manager that the Christians are an audience to be desired (see 5A.8 Films).

(iv) Try 'Its a Knockout' – an international version with a church team from France where one church in your area has a missionary. Or the physically safer 'Superstars' Programme.

(v) Instead of one church float in the town pageant why not a pageant all to yourself? A pageant of church life with twenty floats.

(vi) Recent years have seen a number of new Christian musicals. Inter-church evangelism can discover the depth of talent to present a professional production.

Saturation evangelism

It is possible to set a whole area talking about Christianity. It has been done before (Acts 17:6 and 19:29). It can be done again. Here is the formula.

(i) Start by defining the area to be covered. Tackle a population area of 10-15,000.

(ii) Find your full-time organiser. You will need him or her, for this is going to stir the whole city for Christ. Your co-ordinator may be able to recruit a number of volunteers, e.g. unemployed young Christians. Indeed, take the whole thing up with governmental job schemes. What does your organiser co-ordinate? Simply this, a two-week invasion of your town by 200-300 Christians. A 1:50 ratio gives a real chance of getting everyone to hear the message.

(iii) Persuade at least 50-100 local believers to take two weeks of their holiday to be part of the project.

(iv) Persuade every Christian home to provide accommodation for at least one of the Christian visitors from other towns. An extra Christian in the home motivates every home to be involved.

(v) Catering for such a huge army of Christians is a mammoth task. It is possible however to run on Bed and Breakfast and Evening Meal with just a drink and crisps at lunchtime. Or you can line up all the fish and chip shops in town to cook for you on Tuesday lunchtime. Just think of the publicity you can make out of that.

(vi) What do you do with an army of 300 Christians? Every morning you pray and have a devotional/encouragement talk about witnessing. Every lunchtime you send out teams to visit every club, every pub, every shopping area. In the afternoons you call at every home. You arrange visits to every school and every work place. If there is no opportunity to go inside, you witness at the work's gates. You do it every day. Every church board has a poster about the Jesus Time. Every Christian home has a temporary notice board in the garden – you need some unemployed carpenters for that job.

You simply occupy the area for Jesus. Every night there is a packed church listening to the message of the gospel and a packed prayer meeting running at the same time. It is possible by means of on going inter-church evangelism to get a whole area talking about Jesus. Think big and then think bigger. Do it once and then remember that it's easier to do something a second time. Do it for God's glory.

5A.16

Celebration evangelism

Celebration evangelism is simply presenting the good news of Jesus through his own praising people. The Bible includes many lovely illustrations of the power of praise to influence the unbeliever as well as blessing the believer.

Why?

(a) Defeats enemy

2 Chronicles 20:18–22 is a lovely story of a leader's obedience to a prophetic word from the Lord. The people of God didn't have to fight at all, only to sing, 'Give thanks to the Lord for his love endures for ever'. The enemy destroyed themselves as the people of God praised the Lord. So celebration evangelism sets the devil to flight.

(b) Enthrones the Lord as King

Psalm 22:3 declares that, 'the Lord is enthroned as the Holy One on the praises of his people.' Sometimes in evangelistic services people have got hold of the mistaken idea that they would be doing the Lord a favour by becoming one of his followers. Even worse has been the idea that you only have to believe and your problems are over. None of that can happen in true celebration evangelism. The Lord is lifted up on high by the praise, and people realise that repentance and faith involves a submission to the King. Isaiah had the same experience (Isa. 6). The Lord, high and lifted up, made Isaiah aware of his sinfulness.

(c) Convicts of sin

Nothing is more likely to bring conviction of sin than when a person finds himself in the middle of the Lord's praising people, realising that he cannot praise in that way because his own hands are not clean.

(d) Church growth

The Bible indicates that one of the features of the early Church's growth was celebration evangelism. Luke records this in the closing words of his gospel: 'Then the disciples worshipped and returned to Jerusalem with great joy. And they stayed continually at the temple, praising God.'

Later we are told that, 'a large number of priests became obedient to the faith' (Acts 6:7). They had been exposed to celebration evangelism. Acts 2: 46–7 tells us plainly that the early disciples continued to meet daily in their homes for fellowship and teaching and that they also met daily in the temple courts to praise God and so the Lord added to their number daily those who were being saved. The link between the daily conversions and the daily praise is not to be missed. Clearly the celebration style of meeting was in operation at the church at Corinth (1 Cor. 14:24–6). Peter also commends, or is it commands, such an approach when he writes 'declare the praises of him who called you out of darkness into light' (1 Pet. 2:9).

(e) *Sets scene for evangelism*

Celebration indicates an atmosphere of joy; there is an underlying sense of excitement. The act of celebration doesn't do the work of evangelism. That is a work which only the Holy Spirit can do. Celebration, however, sets the scene in which the Spirit can do his work.

Ingredients

The ingredients of celebration evangelism have evolved over the last few years.

(a) *Speaking*

A stating or proclamation of the good news has a part. 'How can they hear without someone preaching to them' (Rom. 10:14) still remains true. There is an element of every celebration evening which sets forth that which God has done by his grace. There is a place where the facts must be stated in understandable language. Where better, than within the context of love, in a meeting where the people of God are praising God.

(b) *Drama*

The happenings of God have always been dramatic. Some people need to be stabbed awake by some vivid presentation of the facts.

(c) *Dance, Mime and Poetry*

need to be used. Both portray moods and feelings of joy and sadness in gesture language. A language understandable to even the deaf and dumb.

(d) *Visual*

The use of film or a single photographic slide can be very effective.

(e) *Music*

The talents of a group of instruments and instrumentalists, leading the singing of the people of God is wonderful.

(f) *Prayer*

In an ideal situation all the participating people for a celebration evening are able to meet for an extended period of prayer beforehand. If they are all able to mention their possible contribution without any feeling that their 'item' must be included, then you have moved some way towards rich blessing.

The evening

Mixing the ingredients on the actual day is far to be preferred over having a 'programme'. And if, in the mixing, someone is used more than once and someone else not used at all, then both must recognise the leading of the Lord in this. Dr Paul Rees of America gave sound advice, 'Stay flexibly in touch with the Holy Spirit'. Try and do that.

Appoint a linkman/continuity person to lead the celebration through. It doesn't have to be the speaker but it does need to be someone with a recognised gift of discernment. Such a leader can sense the leading of the Lord as the ingredients of the meeting are mixed. Never be afraid to repeat an item if that is the Spirit's prompting. Every individual contributing must always aim at the best. That means rehearsals and more rehearsals. It does us all good to submit to such discipline and indeed to be open to exploring what the Lord is trying to say or wanting to say or trying to mould and modify. Celebration evangelism holds its breath waiting for the 'holy moment' – the moment when the Lord seems to move among the people. Never be afraid of silent periods; they can be powerful in a noisy world.

When it comes to an invitation or an appeal for repentance and faith at the end of such a celebration meeting it is an invitation to be involved with the people of God in acclaiming Jesus as Lord. If an invitation is given to stand as an act of surrender and welcome to the Lord Jesus, then it is possible to involve the Christians near to any who stood as a 'counselling cluster'. Nothing brings assurance more clearly than being welcomed into the family by new brothers and sisters. Celebration evangelism can be an event over several days, good publicity is expensive and it takes as much to advertise one evening as to advertise five or more. Or it can be tied in with the special Christian feast days. Celebration can become a feast day happening. So often these major opportunities for evangelism are neglected simply because they appear each year on the Church's calendar or because we gear the day for the benefit only of the believers.

It is natural to feel some hesitancy about moving out into this style of evangelism. It demands so much more effort than an ordinary evangelistic rally. It requires far more professionalism and rehearsal. It needs so much more sensitivity to one another and to the leading of the Spirit of God into an expression of praise and worship. Within that event there is a communication of love which surrounds and envelops the unbeliever. The evil one will do all that he can to prevent such a happening. There are more risks but also more remarkable results.

The exciting reaching out programme of celebration evangelism results in a surge of excitement amongst the members of the organising church or churches. This is not simply amongst the young people, although we often give our Christian teenagers too little to shout about. Why shouldn't they shout about their discovery of eternal life. It is when Christians are seen to be thrilled with what is happening that more and more non-Christians pay attention. Nothing commends the Christian faith more than the radiant faces of young and old as they truly praise God.

O give thanks to the Lord, all you His people
O give thanks to the Lord for He is good
Let us praise, let us thank, let us celebrate and dance
O give thanks to the Lord for He is good.

5A.17

Co-operative ventures

Most of us find one-to-one evangelism very demanding, and getting other people involved is often difficult. Co-operative ventures try to ease these problems by getting people to tackle the task together. Through a programme of practical training, with a strong emphasis on mutual support and encouragement, many people who would not normally get involved in evangelism are drawn into the task of sharing their faith.

Co-operative ventures are not big public events. They're much more grass roots evangelism, built on a local church or fellowship. As such, they have certain natural advantages:

contacts are built up year in and year out

the lively local fellowship gives living proof to the power of the good news to change people

follow up becomes a natural part of the local fellowship, and doesn't need a big machine to handle it

other non evangelistic gifts, released through the co-op, can be immediately channelled into the local fellowship.

If you've never been involved with a co-operative venture, here is a brief glance at two which are operating in the country at the moment.

Co-op 1. 'Breakthrough'

It's good that we have experts in evangelism, but human nature uses experts as an excuse *not* to evangelise! The cry goes up 'We can't evangelise because we don't have an expert available!'

The Breakthrough Training Kit has tried to overcome this problem by producing a course which is totally self-help in nature and content. The vision is that groups of people will take the kit and use it in whatever way they want. The principles behind it are:

(i) 'You bring your desire and enthusiasn – we'll supply the rest!' The course contains everything needed to run a training course, including overhead projector slides, and pre-recorded cassettes. Even the most inexperienced and poorly equipped group ought to be able to use it.

(ii) 'Go as far as *you* want!' The course is designed to be shaped to the needs of the users, and not vice versa. All the options are laid out in the 'span of evangelistic activity', and users decide how far they want to go. They then use the appropriate sections of the course. Breakthrough recognises that different groups have different desires, and different ability levels. This has been taken into account at the compilation of the course. There is no regular pattern of sharing, as there is in Evangelism Explosion, but there are sharing challenges, and the group is encouraged to take these on together. Breakthrough also recognises that not everyone can *remember* a gospel outline. To help overcome this, ways of using an evangelistic leaflet as a sharing tool are explained.

(iii) 'When are you free!' In the introduction to the course there are a variety of ways of running a course – evenings, weekends, Saturday mornings etc. Users are encouraged to find a time that suits them. What is suitable will differ from place to place.

(iv) 'Nine or ninety?' Breakthrough has not only faced the fact that one evangelistic leaflet cannot be suitable for all ages – it has done something about it! Evangelistic literature aimed at different ages has been produced, and a sample of each is included. Extra material can be ordered separately.

(v) 'The all-age course'. Breakthrough can be adapted to suit all ages, and part of the vision is that those who benefit from the course can, in time, train others to share Jesus as well.

Breakthrough is now being increasingly used in England in many different situations – training teenagers to share at school, training adults to share at work and at home, training people to counsel and follow up at large missions and crusades. It's freedom, flexibility and twentieth-century feel make it a co-op worth looking at for yourself.

Co-op 2. 'Evangelism Explosion'

Evangelism Explosion, (now better known as Teach and Reach) is a church based co-op. It is much more directive in its training course than Breakthrough. Members enrolling on a local Evangelism Explosion course will be committed to sixteen weeks of training, with a fairly definite pattern to it. Like Breakthrough, Evangelism Explosion seeks to help lay people take on the task of sharing Jesus. Over the years it has proved very effective. Its basic principles:

(i) Local church based courses are run over a period of sixteen weeks and it is expected that those on the course will turn up, will participate fully in the training, and will do the homework.

(ii) Each week is a mixture of classroom teaching/training, which lasts forty-five to sixty minutes, and 'on-the-job training'.

(iii) On-the-job training is what makes Evangelism Explosion so special. It is, in essence, the industrial apprentice model, transferred to evangelism. Each week, after the training, the teams each consisting of three people, go out to visit, with the intention of sharing the good news. One member of the team is experienced in this task, while the other two are learning. They learn, not only in the classroom, but by watching the more experienced team member in action. As the weeks go by, so the roles are reversed, and the 'trainees' do more and more of the sharing, but the 'trainer' is always right there, to help and encourage should things get difficult.

(iv) Follow-up is an integral part of the course, and each member is taught to handle immediate follow-up. Long term follow-up is also taken very seriously.

The sixteen-week courses keep repeating, at a rate of two(or maybe three) a year. This takes the pressure off slow learners, and gives a feeling of continuity.

Evangelism Explosion has certain advantages in its approach, which those who denegrate methods are sometimes slow to observe:

● its gospel, using the 'eternal life' approach, reaches many church people who have become innoculated to other forms of gospel presentation

● its 'eternal life' concept is very relevant to a soceity that has a very deep fear of death

Evangelism Explosion is a training tool, as well as an evangelising one. Trainees are encouraged to become team leaders after they have completed one or more training courses. So the pool of workers is constantly being enlarged.

Evangelism Explosion is a co-operative with a proven world-wide track record. There are many bright ideas in evangelism, but not many of them can claim this kind of record. This makes Evangelism Explosion worthy of closer consideration.

The Problem of Cults and Evangelism

'The Spirit says clearly,' warned the apostle Paul, 'that some people will abandon the faith in later times; they will obey lying spirits and follow the teachings of demons (1 Tim. 4:1). Peter concurred in this forecast: 'They will bring in destructive, untrue doctrines,' he agreed, 'and will deny the Master who redeemed them. . . Even so, many will follow their immoral ways; and because of what they do, others will speak evil of the way of truth' (2 Pet. 2:1–2).

No prophecy in the Bible has proved more true. All through Church history, but especially in the last century and a half, organised Christianity has been plagued by a multiplicity of fringe religious groups – some originating within the Church, others exotic imports from alien religions – each claiming to represent the real truth about God and ultimate reality. Often called 'the cults' (although the term is dangerously imprecise), they pose several problems for Christians involved in evangelism.

(i) How do we tell 'destructive, untrue doctrines' from what is simply an original slant on Christianity? How can one distinguish reality from falsehood?

(ii) How do we prevent a situation in which 'others speak evil of the way of truth? How can we distinguish our evangelistic endeavours from theirs?

(iii) If 'many will follow their immoral ways', how can we prevent infiltration? Can we stop them snatching away our young, immature converts?

(iv) What about those who 'follow the teachings of demons'? Are they irredeemably lost, or is there a means of evangelising them?

This article will suggest some brief answers to these questions. But first there is a more basic question to face: how much do we actually need to know about these groups?

How much do we need to know?

There are, of course, Christians who pride themselves on being amateur 'cult bashers'. They have a pedantic knowledge of every facet of doctrine of the Mormons, or the Jehovah's Witnesses, or the Moonies. But not everybody has the time or interest to do this; and anyway, such Christians tend not to be among the more mature or gracious members of their church.

The Bible's injunction is to 'expose the darkness *by means of the light*' (Eph. 5:11). Far more important than knowing everything about everyone – impossible, anyway, in a day of such religious pluralism as ours – is having a firm grasp of the foundations of genuine Christian faith. The mature Christian with a stable footing in biblical doctrine will not easily confuse the fake with the real (Eph. 4:13–14). Even when dealing with a cult he has never heard of before, he will be able quickly to disentangle the cobweb of ideas presented to him and extricate the main issues of truth and falsehood.

However, anyone involved in evangelism ought to know a *bit* about the main alternatives to his own message. It is only intellectually honest, after all, to study the other man's version. The amount you need to know will vary depending on your own capacity to absorb information, the extent to which you are likely to encounter cult problems in your evangelism, and the degree of interest you have in the subject. But I would personally consider an evangelist ill-equipped if he did not have a working knowledge of the basic concepts of Eastern thought (vital for understanding Hindu- and Buddhist-based groups such as Divine Light Mission, Scientology, Transcendantal Meditation) and a sound understanding of the key ideas of the most influential Christian-based groups: the Mormons, the Jehovah's Witnesses, and the Spiritualists. I would stress 'key ideas'; don't waste time in muckraking through details of Joseph Smith's plural marriages or Charles Russell's false testimony in court.

There are some New Testament passages which anyone encountering cult members should study deeply and know virtually backwards. My personal list would be Galatians 3 (law-keeping and liberty), Hebrews 1 (the status of Jesus', I John 4 (definition of a false prophet), 2 Peter 2 (marks of a corrupt teacher), Ephesians 2 (salvation by faith).

Finally, much more important than knowing all the doctrines of a group is understanding how it feels to be a member. You will not reach a cult member by impressing him with your encyclopaedic knowledge of everything he is rumoured to believe – but by relating to him as a person, seeing the world through his eyes and finding common ground from which to begin talking. Hence it may be much more rewarding to read books like Erica Heftmann's *The Dark Side of the Moonies*, or W. C. Stevenson's *Year of Doom 1975* – which give an honest account of the thoughts and feelings of ex-members. Better still, find a member and talk to him or her; and spend more time listening than talking.

How do we tell real Christianity from spurious cult teaching?

There are so many small, independent evangelical causes around – house churches, evangelistic organisations, racially distinctive churches – that it is easy to dismiss anything different from ourselves as false. But that could be throwing out the baby with the bathwater. How do we tell who is with us, and who against?

Eastern-based groups are sometimes easy to spot because of their overtly non-Christian stance (e.g. Krishna Consciousness, Bhagwar Rajreesh), but sometimes Eastern teachings can masquerade in Christian language (e.g. Christian Science, the Unity School of Christianity) or present themselves as neutral and not really religious (e.g. TM). Here the solution is to understand clearly the difference between an Eastern world-view and the Christian one.

We believe that God is a person, not an impersonal force; that life ends in death and judgement, not reincarnation; that the material world is real, not illusion; that Jesus was the unique son of God, not one of many manifestations; that man is separated from God by sin, not ignorance. Any group which will not assent to these propositions is certainly not a Christian one.

Christian-based cult groups can be spotted by asking three basic questions about their teaching.

do they accept the Bible as their source of authority – or is there some extra source? (This could be a book, such as *Divine Principle* or the 'standard works' of Mormonism; or a prophet, such as David Berg of the Family of Love)

do they accept that Jesus Christ was both fully human and fully divine?

do they believe in salvation through faith alone – or do they insist on some form of 'works' in order to secure a home in heaven?

How do we distinguish ourselves from them?

Never try to explain the difference between yourself and the cults by:

outlining the theological differences. A non-Christian man in the street isn't interested in what he sees as fine points of God talk

vilifying the cults.

There is a lot of idealism, honesty and integrity tied up in some very strange groups. Don't poke fun, retail salacious stories about the group's activities, or spread second-hand, unchecked information. What then *will* impress the man in the street that you are not like the cults?

Normality and a sense of humour – often lacking in the fever-pitch intensity of cult salesmanship. Be real, be relaxed.

Lack of interest in making money for your cause.

Local roots – the fact that your evangelistic enterprise is identified with local churches and has a stake in the community. You are not a fly-by-night spiritual 'blitz' operator.

The interdenominational nature of your message – the fact that you are not peddling a sectarian gospel, but one which the mainstream churches of the area would recognise as theirs.

How do we prevent infiltration?

2 John 10–11 is a passage often used by Christians to teach that it is somehow dangerous to allow cult members over the threshold of one's house. This is a sad misconception. The epistle is really written to a house *church*, and is warning about the dangers of accepting wandering teachers

(of whom there were hundreds in those days) into the church without careful examination.

Fair enough; few of us would invite a Mormon missionary to take our Sunday morning service. But are there other things we need to do to prevent cult teachings creeping in unobserved?

(i) We should be careful about our personal association with cult members. We will never win them without befriending them; but some groups, such as the Moonies, have exploited friendships in order to reach immature Christians via their leaders. Be careful that you do not seem to be endorsing falsehood by mingling with its exponents.

(ii) We should build doctrinal foundations into new Christians' lives as quickly as possible – not leave them to pick up what scraps of information they can haphazardly glean from a diet of Sunday sermons.

(iii) We should never, never allow anyone to counsel enquirers at the end of an evangelistic event unless we are certain of his qualifications and aptitude.

(iv) We should keep a watching brief on cult movements in the local area, and keep a file of information open on new ones as we hear of them. It can be useful to be on the mailing list of one of the specialist Christian groups involved in research on the cults.

Finally – can cult members be evangelised?

Absolutely *yes*. For far too long, the Christian Church has missed a significant mission field here! Cult members in general are idealistic people, intent on finding and serving God. Many of them realise, deep down, that they are unhappy with their religious experience so far; but they remain in the cult because they know nowhere else to go. A loving, faithful Christian witness can be the key which unlocks the prison door for them; but all too often the only Christians they encounter are fearful, suspicious and occasionally vindictive.

(i) Be gentle and loving in your approach to the cult member; he has had religion sold hard to him once already. Be sensitive to what will pain him; do not attack his leader, or his methods, unless you have to, and always apologise in advance for anything hurtful you have to say. Do not be tempted into heated argument; do not heap scorn upon his point of view, however crazy it seems to you; insist firmly on the truth, but do it without rancour.

(ii) Make sure your information is up to date. Never pretend to knowledge you don't possess. He will respect honest ignorance more than glib superficiality.

(iii) Stick to the main points – don't allow yourself to be sidetracked into discussing 'red herrings' such as blood transfusions with a Jehovah's Witness, the authorship of the *Book of Mormon* with a Latter Day Saint, fund-raising techniques with a Moonie. Resist any temptation to score cheap points.

(iv) Realise that members of some groups (e.g. the Family of Love and Unification Church) are inoculated against the standard evangelical approaches. Be original. Avoid jargon. Don't come straight out with your testimony, but be mysterious about your own beliefs if necessary, until you are *asked* to explain where you yourself stand.

(v) Recognise that in *some* cases a degree of 'mind manipulation' has taken place; doctrine has been implanted by psychological violence; and consequently the cult member will come up with stock answers in a conditioned, repetitive way. Keep plugging away to try to find the key which will unlock his thinking. But realise that it may take a long time and much patience.

(vi) Remember that in the case of many groups, the cult is 'home' to the member. Should your contact decide to leave, you will need to have ideas about where he can go. It must be a warm, accepting environment, where he can simply relax and begin to sort out his head for himself, without being pressured to accept Christ or attend church. What he needs at this stage is Christian care and love; if this is shown genuinely, it will lead him to Christ of itself.

'The Lord's servant must not guard' Paul insisted. 'He must be . . . gentle as he corrects his opponents, for it may be that God will give them the opportunity to repent and come to know the truth' (2 Tim. 2:24–5). It may be. It really can happen.

Useful addresses

Christian Response to the Occult, 7 London Road, Bromley, Kent
FAIR, BCM Box 3535, PO Box 12, London WC1N 3XX
Christian Information Outreach, 92 The Street, Boughton, Faversham, Kent
Spiritual Counterfeits Project, Box 4308, Berkeley, CA94704

Material resources

Video training course: NIE, 146 Queen Victoria St., London EC4V 4BX
Cassette series by John Allan: Scripture Union, 5 Wigmore St., London W1
The Kingdom of the Cults, W. Martin (Bethany Fellowship)
Cults and New Faiths J. Butterworth (Lion)
The Challenge of the Cults M. Burrell, (IVP)
TM Yoga, The Rising of the Moon, J. Allan, (all IVP)
The Mystical Maze, P. Mears, (Campus Crusade)
The Mormon Illusion, F. McElven (Gospel Light)
How to Witness to Jehovah's Witnesses W. Schnell, (Baker)

Ethnic Minorities

Introduction

Britain has received many immigrants during recent years, representing many different countries. These ethnic minorities are generally concentrated within the inner areas of our cities. However, these are the very areas where the churches are experiencing a rapid decline in membership, with a increasingly large proportion of the congregations living outside the immediate neighbourhood.

Educating the church

It is necessary to teach the Church how to grasp the opportunities there are to witness to people from many different backgrounds and religions. Christians must be aware of the people living around them; their places of origin, the cultures practiced, the religious beliefs, and the languages commonly used. A knowledge of these basic characteristics is essential if we are to adequately and relevantly present the gospel to them. This can be done through the following ways:

(i) A weekend conference for the church on the background, culture and beliefs of the various ethnic minorities represented in the community.

(ii) A series of mid-week meetings covering the same topics in greater depth. Filmstrips and discussion groups are useful.

Background and culture

Religion is frequently an integral part of the life of the immigrant. West Indians are from a predominantly Christian background. In the West Indies 80 per cent of the population attend church; it is vital that we should recognise the great spiritual potential of these peoples. It is probably a sad reflection on our churches that less than 20 per cent of the West Indian people meet to worship God in this country. In contrast Asian families do not, in the majority of instances, have a Christian faith. Their community is rich in its diversity of cultures, practices and religions, encompassing Pakistanis, people from Bangladesh, Indians from the Punjab, other parts of India and East Africa.

Major religions of the Asian

Perhaps the main religion of Asians is that of Islam, although Hinduism and Sikhism are also strongly represented in most Asian communities.

(a) *Islam*

Muslims follow the religion Islam. They worship in mosques and pray towards Mecca where their founder, Mohammed, was born in 610 AD. Their holy book is called the Qur'an and every Muslim believes in the following six articles of faith: the oneness of Allah, angels, the scriptures, the prophets, the day of judgement, and the decrees of Allah. Each true follower of Islam also practices the five duties, or 'pillars', of their faith: recital of the creed, prayer, fasting, almsgiving and a pilgrimage to Mecca.

(b) *Hinduism*

Hinduism is the dominant religion of India and there are numerous forms. It has no historical founder and reflects a mixture of philosophy, ritual, ancient customs and traditions emerging over a period of some 5,000 years. The Hindu believes in many gods, one god, or an impersonal force called Brahman.

(c) *Sikhism*

The majority of Sikhs come from Punjab, Northern India. Sikhism emphasises love and devotion, and displays an amazing tolerance towards other people. It originated from Guru Nanak who was born in 1469 AD. Coming from a privileged family, he rejected Hindu beliefs early in life and founded a religion simple enough for anyone to follow. He believed that everyone should have direct communion with God and that all people should be equal under the fatherhood of God. Salvation was to be found by living a good, honest life of kindness and generosity. Having travelled widely with his message, Guru Nanak died at seventy.

Our approach

(a) *Attitudes*

Our attitude to those of other ethnic backgrounds is very important. If they sense a hint of coolness, of prejudice, of paternalism then our work will easily be nullified. Beware of reserve as it can often be mistaken as an expression of superiority; rather show friendliness. As confidence is won fears may be overcome, demonstrating that although we are culturally and racially different from each other, all people are equal in the sight of God. When this takes place and is followed by the proclamation of the gospel, the heart prepared often responds to God's love.

(b) *Sensitivity*

We must always have a sensitivity towards one another's culture and beliefs. Our approach should always be polite and expressing our Lord's great concern for all peoples.

(c) *Responsibility*

We have a responsibility not only to tell every man, woman and child about Christ Jesus (as commanded in Matt. 28), but also to demonstrate love and compassion practically.

(d) *Openness*

Do not be surprised if you are asked personal questions. Answer them without embarrassment, otherwise it may appear as showing a lack of confidence in the other person. Be truthful and open about your experience of Jesus; personal testimony can be far more valuable in helping someone to understand the nature of God's love and salvation than theological argument.

(e) *Scripture*

Aim to leave portions of scripture with individuals who are interested in knowing more about Jesus. God can speak through his words long after our visit has been forgotten.

Types of Evangelism

(a) *Friendship and service*

Immigrant groups face many problems within the host society; often problems of racial prejudice, difficulty in speaking English, or understanding governmental and institutional systems and procedures. There are many ways we can show friendship to others. We can offer practical help with the filling out of forms, helping with odd jobs that need to be done, taking care to explain our culture and traditional practices, helping children with their homework and opening our homes to neighbours of other ethnic groups.

(b) *Literature visitation*

Many of the homes may be recognised by the name of householders on the electoral roll, which is available for use in the main public libraries. When engaging in visitation it is important that teams are composed of married couples, or if this is not possible, either two men or two women should visit together. This avoids many complications, particularly as the Asian community considers it improper for members of the opposite sex even to talk to each other. There are Gospels, Bibles and other Christian literature available in many different languages as well as in English. Literature should be handed personally to those who are interested, and the Christian message shared whenever the opportunity arises. A Hindu may well ask if Jesus is only one way to God, whilst the Muslim will question your belief in the Son of God and the validity of the Bible. When visiting West Indian homes talking about the Bible and the Lord Jesus is often readily accepted. If there is a West Indian church or Christian fellowship involving other ethnic peoples in the neighbourhood, it may be possible for your church to share in such outreach with them.

(c) Discussion and dialogue

A dialogue may be established between Christians and leaders of another religion to discuss and consider action on particular social problems troubling the community. This encourages understanding and tolerance amongst all concerned. In the West Indian situation, relationships between black-led churches and white congregations should be encouraged. This may be done by: the exchange of pulpits, ensuring that the West Indian believers are represented on local fraternities and Council of Churches, and a sharing of mission.

(d) Special meetings

Social events such as 'international evenings' with food, music, dance, poetry and art can provide a setting for presenting the Christian message. Coffee mornings for mothers and their children, youth clubs with a Christian emphasis, cookery demonstrations and ladies' English classes can all provide openings for sharing the gospel. Evangelistic meetings may be arranged, however it is often difficult to encourage Asians to enter church premises. Evenings involving Asian music, Punjabi Christian choirs, and films in Urdu, Gujarati and other languages may be helpful in creating an openness amongst ethnic minorities to the message of Jesus.

The Do's and Don'ts

(a) Misunderstandings

It is important that we understand the culture and religion of the people we are seeking to reach, otherwise we may cause offence and misunderstandings that could be avoided. We must also realise that most Asians consider British people all to be Christians, therefore it may be more appropriate to introduce ourselves as 'followers of the Lord Jesus Christ' rather than as simply Christians.

(b) *Terminology*

Be careful not to use Christian phrases and terms that may be misinterpreted. Try to express biblical truths in simple meaningful language.

(c) *Appearance*

Our appearance should be carefully considered; dress should be modest. Muslim ladies are expected to dress in such a way as to not reveal the shape of the body, and Christians should respect this point of view.

(d) *Receive hospitality*

Do enter the home if you are invited in, however it is advisable for a woman only to enter the home if the wife is present, and a man if the husband is present. Accept cheerfully and thankfully any food and drink you may be offered.

(e) *Respect for the Bible*

It is important that the Bible used is not dog-eared, or heavily underlined, as Asians in particular have a great reverence for their holy books. Always handle the Bible with respect and never place it on the floor.

Conclusion

Today must be our time of action. It is already evident that the members of the various ethnic communities in Britain are beginning to follow one of two trends. Some are becoming Westernised and adopting many of the attitudes of the host society, including the hardening of heart towards Jesus. Others are increasing their commitment to their own religion and becoming radical believers, which vastly restricts their openness to the gospel of Jesus Christ. We must act today for tomorrow may be too late.

Resource materials

1. Suggested filmstrips are:

The way of Islam – part 1 beliefs and practices, part 2 customs and culture

The way of Hinduism – beliefs and practices

The way of Sikhism – beliefs and practices

These can be obtained from In Contact Ministries, St Andrews Road, Plaistow, London E13 8QD

2. Literature – Bibles, scripture portions and other Christian literature can be obtained from:

The Bible Society, 146 Queen Victoria Street, London EC4V 4BX

Scripture Gift Mission Inc., Radstock House, 3 Eccleston Street, London SW1W 9LZ

Evangelistic literature is available from St Andrews Christian Bookshop, St. Andrews Road, Plaistow, London E13 8QD and from Christian Literature Crusade, 51 The Dean, Alresford, Hampshire SO24 9BJ

3. Films. These may be gained from International Films, 235 Shaftesbury Avenue, London WC2H 8EL

4. Evangelistic cassettes and records. These may be obtained from Gospel Records Fellowship, Morelands Training Estate, Bristol Road, Gloucester GL1 5RZ

Leading Individuals to Christ

6.1

The Witness

I've been involved in evangelism long enough to know that there are many different ways of sharing the gospel, many different situations in which it is shared, and many different starting points. But there is one common feature. By the Holy Spirit's power, we do have to lead people to a living relationship with Jesus Christ. How do we do it?

In this final section of the manual, we're going to look at what can be done when faced with a person who wants to know Jesus, and who wants to respond in some way. Space is limited, but wherever possible there are at least two alternatives given as to what can be done. Wider research will yield other possibilities.

1. Let's start at the very beginning

When we find ourselves in the position of sharing Jesus, with the desire to see a response, there are a few 'ground rules' to consider.

(a) The pressure is on us

There are forces which work against the sharing of the good news of Jesus, and when we find ourselves in a one-to-one situation, they're very definitely focused on us. So be prepared for the unexpected – from feeling ill or angry or depressed, to the phone, door bell, baby waking etc. Recognise these things for what they are.

(b) It's not our decision

No matter how much we long to see our listener come to Christ, it's not up to us to force the pace, or 'arrange' a response. This doesn't rule out determination on our part, but it does call for a close walk with the Lord, and a listening to his Spirit.

(c) Ambassadors for Christ

Grace and sensitivity should be the keynote of our sharing. We are ambassadors for Christ, and as such our job is to present his claims – not our own – as clearly as possible. This doesn't stop us being firm and direct in what we say but we must avoid being aggressive.

Ambassadors are also expected to keep confidences. When someone responds to Christ, it's not for us to shout it from the housetops, yet this is all too often what happens in Christian fellowships, and can be so damaging to new believers. It's for them to share what God has done for them, and although we might encourage them to do so, we must learn to keep the confidence until they speak.

2. Getting started

It's not much good having a great story to tell if we can't get into it, yet many people never get into sharing their faith because they can't surmount this first hurdle.

If we consider a one-to-one situation, what can we do to help us get into sharing? Here are three practical suggestions:

(a) The direct approach

Spend some time getting to know each other. It's hard to share our inner feelings with a stranger, so spend time becoming friends. When the moment feels right, ask 'Do you mind if I move the conversation on to spiritual matters now – that's really why I've come to talk to you.' It might look corny in print, but if we really love someone enough to want to share Jesus with them, then this conviction will come across in our voice.

(b) The Evangelism Explosion approach

This is a very simple and effective lead in to the gospel. In the following order the conversation would cover

their secular life (the friendship making process again)

their church background – (Have you ever been to church/our church?' (This moves the conversation from the secular to church).

our church – 'Well at our church there are many people who have had their lives changed . . . can I tell you how my life has been changed?' Then follows personal testimony. The conversation has now moved to the spiritual level.

(c) The Breakthrough approach

This is similar to EE, but doesn't have 'our church', and leads to a different style of testimony. The conversation follows this pattern.'

their secular life

their church background . . . 'Have you ever been to church? Had church links?'

testimony

Breakthrough links the testimony with the giving of a suitable leaflet for those who feel they cannot manage a gospel presentation. Occasionally our listener will give us the lead in: What's that badge you're wearing?

Did you have a good weekend?'
Do you believe in an after life?'

and so on. These are gold nuggets but they come rarely, and it's easy to be so amazed that we forget to say anything! Be prepared.

3. Keeping going

There are 'tricks' in every trade, and communicating the good news of Jesus is no exception. Here are some things to keep in mind as we share Jesus.

(a) Don't sermonise or lecture

It's very easy to do this, either because we're used to giving lectures, or because we're so nervous that it all comes tumbling out in one long rush. The following type of comments directed to our listener help turn monologue into dialogue:

What do you think?
Have you ever thought?'
Do you think people feel that . . . ?
Does that strike you as unusual?'

If your listener interrupts with a question, use it as an opportunity to generate dialogue:

What do you mean exactly?
That's a good thought, but what about . . .?

(b) Pray at all times

Conversations about Jesus must be led by the Spirit. If things aren't going well – or even if they are – pray. It's amazing how often we forget to pray as we go along, yet many conversations are revolutionised by a short unspoken prayer.

(c) Don't get into an argument

We might easily win the argument, but will probably lose the chance to share further. These kind of statements turn away anger and the negativeness that comes with it:

I'm glad you feel free to say that to me
That needs some thinking about
I've often wondered that myself
Many honest people have that view
I just don't know the answer to that . . .

(d) *Be aware*

Sometimes, when we're sharing Christ, or wanting to, we become oblivious to the obvious. No mum will ignore a crying baby, a telephone won't go away, nor will unexpected guests. A man getting ready for work, a cooking meal, a set table, a running bath – all these things suggest that the time might not be right. When we ignore these signs, we're not ambassadors, we're liabilities! Learn to assess the situation, and learn to say 'It's obviously not convenient to talk now . . .'

(e) *No need to apologise*

Be gracious, but be careful that this doesn't stray into constant apologies, and even an apologetic attitude to Christ

(f) *Watch your language*

It's very easy to spoil communication because we start using language which is unintelligible to our hearer. What, for example, does our listener make of:

Alleluia

saved by the blood

born again

filled with the Spirit

Christian

These words mean a lot to us, but they don't convey much to our hearers. If we really want them to understand Jesus, we must make every effort to be as plain and clear as possible.

4. Testimony

The story of how we came to know Jesus, and what he means to us today, is one of our most powerful weapons in evangelism. Our testimony brings Jesus out of the pages of the Bible, and away from the Church, and shows him alive and working in the twentieth century. It's a story unique to each one of us, and it makes a tremendous impression to our hearers. They might be able to dismiss the Bible and the Church, they might even think that we're misguided, but they can't deny the reality of our experience for us. We're the evidence that just won't go away.

We're not all called to be evangelists, but we are all called to be witnesses of what Jesus is doing in us and for us. It's important that our testimonies should make the reality of Christ clear for our hearers, and to make this happen, we need to do some thinking, and some advance work. Here's one way to get a testimony clear, but before we look at it, be warned of some pitfalls:

some testimonies contain too much irrelevant detail about the past. Our hearers are living in the present.

Some testimonies stop short of sharing an example of what God's doing this week. Try constantly to update testimony.

Sometimes it seems that testimonies have been written with Christians in mind. Try to hear the testimony from the listeners point of view. Style? Language? Idiom?

(i) Before giving a verbal testimony, it helps to write it down. Write down the story of how you came to know Jesus. It doesn't have to be neat – short phrases and words will do. Make sure you include:

how you started to think about God

how you came to know Jesus

what difference knowing him made to your life

what difference he makes today, with one example from the last two weeks.

(ii) Leave that list in a safe place for a few days

(iii) Come back to your list and read it through. Is there anything you want to change? Then do it.

(iv) Now write it in long hand, and leave it for a few days.

(v) When you come back to read your lifeline, ask yourself:

how long did it take to read?

could I use it with my friends – would they get bored?

are there one or two good illustrations?

(vi) Find a Christian friend, read it to him/her, ask them what they thought, and make any changes that you both think will improve it.

(vii) Practise saying it a few times, until you can say it without notes. By the way, some of us don't have a 'before' section to our experience of Jesus. So our testimonies begin, 'There's never been a time that I haven't known Jesus . . .' and then continue with the up-to-the-minute section.

I have a vision that every Christian in England will be able to:

start a spiritual conversation

give a personal testimony

then give an evangelistic leaflet to round the conversation off. Not a staggering vision I know, but think what a difference it would make to the work in England.

6.2

The Message

1. Basic message

When considering the task of sharing the basic message of Jesus, we're not only faced with a content question, but also with a communicating one. It is possible to develop a basic message that says everything, but such an outline would be almost impossible to communicate. On the other hand, there is little value in developing a gospel outline that communicates really well yet has no content.

We're going to consider content and communication now, but before we do, a useful exercise is to make up your own outline. What would you include? This will help you be more sympathetic with those who have already tried to develop a good communicating outline!

By the way, some people find learning and sharing a gospel outline too hard. Why not get them to write a lead in, a testimony, and then help them develop a sharing pattern based in their favourite evangelistic leaflet. This way, they'll grow in confidence, and will always have something to give away even if they can't share in full.

(a) *Content*

Space necessitates brevity here.

> The age of fulfilment has dawned, as the scriptures foretold. God has sent his Messiah Jesus. He died in shame upon the cross. God raised him again from the tomb. He is now Lord at God's right hand. The proof of this is the Holy Spirit, whose effects you see. This Jesus will come again at the end of history. Repent, believe and be baptized. (C. H. Dodd quoted in *Evangelism, Now and Then* by Michael Green.)

Michael Green goes on to develop this, and I recommend a reading of this section of his book.

A slightly fuller gospel outline is to be found in *Out of the Saltshaker* by Rebecca Manley Pippert. It reads:

God   God loves you (John 3:16).
God is holy and just, he punishes all evil and expels it from his presence (Rom. 1:18).

Man   God, who created everything, made us for himself to find our purpose in fellowship with him (Col. 1:16).
But we rebelled and turned away from God (Isa. 53:6). The result is separation from God (Isa. 59:2). The penalty is eternal death (Rom. 6:23).

Christ God became man in the person of Jesus Christ to restore the broken fellowship (Col. 1:19–20)

Christ lived a perfect life (1 Pet. 2:22).

> Christ died as a substitute for us by paying the death penalty for our rebellion (Rom. 5:8).
>
> He arose (1 Cor. 15:3–4) and is alive today to give us a new life of fellowship with God, now and forever (John 10:10).

This outline is designed as a useful summary to be kept in mind. It goes on to consider response, which we'll look at later. How does this compare with your basic message?

(b) *Communication*

Evangelism Explosion and the *Breakthrough Training Kit*, have also given much thought to content, but they have gone further and have tackled the communication and training side of the basic message. Both courses expect their outlines to be learnt, and have aids to learning included in the course. They also have a host of illustrations and Scripture to back up the content. The use of illustrations is vital. Not only do they bring the gospel to life, but they also live on in people's minds long after we have left. The same is true of Scripture, which has a power of its own to convince, and to live on, but its use needs to be carefully thought out.

The habit of using Scripture in conversation, without quoting chapter and verse ('The Bible tells us that all, like sheep, have gone astray' rather than 'It says in Isaiah chapter 53 verse 6 all we like sheep have done astray') tends to be more effective.

Here are the *Evangelism Explosion* and *Breakthrough* outlines. They are designed to be easily learnt, easily and naturally spoken, and above all easily received by an interested listener. Again, compare them with your outlines.

Evangelism Explosion

Grace	Heaven is a free gift
	It cannot be earned or deserved
Man	Is a sinner
	Cannot save himself
God	Is loving and doesn't want to punish us
	Is just, and must punish sin
Jesus	Who he is
	What he has done (Calvary/paid for our sins)
Faith	What it isn't
	What it is

(Response section follows)

Breakthrough:

It's God's world. He made it, and he's really there.
He has given control of the world to Jesus
He proved this by raising Jesus from the dead.
God calls on everyone to submit their lives to Jesus.

People do what you might expect – rebel against the idea that anyone has control over their lives. Some rebel actively and become atheists. Most rebel quietly. They say, do and think wrong things, which proves that they are rebels, as God doesn't want these wrong things.

God does what you might expect. He calls on people to stop rebelling and to accept Jesus as Lord.

What if I do? Then I am treated as though I had never rebelled.
God can do this because of Jesus' death on the cross. On the cross, Jesus took all our rebellion against God on himself.

What if I don't? I'm ruined. God has the right to condemn me, not because he enjoys making me feel miserable, but because he really is Lord of history. If I take him on, I'm bound to lose in the end.
(Response section follows)

Here then is a *very brief* look at the basic message and some ways in which it has been used. In making up your own, consider;

- the content and the communication question
- illustrations
- verses
- ease of remembering
- ease of understanding

2. Getting stuck

Most of us get in a muddle from time to time when sharing Jesus. (In fact, I seem to be in a muddle most of the time!) Sometimes we forget a verse or an illustration gets all mixed up. Sometimes we get the good news itself in the wrong order, or we're thrown out of our stride by something, and cannot get going again. In these circumstances, the best advice is not to panic! Relax, smile, and use something like this:

I don't think I quite got that right!
Sorry – memory not working very well today.
I was afraid you would ask that!
I'm glad you feel you can say that!

These remarks don't look much on paper, but in practise they're very useful – defusing an awkward moment, and giving a little breathing space. The objections people throw at us often give cause for concern, especially to the ordinary Christian lay man or woman. How are we going to cope with these objections? Here are some practical guidelines:

(i) Do they have them? We often imagine that our listeners are bristling with objections to Christian faith. The truth is often far worse – they've probably not given Christ a thought at all. So encourage positive thinking – objections are the exception, not the norm.

(ii) *Prevent them coming up.* Many objections can be avoided by careful thought and presentation. For example:

So you see Mike, God is just and must punish our sin.
Oh no Jim, my God's a God of love.

So now there is an eyeball to eyeball confrontation between Mike and Jim. But:

So you see Mike, God is a God of love, really caring about us, his creation.
But there's another side to him as well – he's just, and must punish sin.

By putting the justice of God after the statement about his love has defused the situation *before* it has arisen.

Many objections can be avoided like this, and it's not a question of slick selling. It's rather a clearing away of the clutter, so that, as good ambassadors, we might present the message of Christ.

(iii) *Answer them later.* Sometimes our listeners will interrupt us with questions that we're going to answer later in our presentation. For example, at the very beginning of sharing, we might get, 'Yes. But it's not fair, God condemning people, is it?' A simple answer to this might be 'I'm glad you feel free to ask that, and I think the answer to your question will be given in what I'm going to say later.' People don't mind us saying this – after all, questions are answered by the good news of Jesus. So let's get on and present it.

(iv) *Answer them.* There are only a few basic objections to the gospel. (*See* Paul Little *How to give away your faith*, Jim Smith *Breakthrough Training Kit*) Learn the simple answers, and give them if possible, but be careful not to be side-tracked *away* from the good news.

(v) *I don't know.* No shame in saying this. On the contrary, people are often amazed at our honesty. But use 'I don't know' like this:

I'm sorry Mike, but I just don't know the answer. But I know someone who does, and I'll check with them and tell you what they said. Can I carry on now, or would you rather talk to my friend at another time?

3. Response

The Bible tells us that the gospel is 'the power of God for the salvation of everyone who believes' (Rom. 1:16). Therefore, it follows that it is impossible for our hearers *not* to make some kind of response, even if it's 'I'll go away and think about it' or 'No thanks'.

But handling response is not easy. There are fears that people are being pushed or manipulated, and fears that people are responding to please us, and not Christ. Add to this Satanic pressure that comes on us at this moment in our sharing, and there's a 'panic' situation in the making! The panic can be averted by having a simple set of guidelines which will help us understand where our listener really is, and will help our listener understand just what it means to follow Christ.

Here is one set of guidelines:

(a) The clearing up question

'Do you understand what I have been telling you?' This is a totally straight forward question, with no hidden traps. It allows our listener to talk freely about what has been said, and can often bring to light bits of the good news that he/she didn't understand.

(b) The response question

'Would you like to make Jesus Christ your Lord and Saviour?' It's not up to us to answer this question. It has to be put, and we must wait on the answer.

(c) The making sure stage

'Let me explain what it means to accept Jesus as Saviour and Lord.' It's very important that we clarify what it means to respond to Jesus, and it's vital that it's done at this point, before any decision is made. Our listeners need to know what they are committing themselves to, and we avoid the problems of 'easy-believism' or premature commitment. All through this stage it's worth saying again and again 'Is this what you want to do?' Our listeners will feel than that they can back off if they want to.

There are three elements in the making sure stage:

Jesus as Saviour – delivered us from the consequences of our sin

Jesus as Lord – with the right to make and expect a different life-style

Jesus – the *cost* – what it means in terms of discipline/ridicule to follow.

There are different ways of spelling this out. The ABCR is easy to remember, and does the job adequately:

A Admit
That in God's sight you are a wrong-doer, and that he has the right to have nothing more to do with you.

B Believe
Everything that I've told you about Jesus is true. He lived, died on the cross, came back to life again, is alive today and wants you to follow him.

C Count the Cost

Following Jesus is costly. It means putting him first in your life, letting him have complete control of your life, it means being willing to read your Bible, say your prayers and go to church. And maybe your friends will make fun of you.

Knowing Jesus is worth the cost, and much, much more, but you ought to know it is going to cost you.

R Receive

Receive Jesus into your life. As he comes in he will bring two precious gifts – first forgiveness and the second, the Holy Spirit, who will help you in your walk with Jesus.

(d) The prayer of faith

Many people still hesitate at this point – still fearing to push people where they don't want to go. This quite natural hesitation (which I used to share) can be overcome using this little guideline – the 'Three Ways' technique:

Now Mike, there are three choices I can offer you now; I can *give you a booklet* which will tell you more about Jesus, and when you've read it, perhaps we can talk some more; or I could give you a *booklet* with a prayer in the back, which you can use to give control of your life to Jesus. You can use that prayer when you're alone; *or we can pray now.* Jesus is with us, and we could go to him in prayer, and together tell him that you want to give yourself to his control. Which would you like to do?

The advantage of this is that it relieves us of the responsibility, and gives our hearers a genuine choice.

Suppose they want to pray with us, what do we do then?

It's most important that we know what we're going to do, and that we make this clear to our listener. There are many different ways of handling this situation. Here's one sample pattern. Why not try writing your own prayers before you read this.

OK Mike, let's pray together. First I'll pray, and then there will be a prayer for you to give control of your life to Jesus – will you make this up, or shall I lead you a phrase at a time? Then I'll pray again afterwards.

1st prayer

In this prayer, summarise the gospel again, simply and briefly.

2nd prayer

Dear Lord, I'm sorry for the past, for ignoring you. Please forgive me. Thank you for dying on the cross for me. I want you to be my Lord. Please come into my life right now. Help me serve you faithfully and grow like you every day of my life. Amen.

3rd Prayer

A thank you prayer – thanking God for accepting Mike. This prayer provides a good opportunity to begin follow up.

Make these prayers slow and easy. Leave plenty of gaps and silences, so that there's time to be conscious of what's going on.

(e) *Welcome*

What do we do after the prayer has been prayed? Again it's a very personal moment that needs careful handling. Something like this fits the situation:

Mike, let me be the first to say welcome to the Kingdom of God. You've made the first step in a wonderful journey with Jesus Christ. Welcome!

This looks a bit hackneyed on paper, but something like this makes all the difference when someone has prayed with us, and isn't quite sure what *our* reaction will be.

At any time in this response section, our listener might choose not to accept Jesus there and then. What do we do? There are different types of negative response, and they need slightly different handling:

(i) *'No' – meaning 'Not yet'*. If people want time to think, they've every right to have it. It is a major life-changing decision we're inviting them to take, and sometimes a little 'thinking time' is needed. Be willing to allow this, and offer books/booklets/and further help wherever possible.

(ii) *'No' – meaning 'Not here'*. Sometimes the place isn't convenient, or there are people present that make a response difficult. The 'three ways technique should avoid this problem, but let's be aware of it. We English are easily embarrassed, and may be what our listener is saying is 'not even in front of you!'

(iii) *'No' – meaning 'I haven't really understood'*. Again, isn't it better that we let people back off, rather than plunge ahead when they haven't understood? The Lord is sovereign in evangelism, and perhaps we're only the link in a long chain of bringing our listener to him.

(iv) *'No' – meaning 'No!'* Again, our listeners have the right to reject Christ, but it's our responsibility to lovingly explain that a rejection has consequences. As *Breakthrough* explains, 'If you don't stop rebelling, you will be ruined. Not because God is an ogre, who likes punishing people, but because he really *is* the Lord of history. If you take him on, you're bound to lose in the end.'

Sharing the bad news is never easy, but if we really love people, we won't shrink from lovingly sharing it.

6.3

Follow through

Bringing up a new Christian in the ways of Christ is a heavy responsibility, but it's one we avoid at our peril. The aim of evangelism is to make disciples, not converts. If we forget this, then at worst our new believers will fall away, and at best we'll be left with a Church full of baby Christians, who will be unwilling to share with us the heat and burden of the day.

We can only look briefly at follow through here, and as we do, let's remember that the greatest aids to successful follow through are personal friendships, and a warm and caring fellowship of God's people. These are presupposed in all that follows.

1. Immediate follow-up

When someone comes to Christ, the *minimum* we should attempt is:

(a) *Give biblical assurance of Christ's acceptance.*

This can be done in a number of ways, but it's most successful when they do it. For example:

> Now Mike, I'd like us to look at something Jesus said about what you've just done. It's here in John 6 verse 37 – let's read it. Jesus said 'All that the Father gives to me will come to me, and whoever comes to me I will never drive away.' Mike, have you just come to Jesus in your prayer? Then what does Jesus promise he will never do to you?

We then let our listener discover the biblical truth for himself/herself – 'never cast me away'.

(b) *Give a booklet to help*

There is great advantage in giving something with a summary of the Christian faith, with pointers to the future. If it's got a simple Bible study in it, then so much the better.

(c) *Fix another meeting.*

This is the beginning of the 'personal friendship' touch. Something like

> Mike, I will always be willing and ready to help you all I can. Shall we meet again, when you've had time to read this – then if you've any questions, I'll try to answer them for you.

Distance might prevent us making this kind of offer. But there's always the phone or post, and there's sure to be a local fellowship nearby that can help. Try getting in touch with them. There's so much more that could be done, but if we've been talking for an hour or so already, and there's been prayer, then the time has come to leave. At the subsequent meeting, Bible reading, prayer, witness, Satan, church can all be discussed, and they come more naturally after a little time has elapsed.

2. Long term follow-up

We cannot manage this task alone. The local fellowship, a small home group, books, tapes, videos, and anything else available has to be drawn into the task. But what is the task? In the long term it's discipleship, but in the short term (1-2 years) there are at least four main areas that have to be covered: The Bible, prayer, church, and linking faith to everyday life. Here's a brief outline of these four areas, and as we consider them, it's worth bearing in mind that *we* know that new Christians have to grow, but they don't necessarily realise it. Helping them understand the need for growth is part of our task.

(a) *Bible*

This has to cover the use of a basic follow up booklet, the daily use of the Bible, with daily notes, and the application of the teaching of the Bible to everyday life.

(b) *Prayer*

This has to cover the daily prayer time, intercession for the needs of others, and the ability to see God's answers to prayer.

These two 'truths' are not quickly taught, or easily learnt. Small home groups are a great help here, but the finest way to teach these is to let a new believer share our Bible reading and prayer times at least once a week.

(c) *Church*

We, who are regular at church, forget what a daunting barrier the church door is to those unused to passing through it. Hymns, prayer books, choruses, the right way of doing things – all these are unfamiliar. Then there is the feeling of being a stranger amongst friends. We will have to work really hard here to

help new believers get to church. Offer to pick them up, or meet them outside

help new believers settle into church. Introduce them to our friends, and never abandon them during the after-service coffee time

help new believers to find their area of service within the church.

(d) *Everyday life*

This is where it really matters in the life of a new believer. He or she is walking hand in hand with Jesus for the first time, and there's so much to unlearn, relearn and learn for the first time. Regular contact from us, and regular membership of a caring fellowship will help in:

learning to recognise God's presence with us

seeing answered prayer, and growing bolder in prayer

learning to recognise God's leading and guiding

learning to change attitudes

and this last one is the real cruncher. What, for example, should be the new believer's attitude to:

other people?

family?

material things/money?

personal failings?

life in general?

past/future?

This is where it really matters to be a Christian, and where it really hurts. We can expect many traumas, heartaches and tears, but we are doing it for the Lord's glory and in obedience to his command, and that should make it all worth while.

Then Jesus came to them and said, 'All authority in heaven and on earth has been given to me. Therefore go and make disciples of all nations, baptising them in the name of the Father and of the Son and of the Holy Spirit, and teaching them to obey everything I have commanded you. And surely I will be with you always to the very end of the age' (Matt. 28:18–20).

Resource material

Breakthrough, CPAS, Falcon Court, Fleet Street, London
Evangelism Explosion

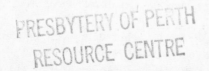